The Evolution of U.S. Military Policy from the Constitution to the Present, Volume II

The Formative Years for U.S. Military Policy, 1898–1940

SEAN M. ZEIGLER, ALEXANDRA EVANS, GIAN GENTILE, BADREDDINE AHTCHI

Prepared for the United States Army
Approved for public release; distribution unlimited

For more information on this publication, visit www.rand.org/t/RR1995z2

Library of Congress Cataloging-in-Publication Data is available for this publication.
ISBN: 978-0-8330-9849-8

Published by the RAND Corporation, Santa Monica, Calif.
© Copyright 2020 RAND Corporation
RAND® is a registered trademark.

Limited Print and Electronic Distribution Rights

This document and trademark(s) contained herein are protected by law. This representation of RAND intellectual property is provided for noncommercial use only. Unauthorized posting of this publication online is prohibited. Permission is given to duplicate this document for personal use only, as long as it is unaltered and complete. Permission is required from RAND to reproduce, or reuse in another form, any of its research documents for commercial use. For information on reprint and linking permissions, please visit www.rand.org/pubs/permissions.

The RAND Corporation is a research organization that develops solutions to public policy challenges to help make communities throughout the world safer and more secure, healthier and more prosperous. RAND is nonprofit, nonpartisan, and committed to the public interest.

RAND's publications do not necessarily reflect the opinions of its research clients and sponsors.

Support RAND
Make a tax-deductible charitable contribution at
www.rand.org/giving/contribute

www.rand.org

Preface

This report documents research and analysis conducted as part of a project entitled "History of United States Military Policy from the Constitution to the Present," sponsored by the Deputy Chief of Staff, G-8, U.S Army. The purpose of this volume is to provide the Army with a history of the evolution of the major laws that govern the Army that were written between 1898 and 1940.

This research was conducted within RAND Arroyo Center's Strategy, Doctrine, and Resources Program. RAND Arroyo Center, part of the RAND Corporation, is a federally funded research and development center (FFRDC) sponsored by the United States Army.

RAND operates under a "Federal-Wide Assurance" (FWA00003425) and complies with the *Code of Federal Regulations for the Protection of Human Subjects Under United States Law* (45 CFR 46), also known as "the Common Rule," as well as with the implementation guidance set forth in DoD Instruction 3216.02. As applicable, this compliance includes reviews and approvals by RAND's Institutional Review Board (the Human Subjects Protection Committee) and by the U.S. Army. The views of sources utilized in this study are solely their own and do not represent the official policy or position of the U.S. Department of Defense or the U.S. government.

Series Introduction

The current institutional arrangement of the Army, which comprises a Regular Army and two reserve components—the Army National Guard of the United States and the U.S. Army Reserve—has been the same since 1940. As a result, a conventional wisdom has developed that this structure is appropriate to the time and unchangeable. When debating the Army's size, appropriate roles and functions, and the laws required to authorize, empower, and govern the Army, U.S. policymakers often think about evolutionary institutional modifications and rarely question the underlying assumptions that led to this structure. It is easier to tinker with the existing Army than to consider fundamental changes to the Army's statutory foundation. This four-volume history of U.S. military policy argues that little about the Army's organization is unchangeable or constitutionally mandated, a fact that should give policymakers license to explore a wider range of options for the Army of the future.[1]

The National Commission on the Future of the Army (NCFA), which Congress established as part of the National Defense Authorization Act of 2015, is a case in point.[2] Congress gave the NCFA the mandate, among other things, to examine the assumptions behind the Army's current size and force mix. Despite this mandate, the

---

[1] Prominent American military historical surveys are Emory Upton, *The Military Policy of the United States*, 4th ed., Washington, D.C.: U.S. Government Printing Office, 1903, pp. 83–84; William Winthrop, *Military Law and Precedents*, Boston, Mass.: Little, Brown, and Company, 1896; Marvin A. Kreidberg and Merton G. Henry, *History of Military Mobilization in the United States Army, 1775–1945*, Washington, D.C.: Department of the Army, 1955; Richard H. Kohn, *Eagle and Sword: Federalists and the Creation of the Military Establishment in America, 1783–1802*, New York: Free Press, 1975; Allan R. Millett, Peter Maslowski, and William B. Feis, *For the Common Defense: A Military History of the United States from 1607–2012*, New York: Free Press, 2012; I. B. Holley, *General John M. Palmer, Citizen Soldiers, and the Army of a Democracy*, Westport, Conn.: Greenwood Press, 1982; Eilene Marie Slack Galloway, *History of United States Military Policy on Reserve Forces, 1775–1957*, Washington, D.C.: U.S. Government Printing Office, 1957; Russell Frank Weigley, *Towards an American Army: Military Thought from Washington to Marshall*, New York: Columbia University Press, 1962; Russell Frank Weigley, *History of the United States Army*, New York: Macmillan, 1967; Russell Frank Weigley, *The American Way of War: A History of United States Military Strategy and Policy*, New York: Macmillan, 1973; U.S. House of Representatives, *Review of the Reserve Program: Hearing Before the Subcommittee No. 1 of the Committee on Armed Services*, Washington, D.C.: U.S. Government Printing Office, February 4–8, 18–21, 1957. A reference guide for the legislation behind the military policy can be found in Richard H. Kohn, *The United States Military Under the Constitution of the United States, 1789–1989*, New York: New York University Press, 1991.

[2] Public Law 113-291, National Defense Authorization Act for Fiscal Year 2015, December 19, 2014.

NCFA elected not to reconsider the Army's statutory authorities and responsibilities and instead focused on ways to refine and improve the existing force. The commission's published report argued that the nation has "one Army" and a "traditional military policy" for sound "historical, cultural, legal, operational, and strategic" reasons.[3] By using this phrasing, the NCFA reinforces the idea that a coherent and constant "traditional military policy" has governed the Army from the earliest days of the Republic. The NCFA's report offers 63 recommendations for such things as improving Army training and readiness, refining the mix of forces and capabilities, and improving personnel management. Yet none of the 63 recommendations calls for a reconsideration of the fundamental laws that authorize, empower, and govern the Army, or the Army's three-component construct.

The notion of a coherent and constant *traditional* military policy stretching from the earliest days of the Republic to today is, however, a myth. U.S. military policy evolved substantially between the writing of the Constitution and 1940, and very little has changed since. Indeed, the term *military policy* was not used in the United States until the late 19th century, when Brevet Major-General Emory Upton introduced the term to Army thinkers. As used by Upton, the term *military policy* connoted matters pertaining to the U.S. Army, such as the laws that govern the institution and the policies for wartime expansion. Today the term continues to refer to Army matters to the exclusion of the other Services. The term *traditional military policy* first appeared in the 1940 Selective Service Act.

We highlight the etymology of the term to underline the fact that today's military policy is not the result of a coherent tradition but rather the distillation of over two centuries of debates and compromises between various competing interests, many of which arguably reflected the political and cultural debates of the day at least as much as the need to meet the military requirements of the nation's security. For each generation since the writing of the Constitution, ideology, political culture, and institutional momentum have limited the discourse on military policy and constrained the range of options available for serious consideration. Indeed, the current force structure is strikingly different from anything the Framers of the Constitution imagined. Although the notion of doing so was once considered anathema, the United States now entrusts its national security in part to a standing, professional force—its Regular Army, augmented by two largely part-time yet highly professional standing reserve components. Once organized to defend a growing nation protected by two oceans, the U.S. Army today is postured to deploy globally on very short notice.

One important example of how the use of the term *traditional military policy* can be misleading is the current Title 32 of the U.S. Code, which states that "In accordance with the traditional military policy of the United States, it is essential that the strength

---

[3] National Commission on the Future of the Army, *Report to the President and the Congress of the United States*, Arlington, Va., January 28, 2016, p. 1.

and organization of the Army National Guard and the Air National Guard as an integral part of the first line of defenses of the United States be maintained and assured at all times."[4] Yet the National Guard's role and status, and the laws governing it, have evolved considerably over time and cannot be regarded simply as a continuation of the 18th century method of producing military ground forces by "calling forth" various types of colonial militias, as the term *traditional military policy* implies. In fact, there is little "traditional" in the evolution of military policy.

One of the more fundamental developments explored in this series of reports is the subtle yet significant shift in the constitutional basis upon which the Army is built. Simply put, the Constitution includes one clause that empowers Congress to "raise and support Armies" and two other clauses that provide for "calling forth the Militia" of the states, as well as the authority to organize, arm, and discipline them "as may be employed in the Service of the United States," for the purpose of executing the laws of the Union, suppressing insurrections, and repelling invasions. The formulation assumed—accurately, at the time—that the states maintained their own militias or at least the means to raise them, even through conscription. Thus, the basic formula was for the country to rely on the "raise and support Armies" clause to maintain a small, standing federal army, but otherwise rely on the states and their militias to provide the bulk of the Republic's fighting forces. The militias evolved, as did their relationships with federal and state governments. In brief, the missions and personnel of militia referred to by the Constitution are not the same as the missions and personnel of what eventually became the National Guard. The evolution of the latter had less and less to do with state governments (and the Constitution's militia clauses) and more and more to do with the federal government (and the "raise and support Armies" clause).

In this four-volume series, we seek to establish an authoritative foundation for the debate over the best design for the future Army force. Drawing on archival research of primary sources and a survey of the historical literature, we trace the emergence of the laws that govern the Army today. This history has policy relevance because it shows that change in military policy is both possible and perhaps appropriate. When senior political and military leaders design Army force structure, thinking should not be constrained by such historically and politically loaded terms as *traditional military policy*. When imagining a future force, senior political and military leaders should recognize that current statutory foundations could be further defined and refined to enhance the Army's ability to meet the nation's dynamic security needs.

Figure S.1 depicts the evolution of U.S. military policy across a timeline from 1775 to the present. Along the top of the figure, we provide the strategic context across five periods—emerging America, the Civil War and the war with Spain, the World Wars, limited wars, and the Global War on Terror—as well as the nature of the Army in these periods. Along the bottom of the timeline, we highlight the specific historical

---

[4] U.S. Code, Title 32—National Guard, Section 102: General Policy, 2012.

Figure S.1
The Evolution of the U.S. Military Policy, 1775–Present

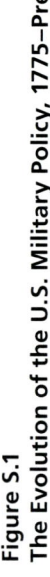

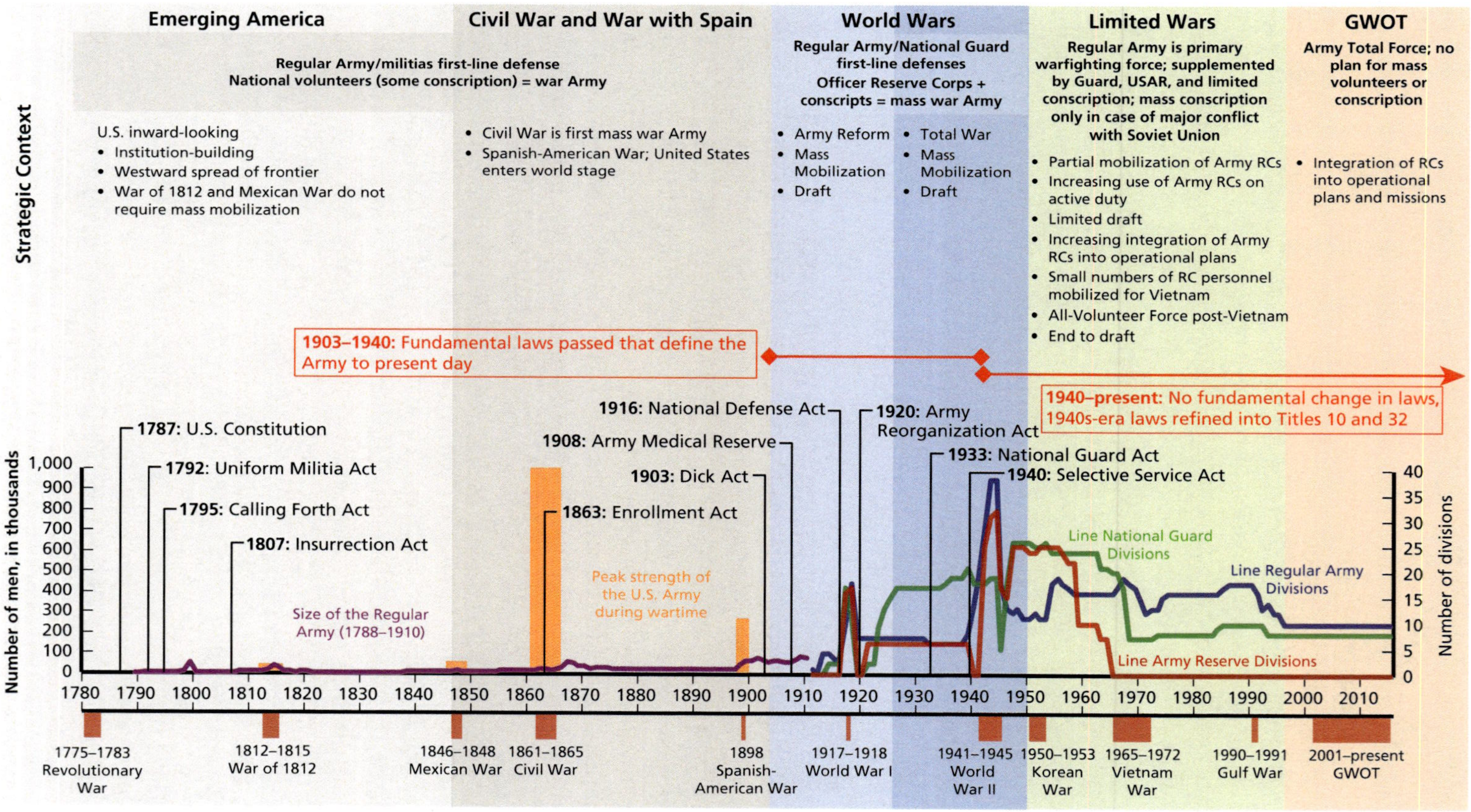

NOTES: USAR = U.S. Army Reserve; RC = reserve component; GWOT = Global War on Terror.

RAND *RR1995z2-1*

context in these periods, including the major wars fought and the size of the Army as it evolved over time in terms of the number of soldiers (the left axis) and the number of divisions (the right axis). In the middle of the timeline, we highlight the major relevant pieces of legislation that affected the evolution of the Army. The laws passed between 1903 and 1940, like the laws bearing on military policy before and after, reflect the debates and challenges of a particular historical period that differs greatly from the security environment that the nation confronts today. The laws nonetheless have remained virtually unchanged since 1940, as indicated in the figure by the thick red lines, despite significant changes in the geostrategic environment and the nation's increasing global interests and commitments.

In Volume I, *The Old Regime: The Army, Militias, and Volunteers from Colonial Times to the Spanish-American War*, we trace the history of military policy from the colonial era through the Spanish-American War. This period is critical for understanding the genesis of the basic structure of today's Army and the various factors that informed that structure. For a combination of strategic, cultural, economic, ideological, and political reasons, the Republic decided against establishing a standing army large enough to handle a major conflict and instead relied on a variety of mechanisms for raising volunteer units and marshaling state militias to expand or augment the Army. There was a basic split between proponents of a professional federal force, who judged the state-provided militias as militarily ineffective and too often contributing to an irresponsible loss of American lives, and those who opposed or feared the idea of a standing federal force (and its costs) and wanted to rely on "the people at arms," i.e., the citizenry organized by the states as militia units. The result was a compromise—an increasingly professional yet small Regular Army and various kinds of volunteer forces and state militias upon which the federal government would rely when the Nation needed to field a much larger force. However, authorities and responsibilities between the federal government and the states regarding the militias were not well established, nor were any mechanisms to ensure that the militias were ready and well trained when "called forth." Nor was there any mechanism to ensure the militia forces from one state were organized, trained, and equipped like the forces of another state to facilitate their integrated employment.

Problems with military effectiveness and recruitment contributed to an evolution in the militia system. The state militias shifted over the course of the 19th century from a colonial-era compulsory force (more compulsory in some communities than others) of all able-bodied white males between certain ages to entirely volunteer units with ambiguous relationships to their state governments. States that provided funding to their community militias tended to exercise more oversight and control. The compulsory militias were all but defunct by the time of the Mexican War (1846–1848), and volunteer militias provided much of the bulk of the Union Army during the Civil War. Postwar, those same volunteer militia units—increasingly referred to as "National Guard"—began to receive more support from state governments (with some federal assistance) and evolved into today's National Guard. Still, their status remained vague, as did their relationship with the federal government and the Army. Mobilization remained largely ad hoc, and the country still lacked anything resembling the large and rapidly expandable militaries fielded by France and Germany in 1870.

The Spanish-American War (1898) was a major turning point. The nation mobilized much as it had for the 1846 Mexican War, using a combination of Regular Army troops, volunteers from states and territories, and state militias. Small Regular Army units were rapidly assembled from small outposts distributed mostly throughout the central and western states, where they rarely trained for any contingencies other than fighting any remaining Native Americans who had not been pushed out of the way and onto reservations and preserving the local peace. Because of concerns associated with the constitutional limitation of militia use beyond the nation's borders, some individual state militia units voted to decide whether they would be mobilized (federalized) for the war with Spain. Some agreed, and some declined. If the unit agreed, the militia unit was brought into federal service as a volunteer unit. Other units were raised purely as federal volunteers (e.g., Teddy Roosevelt's Rough Riders), bypassing the state militia system entirely. A large-enough Army was eventually raised under the "raise and support Armies" clause, but profound problems were identified across the force. All elements of the Army were largely unprepared for fighting as larger organized units. Many units were ill-equipped, the Army's logistical capabilities were inadequate for deploying and sustaining forces overseas, and the tiny Medical Department was overwhelmed by infectious diseases that spread quickly through the ranks. The Army's difficulties were so bad that, in spite of winning the war, the Secretary of War was dismissed.

The volunteer militia units varied considerably from state to state, with little consistency in terms of readiness, quality, equipping, tactics, etc. Interoperability among or between them and the Regular Army was far from assured. There was, moreover, no established mechanism for generating forces to serve overseas for lengthy periods of time. This became a problem when the United States found itself occupying the Philippines and then fighting an insurgency there. Now the nation required an expeditionary capability, and it needed a force large enough to sustain a long-term occupation.

Heavily influencing the military policy of the late 19th century and early years of the 20th century was the maturation of the National Guard as a political force. Influential members of the Guard in 1878 created a lobby group, the National Guard Association, that enjoyed considerable sway with the public and in Congress. Because of the Guard's political influence, military policy debates and the relevant legislation passed in the 20th century often represented political compromises between the National Guard and the National Guard Association, the Regular Army and War Department, Congress, and the President.

As we shall see in Volume II, *The Formative Years for U.S. Military Policy, 1898–1940*, the challenges associated with the Spanish-American War stimulated new Secretary of War Elihu Root to promote reform through a series of laws beginning in the first few years of the 20th century. These laws, the most important among them being the Efficiency in Militia Act of 1903 (also known as the Dick Act of 1903, named for Ohio Congressman Charles Dick, who simultaneously served as chairman of the House Militia Affairs Committee; president of the National Guard Association; and commander of the Ohio Division, National Guard, with the rank of Major General), swept aside the Uniform Militia Act of 1792. They recognized the National Guard (i.e., the state volunteer militia units that had emerged after the Civil War), needed to be organized, trained, equipped, and disciplined along the lines of the Regular Army. This was the first step toward what in 1970 would become the Total Force Policy, and it added substance to the federal government's relationship to the National Guard, including both funding and regulations. These laws and subsequent legislation passed in 1916, 1920, and 1933 made the Guard largely a creature of the federal government, but one that still retained at least a formal connection to state governments—a dual status that in previous decades would have been anathema to Guard advocates. The laws of this era also established what would become today's Army Reserve, starting with a medical reserve cadre and the Reserve Officers' Training Corps. These congressional initiatives improved the Army's ability to expand and gave the Army access to trained specialists of the sort that were in short supply in the war against Spain. Although the new legislation greatly facilitated the nation's relatively rapid and orderly mobilization for World War I, some problems remained, and new ones emerged. Like all previous defense laws dating back to the Constitution, the legislation passed in 1916, 1920, and 1933 represented compromises. Debates of the era focused on how best to meet the nation's security requirements given a still deep-seated resistance to the idea (and cost) of maintaining a seemingly large standing peacetime Army, especially in light of Southern memories of federal forces being employed to enforce civil rights during Reconstruction. There was a grudging acceptance that, in the wake of the Spanish-American War, America required something more robust than the 19th century state-centric method for Army expansion; but there was little agreement over the details.

Volume III, *Another War and Cold War*, covers the period from 1940 to 1970 and examines how the Army, while retaining the basic legal underpinnings established by 1940, evolved in light of the radically different security requirements associated with the nation's emergence as a superpower and the need to maintain forces overseas and to rapidly respond in support of alliance commitments. Through this period—marked above all by the wars in Korea and Vietnam—there were vibrant debates regarding how best to generate the required forces, as well as different attempts by policymakers to balance military requirements with political concerns. These experiences led ultimately to the development of Total Force Policy, which was an effort to eliminate the need for conscription, except in special circumstances, and to further professionalize U.S. military forces.

Volume IV, *The Total Force Policy Era, 1970–2015*, covers the period from 1970 to 2015, from changes to U.S. military policy that resulted from the Vietnam War through years of persistent conflict following the September 11th, 2001, terrorist attacks. In spite of significant changes in the strategic context during this period, the fundamental laws underpinning U.S. military policy remained largely unchanged. Military policy did evolve through Army policy changes and congressional appropriations, although these generally reinforced the existing tripartite structure of the Army. To deal with the strategic, domestic, and financial constraints of the 1970s, the U.S. Department of Defense adopted the Total Force Policy. In its implementation of the new policy, the Army adapted the force mix within its three components to, when combined, fulfill the demands of war plans. The Regular Army was designed predominantly around combat forces to meet contingency timelines, while increased reliance was placed on support forces in the U.S. Army Reserve and Army National Guard to augment the Regular Army and to serve as a strategic reserve. Additional combat forces were maintained in both the U.S. Army Reserve and Army National Guard. Total Force Policy endured even as the nation's strategic circumstances dramatically changed again at the end of the Cold War.

Volume IV also discusses how the demands of persistent conflict since the 9/11 terrorist attacks have led to increased use of individuals and units from the reserve components. For example, as of June 2017, about 25,000 of the 542,000 soldiers of the Army Reserve and Guard are mobilized (federalized), with many serving in Afghanistan and Iraq. Army access to its reserve components has been simplified, and the American public largely supports their regular use, even in combat zones of the type experienced since 9/11.

Contents

Preface iii
Series Introduction v
Figures and Tables xv
Summary xvii
Acknowledgments xxiii

CHAPTER ONE
Introduction 1

CHAPTER TWO
The Spanish-American War and Early Reform Efforts, 1898–1903 5
Introduction 5
The Messy Victory over Spain 6
The U.S. Army in the Philippines 8
Postwar Debates and the Replacement of the 1792 Militia Act 10
Elihu Root and the 1903 Dick Act 17
Conclusion 24

CHAPTER THREE
Army Reform from 1903 to 1916: The Debates Continue 25
Introduction 25
After the Dick Act: The Debate Continued 25
1908: Amending the Dick Act and Establishing the Medical Reserve Corps 32
The Preparedness Movement 35
John McAuley Palmer and the 1912 Plan for Army Reorganization 43
The 1915 General Staff Plan 47
The 1916 National Defense Act 54
A Test of the 1916 Act: The Mexican Border Crisis 57
Conclusion 60

CHAPTER FOUR
Preparedness, World War I, and the 1920 Amendment to the 1916 National Defense Act ... 63
Introduction ... 63
The Road to War ... 63
The 1917 Selective Service Act ... 66
Bringing the National Guard into Federal Service ... 70
Training the U.S. Army for War ... 73
Demobilizing the Army and the War's Aftermath ... 78
The Army Reorganization Act of 1920 ... 81
The Passage and Provisions of the Army Reorganization Act of 1920 ... 87
Conclusion ... 89

CHAPTER FIVE
Refining Military Policy in the Interwar Years ... 91
Introduction ... 91
The Aftermath of the 1920 Amendment and the National Guard's Drive for Dual Status ... 92
The Challenge of Fiscal Restraint for the Organized Reserves and the National Guard ... 95
The 1933 Amendment to the 1916 National Defense Act ... 98
The Road to War, 1939–1940 ... 103
Conclusion ... 106

CHAPTER SIX
Volume Conclusion ... 109

APPENDIXES
A. Summary Table of 19th Century Militias and Volunteer Forces ... 111
B. Summary Table of Legislation Pertaining to the Evolution of U.S. Military Policy ... 115
C. Taxonomy of Important Terms ... 121

Abbreviations ... 129
References ... 131

Figure and Tables

Figure

1. The Evolution of the U.S. Military Policy, 1775–Present viii

Tables

3.1.	Key Provisions of the 1908 Militia Act and Army Medical Department Act	36
3.2.	Key Provisions of the National Defense Act of 1916 (Public Law 64-85)	55
4.1.	Key Provisions of the Army Reorganization Act of 1920 (Public Law 66-242)	88
5.1.	Key Provisions of the National Guard Act of 1933 (Public Law 73-64)	100
A.1.	Summary Table of 19th Century Militias and Volunteer Forces	112
B.1.	Summary Table of Legislation Pertaining to the Evolution of U.S. Military Policy	115

Summary

The 1898 Spanish-American War was a watershed moment in the development of U.S. military policy. The United States had decided to take a more active role in global affairs, and many believed it needed a larger, more professional army to serve the nation's changing goals. After a century of compromise and ad hoc solutions, the Army's uneven performance in the Spanish-American War forced U.S. policymakers to confront the necessity of enacting significant reforms. The exact nature of reforms, however, remained contested. Led by Secretary of War Elihu Root, a new generation of reformers set out to rewrite the laws and regulations governing and guiding the Army. These reformists, what we refer to as the "professionalist" school, consisted primarily of Regular Army officers, civilian officials in the War Department, some members of Congress, and a coalition of like-minded citizens who envisioned a prominent role for the United States in world affairs. They sought to strengthen the Regular Army by increasing its funding, improving professional education, establishing realistic training, and building a ready and capable federal reserve unencumbered by state politics and the 19th century system of using states and their governors to expand the Army.

At the same time, a second reformist school, drawing on the militia tradition, argued that a strengthened National Guard, not a new federal reserve, would provide the best and most cost-effective mechanism to strengthen the nation's defenses. Backed by fiscal conservatives in Congress—many of whom had personal connections to their state militia forces—National Guard proponents argued for federal recognition of the National Guard as a component of the Army and a first-line reserve during war (i.e., a force utilized before volunteers and conscripts). Represented by its increasingly influential lobbying organization, the National Guard Association, this camp blocked Root's more progressive proposals and solidified a federal reserve role for the state militias.

The battle over the future of the Army was waged in Congress, where the National Guard's political influence and budget-conscious arguments held sway. In 1903, the Dick Act divided the state militias into two categories: the organized militia to be known as the National Guard of the states, and the Reserve Militia comprising all individuals in the constitutionally defined militia, but not in the organized militia. The law also sought to ensure the organized militia had the same organization, armament, and discipline as the Regular Army. The legislation effectively marked the birth of the modern National Guard.

Both reform schools—professionalist and National Guard—were unsatisfied with the 1903 Dick Act, which left the relationship between the Regular Army and the National Guard of the states ill-defined. It did not, for example, specify how the federal government should mobilize state militia as individuals or units, nor did it explain how militia units should be integrated into federal service. The new statute did not satisfy professionalists' concerns about the readiness and proficiency of National Guard units or thoroughly address the shortfalls identified in the 1898 Spanish-American War, so proposals to establish a federal reserve continued, albeit with resistance from the National Guard school.

As a result, Congress amended the Dick Act in 1908, stipulating that National Guard units of the several states were to be brought into federal service in "advance" of other volunteer forces used to expand the Army by the federal government. Since the National Guard was an "organized militia" as established by the Dick Act, this legislation aimed to ensure it would be brought onto active service before the federal government expanded the Army further by raising volunteer forces or turning to conscription. To resolve past issues associated with constitutional limitations on where the National Guards of the states could be employed and for how long, Congress also gave the President the authority to "specify in his call the period for which such service is required, and the militia so called shall continue to serve during the term so specified, either within or without the territory of the United States."

To address medical shortfalls experienced in the 1898 Spanish-American War, Congress also enacted the Army Medical Department Act "to increase the efficiency of the Medical Department of the United States Army" in April 1908, which included the establishment of the Medical Reserve Corps, comprising commissioned doctors, dentists, and veterinarians who could be called to active service in time of war. The first explicitly federal reserve component, the Medical Reserve Corps, laid the foundation for the establishment of the Organized Reserve, Enlisted Reserve Corps, and Reserve Officers' Training Corps in 1920 (and eventually, as Volume III will show, the U.S. Army Reserve).

Professionalist reformers were pleased with the establishment of the Medical Reserve Corps, and they pursued further legislation and War Department planning documents that would secure a reserve force for the Army exclusively under federal control. The outbreak of World War I in Europe catalyzed the emergence of a new popular movement for military preparedness. Dissatisfied with congressional action, a coalition of progressive military officers, businessmen, and lawyers sought to leverage public-private partnerships to promote civilian military training and improve national defenses. With the War Department's backing, the preparedness movement founded summer training camps for college students and businessmen. As the war in Europe continued and the risk of U.S. entry grew, preparedness activists agitated for universal military training. Professionalists and preparedness advocates believed that war would require a mass army of rapidly trained citizen-soldiers.

Under significant pressure from the preparedness movement, Congress passed the National Defense Act (NDA) in 1916. As a result, Congress authorized expansions of the Regular Army and National Guard, and allocated additional federal funds to both. In exchange for the federal funding, the state National Guards were now obligated to implement new standardization measures—and accept federal oversight—to ensure efficient integration into federal service.

The 1916 NDA's most lasting contribution to military policy, however, was its legal redefinition of the U.S. Army. Taking a step beyond the provisions of the laws passed in 1903 and 1908, Congress now defined the Army as comprising the Regular Army, the National Guard "while in the service of the United States," and several new federal reserve entities: an Officers' Reserve Corps, Enlisted Reserve Corps, and a Reserve Officers' Training Corps. Thus, the 1916 NDA simultaneously appeased the National Guard lobby by tying the National Guard legally and institutionally to the Regular Army in wartime and satisfied the professionalists by creating several alternative federal reserve cadres and forces that could facilitate the Army's expansion in wartime.

The 1916 NDA faced its first test two weeks after President Woodrow Wilson signed it into law, as a new crisis on the Mexican border prompted Wilson to federalize some elements of the National Guards of the states. Mobilization was quick, especially when compared with 1898, but some Regular Army leaders argued that many Guardsmen were unfit for service and that Guard units tended to lack sufficient support capabilities. Moreover, the Army was unprepared to integrate Regular Army units with arriving Guardsmen, many of whom lacked sufficient equipment or resources. Nonetheless, the American success in the Mexican crisis provided proof of concept and temporarily quieted calls for additional reforms.

A far greater challenge emerged in April 1917 when, after two years of mediation and neutrality, the United States finally entered the war in Europe. War Department planners quickly determined that the United States needed a much larger Army than allowed by the 1916 NDA. On May 18, 1917, Congress authorized the President "to increase temporarily the Military Establishment of the United States." This act, subsequently often referred to as the Selective Service Act, empowered the President "to raise, organize, officer, and equip all or such number of increments of the Regular Army . . . as he may deem necessary"; "to draft into the military service of the United States . . . any or all members of the National Guard and of the National Guard Reserves"; "to raise by draft . . . an additional force of five hundred thousand enlisted men" and to provide the necessary officers and staff; to order "members of the Officers' Reserve Corps to temporary duty"; "to raise and begin the training of an additional five hundred thousand men"; and "to raise and maintain by voluntary enlistment" a force "not to exceed four infantry divisions," among other provisions. While volunteerism fell well short of expectations, the draft succeeded in quickly and efficiently mobilizing a mass army. Yet, once again, the Army struggled to train and field rapidly its vastly expanded force. It took a year for the American Expeditionary Force's first division to reach the front lines, and Army forces often relied heavily on allied French and British forces for supplies, equipment, and training. The Army and the nation had made improvements in the scale and scope of expansion to fight World War I, but the experience of the war demonstrated that problems remained.

Temporarily suppressed by wartime pressures, the professionalist-militia debate flared up again in 1918. The War Department's decision to demobilize Guardsmen as individuals (instead of entire units, although they were mobilized as individuals in accordance with the Selective Service Act) resulted in the disintegration of National Guard units, and in the early years following the end of the war they struggled to rebuild. Demobilized Guardsmen were free to voluntarily rejoin their former units, but many returning Guardsmen, exhausted by war and believing their civic duty fulfilled, lacked enthusiasm for continued military service. Despite the specific language in the Selective Service Act and convinced that the War Department had intentionally demobilized the National Guardsmen as individuals to purposefully weaken the Guard, advocates of the National Guard argued that the war demonstrated the "militia's" effectiveness and revealed the Regular Army's and War Department's unfounded biases. In contrast, professionalists interpreted the wartime experience as a confirmation of the virtues of an appropriately sized Regular Army that oversaw the expansion of a conscripted and mobilized mass army exclusively under federal control.

All sides now applied new vigor to old questions: Should the federal government continue to invest its resources in state National Guard units, or should new legislation bring such reserves completely under federal control? What was the appropriate force ratio between the Regular Army, National Guard, and Organized Reserve? Should the U.S. military establishment be grounded in the Constitution's armies clause or its militia clause to expand the Army in times of war and crisis? Congress considered a variety of answers to these questions. They ranged from anchoring the state Guards to the armies clause to increase federal control, to establishing a new federal reserve force (and presumably returning the state Guards to local duties). Maintenance of the status quo, in which the state Guards would retain their dual status and its association with the militia clause, was also considered.

Predictably, the final legislation was a compromise that left few advocates and stakeholders completely satisfied. Eager for a return to normalcy, Congress had little appetite for a continuance of prewar reforms; the 1920 Army Reorganization Act therefore was incremental. It clarified, but did not fundamentally alter, the 1916 NDA's definition of the Army by folding the various federal reserve entities into an omnibus category now referred to as the Organized Reserve. It upheld the campus Reserve Officers' Training Corps (ROTC) program and addressed the National Guard's central wartime grievance by stipulating that, upon demobilization, federalized Guard units would return to their previous service as state Guard units and not as individuals. Finally, the law reasserted caps on the peacetime personnel strength of the Regular Army and National Guard, each respective cap to be achieved over the course of the following five years.

Despite (or because of) the isolationism of the interwar period, Congress took up military policy reform again in 1932. The next major legislation, the 1933 amendment to the 1916 NDA (referred to at the time as the "National Guard Act"), gave the National Guard legislation that it had been pursuing since 1926. The Guard was allowed to retain its connection to the states via the Constitution's militia clause while, at the same time, enjoying stronger peace and wartime ties to the federal government via the armies clause. The 1933 National Guard Act established the National Guard of the United States as a "reserve component of the army," and differentiated between the National Guard of the states when under the peacetime authority of the states and governors, and the National Guard of the United States. The 1933 amendment also empowered the Chief of Staff of the Army to "exercise the same supervision and control of the reserve components of the Army of the United States as he does over the Regular Army," and for the first time in statute gave the President the authority to order to active duty "any or all units and members thereof of the National Guard of the United States" (i.e., mobilizing units, not just members or individuals). The 1933 act can therefore be seen as the statutory rebirth of the U.S. Army, comprising the Regular Army, the National Guard of the United States, the National Guard while in the service of the United States, the Officers' Reserve Corps, and the Organized Reserve (later to become the U.S. Army Reserve).

When Europe again descended into war, Congress and President Franklin D. Roosevelt took bold and broad measures to prepare the nation. Yet their preparatory measures did not fundamentally alter the policies established between 1908 and 1940 to expand the Army. Both presidential and congressional attention focused on actions to increase available manpower and place the Regular Army and the reserve components on wartime footing. Those measures reflected the strategic context of the time and the major laws governing military policy that were passed during the first three decades of the 20th century.

Acknowledgments

Throughout the project, our sponsor, Timothy Muchmore of the Army Quadrennial Defense Review Office, provided valuable input with drafts and a deep commitment to this history of U.S. military policy, for which we are very thankful and indebted. We also deeply appreciate Mr. Muchmore's respect for the discipline and integrity of our RAND research, method, and writing process. Sally Sleeper, director of the RAND Arroyo Strategy, Doctrine, and Resources Program, provided us with encouragement and sound advice along the way. We are indebted to RAND Arroyo director Tim Bonds for providing additional assistance at a crucial point in the archival research process. RAND's Terrence Kelly was also hugely influential in the earlier stages of the writing of this history. For this specific volume, we are indebted to the three reviews of this report: Brigadier General Lance Betros, U.S. Army, Retired; Robert Citino, senior historian at the National World War II Museum; and Thomas McNaugher, former RAND Arroyo director. We also thank Professor Brian Linn for an additional and most helpful review of this volume, as well as Jerry Cooper, professor emeritus, for his most helpful reviews of portions of all four volumes in this series. For the digital version of all fours volumes, we thank Tim Strabbing, Grace Rebesco, and Michael Bricknell of Rowan Technologies for their hard and most excellent work in producing the digital publication. Many thanks also go to Tamara Elliot of the U.S. Senate Library, who was always there to help in acquiring primary documents and to provide expertise on American legislative history. Anne Armstrong and Ryan Trainor at the National Guard Museum provided the research team with access to a trove of primary evidence. At the Hagley Museum and Library, we appreciate the assistance of Roger Horowitz and Lucas R. Clawson. Gail Kouril and Betsy Hammes, both senior librarians at RAND, provided very helpful assistance and suggestions for the research done on this project. Lastly, we thank RAND's James Torr for his expert editing and Todd Duft, Mark Hvizda, Marcy Agmon, Martha Friese, Jessica Bateman, Yamit Feinberg, Patrice Lester, and Lisa Sodders for shepherding this report through the publication process.

CHAPTER ONE

Introduction

In the previous volume, we examined how, for a variety of reasons, including American political tradition, the nascent American Republic adopted a military policy characterized by a combined inability and reluctance to sustain a large standing professional army and a preference for relying on a combination of a small standing force, volunteers, and state-controlled militias to generate wartime armies. The system evolved over the course of the 19th century in some important ways. By and large, the same policies dictated how the country responded to crises from the rebellions of the 1790s to the Spanish-American War a century later. There were a number of problems associated with those policies, and competing schools of thought regarding how to deal with them would emerge. Yet, ultimately, the policies remained in place—in large part because they were sufficient for the survival of the nation, regardless of their operational inefficiencies or cost.

The more significant problems with the nation's military policies, as well as measures crafted over time in response to them, had to do with the evolution of the militias and the limitations associated with them. There were two basic types of militias during the 18th and 19th centuries, with two separate traditions. The first variety were often referred to as "common" or "compulsory" militias. These, with roots in English culture, consisted of all able-bodied white men of a certain age, whom Americans considered to owe military service to the community in exchange for the rights of citizenship. The common militias were predominant in the small villages of colonial America, which were underpopulated and frequently threatened by Native Americans and the French. Ideologically speaking, 18th century Americans identified militia service with civic virtues and, eventually, republicanism and patriotism, although at the same time many men who had the means avoided militia service by either paying a fine or paying for a substitute.[1] Americans at this time thought militias better fit their fiscal realities, and offered a far better alternative to placing a standing army in the hands of a central power, something they generally regarded as a threat to liberty. The second kind of

---

[1] For a representative illustration of the substitute system in the 18th century, see Arthur J. Alexander, "Service by Substitute in the Militia of Northampton and Lancaster Counties (Pennsylvania) During the War of the Revolution," *Military Affairs*, Vol. 9, No. 3, Autumn 1945, pp. 278–282.

militia was the voluntary militias, which might be thought of as fraternal organizations or clubs consisting of men who, for whatever reasons, enjoyed aspects of the military life and joined together part-time to socialize and drill.

The common/compulsory militias predominated in the 18th century (when the American population was still quite small and geographically distributed) and were what the Founding Fathers had in mind when they wrote the militia clauses of the Constitution. Members of the common militia, by custom and law, could serve for only limited periods of time, and were typically employed close to home. Moreover, the common militias were, especially in the eyes of critics such as George Washington—whom we characterize as belonging to the "professionalist school"—often unreliable. They lacked discipline and tactical skill, owed primary loyalty to their locales, and could not or would not serve for extended periods. Finally, as the population grew, and as the Native American threat moved West, the state-run militias tended to atrophy, which hindered states' abilities to mobilize them when required. Many professionalists wanted to do away with any reliance on the militias during war and assign them to local duties. In the place of state-run militias, professionalists proposed militias or reserves under federal authority that provided trained fillers to bring Regular Army units up to war strength. However, in the face of political resistance, professionalists argued by way of a compromise for a "well-regulated militia," by which they meant militias that met federal standards of readiness and standardization and were subject to federal authority in time of war. Against the professionalists ranged a coalition of militia advocates, who insisted that the militias enjoy pride of place in the nation's military establishment and the honoring of its lineage and traditions. Furthermore, these advocates wanted to ensure that the respective states maintain a strong constitutional link, thereby guaranteeing control of their militias.

Each of the nation's wars of the 19th century exposed the limitations of the militias and the risks associated with relying on them, as well as the drawbacks of a skeletonized army, although it must be stressed that none of the problems proved fatal. The closest real scare was the War of 1812, when the U.S. government struggled to field a force sufficiently large and competent to repel the invasion of the British Army, and during which three states refused to send their militia forces when called by the federal government. The government's reliance on the cooperation of state governments and the inability of common militias to serve in Canada proved to be liabilities. The New England states were slow to comply with federal requests for militia levies, and in some cases militia officers stood on their constitutionally mandated limits and refused to invade Canada. By the time of the Mexican War (1846), volunteer units already had eclipsed the militias, which was a boon to the federal government because volunteers were not confined to the militia's constitutional limitations and were generally employable for longer terms of service. Also, the gradual professionalization of the Regular Army, above all thanks to the creation of West Point, meant that there were more trained officers available to lead Regular and volunteer units alike.

The Civil War proved a different kind of challenge, mainly the need to generate war armies of unprecedented scale. Congress met this challenge through a variety of measures that altered the system without actually breaking or recreating it. Congress managed to build a massive force, largely out of volunteer regiments, but with some conscription. After the war, the military establishment mostly reverted to its antebellum state, but one major difference was that militias of all types were nearly defunct in the war's immediate aftermath. Another difference was that militia service was no longer restricted to "white" males. Roughly a decade later, however, the volunteer militia units, which increasingly referred to themselves as National Guards, began to enjoy new levels of state and even some federal support.

The National Guard Association formed in 1878 to lobby on behalf of the National Guards of the states and to counter the ideas and proposals of the professionalist school. Over the course of the next 60 years, the National Guard Association, which in 1911 would later refine its title to the National Guard Association of the United States (NGAUS), grew in terms of its lobbying impact and overall role in shaping policy. Indeed, as the following chapters will show, the NGAUS would fight stridently to ensure that the interests of the National Guard of the several states were addressed. The NGAUS was able to develop a tight trinity, so to speak, that linked National Guard units, state governors and their National Guard adjutants general, and supportive members of the House and Senate—many of whom were former or active Guardsmen themselves—into a well-oiled and influential political action machine.

As for the professionalists, in the late 1870s they found a thoughtful champion in Brevet Major General Emory Upton, who, informed and inspired by the Prussian model, proposed developing a large federal reserve force to complement an expansible Regular Army, with much reduced reliance on state-controlled militias. His views were largely informed by his experiences in the costly carnage of the Civil War and his professional travels abroad to observe and assess foreign militaries.

Amid these competing perspectives, U.S. military policy remained essentially unchanged after the Civil War, largely because there was no compelling reason to do otherwise—or, perhaps more precisely, none so compelling as to overcome Congress's tight-fistedness and the widespread belief that a militia-centric military policy was adequate to most likely security challenges, which were predominantly domestic. Europe and Asia and their massive wars were a long way away.

As we shall see, the situation finally changed dramatically in the wake of the 1898 Spanish-American War. Yes, the Army and the nation prevailed once again, thereby apparently validating the nation's military policy. However, the war changed forever the nation's security responsibilities and paradigm. Now, rather than hiding behind two oceans, America was a world power with overseas possessions and potentially aggressive neighbors. The war also placed in stark relief the human and material cost of relying on ad hoc mobilization schemes and an anemic Regular Army that had little capacity to plan, deploy, and sustain expeditionary operations involving large military forces abroad. The much-publicized horror of the Army's decimation by disease alone made clear that things would have to change. The time had come to rethink military policy to provide the nation with a force commensurate in size and quality with the demands of the new century. In the first three decades of the 20th century, planners and legislators of both the professionalist and the militia-cum–National Guard schools engaged in a series of debates and negotiations that would ultimately produce a series of laws intended to do just that.

CHAPTER TWO

The Spanish-American War and Early Reform Efforts, 1898–1903

Introduction

In comparison to the major conflicts of the 20th century, the 1898 Spanish-American War was relatively insignificant. Congress declared war in April; in late July, Spain approached the William McKinley administration to discuss peace terms; and by mid August, the two sides had signed a cease-fire. Congressional deliberation of the peace treaty lasted nearly as long as the active fighting, and the Senate ratified the Treaty of Paris on February 6, 1899.

The speed and decisiveness of the U.S. victory concealed the severe strain that the war had placed on the Army and the nation. The military's skeletal bureaucracy was overwhelmed by the flood of volunteers (including National Guardsmen) and the herculean task of organizing them into a fighting force, deploying them to a foreign theater of war, and sustaining them once there. The Army's swift victory in spite of these structural challenges provoked journalist Richard Harding Davis to conclude in his report of the Cuban and Puerto Rican campaigns that "God takes care of drunken men, sailors, and the United States."[1]

The Army's mobilization and organizational challenges continued to affect its performance in the war's second theater, the Philippines. After Spain ceded the islands, the United States, and therefore the Army, took up the task of occupation. The U.S. acquisition and occupation of the Philippine Islands precipitated an insurgency that lasted from 1899 to 1902 and required three rotations of Regular and volunteer troops. Despite the speedy victory over Spain, the United States still faced the problem of mobilizing sufficient manpower to sustain the Army's fight against a protracted Philippine insurgency and, equally important, to garrison permanently the newly acquired territories.

The challenges presented during the occupation spurred a determined reform movement, which was reinforced by the aggressive and brilliant President Theodore Roosevelt who, among others, was a part of a larger reform movement in American

---

[1] Richard Harding Davis, *The Cuban and Puerto Rican Campaigns*, New York: Scribner and Sons, 1898, p. 96.

society and institutions called Progressivism. Beginning as early as 1900, would-be reformers advanced various proposals to address the Army's perceived problems. Their proposals stirred spirited debate that reflected the long-standing competing visions of U.S. military policy. In the end, the debate led to some of the most sweeping reforms in the Army's history and to laws that frame U.S. military policy to this day.

The Messy Victory over Spain

The Spanish-American War was a major turning point in American military history because it thrust America onto the world stage, bringing the United States into possession of new foreign territories that needed to be defended from powerful rivals, as well as to be governed. The war was also a turning point because of what it revealed about the inadequacies of the U.S. military relative to what it now required. Marshaling manpower was assuredly not a problem: On April 22, 1898, Congress passed a mobilization law—largely a copy of the 1863 Enrollment Act—that asked for state volunteer militias, as well as something new: three federal volunteer cavalry regiments. Legislation in early May authorized more volunteers in the form of a brigade of engineers and ten regiments of infantryman capable of withstanding tropical climate.[2] Public enthusiasm for the war was such that a flood of men came forward. The Army took in more volunteers than it needed or could even cope with and yet still turned away upward of three-quarters of applicants. By the end of May 1898, most of the 125,000 from the April 22 call had been mustered into service.[3]

---

[2] U.S. Statutes at Large, An Act to Provide for Temporarily Increasing the Military Establishment of the United States in Time of War, and for Other Purposes, Fifty-Fifth Congress, Session II, Chapter 187, April 22, 1898 (30 Stat. 361); U.S. Statutes at Large, An Act to Provide for a Volunteer Brigade of Engineers and an Additional Force of Ten Thousand Enlisted Men Specially Accustomed to Tropical Climates, Fifty-Fifth Congress, Session II, Chapter 294, May 11, 1898 (30 Stat. 405); Marvin A. Kreidberg and Merton G. Henry, *History of Military Mobilization in the United States Army, 1775–1945*, Washington, D.C.: Department of the Army, 1955, pp. 162–163.

[3] Secretary of War Russell Alger recalled that only 24 hours after the April 22 call, "the nation was aflame. Tenders of service came by the hundreds of thousands. It is safe to say that a million men offered themselves where 125,000 had been called" (Russell Alexander Alger, *The Spanish-American War*, New York: Harper & Brothers Publishers, 1901, p. 7). In his view, the martial enthusiasm was "the apotheosis of patriotism." Newspaper accounts in the weeks after were similarly hyperbolic, but the fact remains that the rush to arms was considerable. "122,120 Volunteers in Service," *New York Times*, May 31, 1898, p. 3; "Anxious to Volunteer," *Washington Post*, May 8, 1898, p. 2; "The Volunteer Army," *Los Angeles Times*, May 22, 1898, p. B4. On the early mobilization of volunteers, see Russell Frank Weigley, *History of the United States Army*, New York: Macmillan, 1967, p. 298; Graham A. Cosmas, *An Army for Empire: The United States Army in the Spanish-American War*, Columbia, Mo.: University of Missouri Press, 1971a, p. 116; Brian McAllister Linn, *The Philippine War, 1899–1902*, Lawrence, Kans.: University Press of Kansas, 2000, p. 11; David F. Trask, *The War with Spain*, Lincoln, Neb.: University of Nebraska Press, 1996, pp. 156–158; Kreidberg and Henry, 1955, p. 158; Richard Melzer and Phyllis Ann Mingus, "Wild to Fight: The New Mexico Rough Riders in the Spanish-American War," *New Mexico Historical Review*, Vol. 59, No. 2, April 1984, pp. 109–136; Gerald F. Linderman, *The Mirror of War: American Society and the Spanish-American War*, Ann Arbor, Mich.: University of Michigan Press, 1974.

Although by most accounts state volunteer militias were in better shape than at any point in history, thanks to the support state and federal governments provided to National Guard units in the last decades of the 19th century, the challenge of turning the force that mustered for the war into an effective, organized fighting army remained massive. The Army, moreover, had not planned for an effort nearly so large. Large numbers of men arrived at hastily prepared camps while the Army scrambled to provide basic equipment and other supplies. Unexpectedly, much of the National Guard units' equipment proved inadequate, forcing the War Department to draw from its own stocks.[4] The entire process of staging forces for deployment was chaotic. The deployment to Cuba and the sustainment effort that followed were a logistical fiasco.[5] Once in Cuba, the American invasion force fought well but at a greater cost in human life than might have been the case had it been more proficient in modern fighting techniques and better led.[6] What happened after the famous victory at Santiago de Cuba was worse: Disease destroyed the invasion force (and also ravaged Army camps back on the mainland), and, as leaked news reports fueled public outrage, the Army scrambled to transport survivors to an unprepared hospital camp then being constructed in Montauk, New York. Thanks to a sensationalist press that often politicized problems, these and other calamities received significant scrutiny that prompted investigations, many of them targeting Secretary of War Russell Alger.[7] The inquisition cleared Alger of wrongdoing (but not incompetence), and he resigned shortly afterward. Such probes did serve to point out what by then had become obvious: The Army and the nation were not prepared for large-scale expeditionary warfare.

---

[4] *Report of the Commission Appointed by the President to Investigate the Conduct of the War Department in the War with Spain*, Washington, D.C.: U.S. Government Printing Office, 1899, pp. 94–95.

[5] On the logistical woes and related problems, see Cosmas, 1971a, pp. 139–294; Kreidberg and Henry, 1955, pp. 171–173; Weigley, 1967, pp. 298–304; Ronald J. Barr, *The Progressive Army: The U.S. Army Command and Administration, 1870–1914*, New York: St. Martin's Press, 1998, pp. 32–41; James A. Huston, *The Sinews of War: Army Logistics, 1775–1953*, Washington, D.C.: United States Army Center of Military History, 1997, pp. 273–291.

[6] In total, the Army lost 243 killed in action and 1,445 wounded in operations in eastern Cuba. Cosmas, 1971a, p. 230. For descriptions of the major engagements in Cuba, see Trask, 1996, pp. 194–335; Graham A. Cosmas "San Juan Hill and El Caney, 1–2 July 1898," in C. E. Heller and W. A. Stofft, *America's First Battles, 1776–1965*, Lawrence, Kans.: University Press of Kansas, 1981; Peter S. Kindvatter, "Santiago Campaign of 1898: Joint and Combined Operations," *Military Review*, Vol. 73, No. 2, 1993, pp. 3–14; Jack Cameron Dierks, *A Leap to Arms: The Cuban Campaign of 1898*, Philadelphia, Pa.: J. B. Lippincott, 1970.

[7] Cosmas, 1971a, pp. 286–294; Weigley, 1967, p. 305. For a thorough analysis of sickness and disease during the war, see Vincent J. Cirillo, *Bullets and Bacilli: The Spanish-American War and Military Medicine*, New Brunswick, N.J.: Rutgers University Press, 2004.

The U.S. Army in the Philippines

The Philippines campaign deserves particular attention because, in addition to the problems revealed in the Cuban theater, the conquest and occupation of the Philippines created entirely new challenges. More to the point, the Philippine war witnessed an entirely different wartime manpower organization—the U.S. Volunteers—outside both the "professionalist" and the National Guard agendas. Events during the initial deployment mirrored those of the Cuban expedition. Indeed, looking back on his experience of commanding the first U.S. Army expeditionary force to fight the budding Filipino insurgency, Brigadier General Thomas Anderson suggested that the Army's lack of prewar planning and preparation led to "tardiness in mobilization" of Regular and volunteer troops for service in the Philippines.[8]

The first expedition departed on May 25, 1898, but lacked much of the equipment and many of the troops envisioned by War Department planners. Anderson recalled that his expedition, which consisted of five companies of Regulars and two regiments of militia volunteers (i.e., National Guardsmen who had volunteered for federal service as individuals to circumvent constitutional restrictions on militia service abroad), sailed for the Philippines without a single field gun, horse, mule, wagon, or cart. Moreover, the militia volunteer regiments had arrived understaffed, and several units were sent home to recruit more men. As a result, thousands of minimally trained and unequipped recruits waited in large depots in and around San Francisco before their eventual deployment.[9]

By July 29, 1898, seven convoys had sailed from San Francisco for Manila. This included a July 15 convoy that took the first group of replacements for units already conducting military operations in the Philippines. By month's end, 13,000 volunteers and 2,000 Regular troops, organized as the VIII Corps, had reached the islands.[10] When the U.S. Army attacked Manila on August 13, its forces consisted of four companies of Regular artillery, three volunteer artillery units, parts of three Regular infantry regiments, and portions of eight National Guard infantry regiments.[11]

---

[8] Thomas M. Anderson, "Nationalization of the State Guards," *Forum*, Vol. 30, 1901, pp. 655–656.

[9] Leonard L. Lerwill, *The Personnel Replacement System in the United States Army*, Washington, D.C.: U.S. Department of the Army, 1954; Linn, 2000, p. 12; David J. Silbey, *A War of Frontier and Empire: The Philippine-American War, 1899–1902*, New York: Hill & Wang, 2007, pp. 42–43; Kreidberg and Henry, 1955, pp. 153–161.

[10] Richard W. Stewart, *American Military History*, Vol. I: *The United States Army and the Forging of a Nation, 1775–1917*, Washington, D.C.: U.S. Government Printing Office, 2005, p. 354.

[11] Francis V. Greene, "The Capture of Manila," *Century Illustrated Monthly*, No. 57, 1898–1899, pp. 785–791, 915–936. For a detailed description by an embedded journalist of the expeditionary force from first muster in the United States until shortly after the Battle of Manila, see Francis Davis Millet, *The Expedition to the Philippines*, New York: Harber & Brothers, 1899.

As the need for additional men in the Philippines continued, President McKinley authorized the organization of supplemental volunteer regiments.[12] Unlike the militia units (or the special volunteer regiments, such as the Roughriders formed in 1898 in the territories and not in states), these regiments were mustered in the states and led by officers appointed by the President, not state governors. As a means to fill the new units, the Army established recruiting stations at all demobilization camps. For those interested, returning soldiers could discharge from volunteer units and then immediately reenlist in the newly formed federal regiments for their return to the Philippines.[13]

The U.S. Volunteers, as they were formally named, were recruited, trained, and deployed in roughly four months, thus showing many Regular Army officers at the time that an effective (non–National Guard) citizen force could be quickly mobilized. At 35,000 troops, the U.S. Volunteers were the largest component in the Philippines between fall 1899 and spring 1901 and were largely responsible for the effective regional counterinsurgency campaigns. Many Regular Army officers concluded they were better than those who were then enlisting in the Regulars. Thus, these U.S. Volunteer regiments not only provided a prototype organization that was, if not better than, then certainly equal to the National Guard, but also better than the Regular Army after it had been decimated by disease in Cuba. As a result, the U.S. Volunteers certainly inspired among many Regular Army officers much of the interest in citizen-soldier reserve organizations.

While these U.S. Volunteer regiments were forming for duty in the Philippines, President McKinley, who had fought in the Civil War as an officer in an Ohio volunteer regiment, broke with the senior Army leadership's insistence that U.S. Volunteer regiments be led by old Civil War veterans. They would be commanded instead by the best senior company-grade officers as colonels and lieutenant colonels and even some senior Regular Army noncommissioned officers as company officers, and a sprinkling of recent U.S. Military Academy graduates. It was a unique case of promotion by merit. The great majority of U.S. Volunteer companies, therefore, were led by either graduates of military schools, former Regular Army enlisted, or Regular Army officers. Militia units that volunteered en masse were led by their own National Guard officers. The speed and general excellence of these company officers indicated the potential for commissioning large numbers of officers in a citizen-soldier mass army

---

[12] The legislation calling for volunteers in 1898 was a compromise between advocates and opponents of the National Guard. Cosmas describes the act passed on April 22 as creating a volunteer army organized and offered by the states and made up mostly of National Guard regiments. However, additional legislation in mid-May authorized the enlistment of some 20,000 U.S. volunteers, to be organized and officered by the federal government. Graham A. Cosmas, "Military Reform After the Spanish-American War: The Army Reorganization Fight of 1898–99," *Military Affairs*, Vol. 35, No. 1, 1971b, p. 13.

[13] Lerwill, 1954, p. 153; Linn, 2000, pp. 9–12; Kreidberg and Henry, 1955, p. 162; Robert D. Ramsey III, *Savage Wars of Peace: Case Studies of Pacification in the Philippines, 1900–1902*, The Long War Series, Fort Leavenworth, Kans.: Combat Studies Institute Press, 2007, p. 19.

The Philippine War demonstrated at least two important aspects concerning the marshaling of U.S. manpower for conflict. First, it showed that the United States could rapidly create an effective volunteer military force that did not require significant National Guard participation. Accordingly, the success of these U.S. volunteer regiments served as a warning to the National Guard that it could be replaced. This likely produced a willingness by proponents of the National Guard to work on upcoming important legislation that would be passed in 1903, as we discuss further below. Second, the ease with which Congress accepted a system utilizing the U.S. Volunteers demonstrated that, at the turn of the century, there was no clear recognition of a militia-army "traditional military policy" to provide wartime manpower. An all-volunteer federal reserve/combatant force was widely acknowledged as a viable approach to this problem.

But the system was far from perfect. Of note, only the 35th and 36th U.S. Volunteer Infantry Regiments and the 11th U.S. Volunteer Cavalry Regiment were formed in the Philippines, and none were able to recruit sufficient Filipino veterans—they were filled out with stateside replacements. All the other Volunteer regiments were raised in the continental United States. The haphazard mobilization process and disorganized replacement system, combined with a lack of training and equipment, undermined the Army's operational effectiveness in the first months of fighting in the Philippines. Anderson underscored this point when he attributed his success in Manila to the faintheartedness of the Filipino attackers rather than the effectiveness of the U.S. mobilization effort, which he characterized as "too slow for either offensive or defensive war against a first-class power."[14] Anderson's appraisal echoes the general assessment of the U.S. experience against Spain in 1898 and the Philippine insurgency that followed.

Although the United States had mobilized an effective, albeit relatively small Army, despite its reliance on 19th century expansion methods, the experience was a wake-up call for reformers in the War Department and Congress. Proponents of the Regular Army and National Guard had clashed over the size, composition, and control of national volunteer forces, but the war's aftermath forced both to focus their attention on the underlying challenge: the intrinsic difficulty of an Army expansion policy reliant upon the states to form trained, equipped, and ready volunteer units.

Postwar Debates and the Replacement of the 1792 Militia Act

"The Spanish War was perhaps a good thing for the country," noted a veteran to students at the Command and General Staff College at Fort Leavenworth a decade later. "From that time we began to have a real military policy," he believed, and that meant the nation would "never again be in such a miserable state of military

---

[14] Anderson, 1901, pp. 655–656.

unpreparedness."¹⁵ In fact, an effective military policy would be many more years in the making. The mobilization issues of 1898 were a symptom rather than a cause of the structural problems plaguing the Army. Observers credited the war for generating debate over the neglected issue of wartime expansion, a concern that increased in salience as the country assumed the mantle of an imperial power.¹⁶ The United States had not substantially revised its military policy since the 1792 Militia Act,¹⁷ and serious questions about the organization, size, and purpose of the Army now became pressing. In particular, reformers were preoccupied with the problem of defining the Army's peacetime composition and developing efficient methods for mobilization and force expansion in times of war.

One of the central points in this debate, the Efficiency in Militia Act of 1903 (aka the Dick Act),¹⁸ was the first of many statutory efforts to revise the outdated 1792 Militia Act, which had been the only federal statute up to 1903 that governed the militias. As we shall see, the Dick Act was a landmark law. It established the National Guard in federal law as the "organized militia." Still at issue, however, was the Army's precise composition and how, if at all, organized militias might fit into it.

By the turn of the century, two schools of thought had emerged. The first was the professionalist school. Composed primarily of Regular Army officers and War Department officials, the professionalists were motivated in particular by the writings of Upton, a decorated former officer and noted military thinker. The professionalists called for utilizing the militia for local duties, but not to expand the Army. Rather than utilize National Guard units to fill fighting ranks when needed, proponents of federal control called for the creation of a large pool of federal reserve volunteers under the armies clause of the Constitution. By using this clause, instead of the militia clause, volunteers would be trained by the Regular Army and, in case of war, could be called on to fill its ranks.

In contrast, the militia school of thought acknowledged some of the greater faults cited by the professionalists, but defended the National Guard's structure as a politically viable option and a tool for building local public support. Members of this school viewed the National Guard as a key part of the Army's expansion in war and crisis,

---

[15] Hanson E. Ely, "The Military Policy of the United States," *Journal of the Military Service Institution of the United States*, Vol. 40, 1907, p. 384.

[16] For instance, Brigadier General William H. Carter, a Spanish War veteran and future adviser to Secretary of War Elihu Root, would note two decades after the war: "No one dreamed that a war with Spain would sever the last of her overseas possessions and reopen the whole subject of army reform at the same time, but such was the result, for public opinion was aroused over our shortcomings to a degree that victory could not assuage and still." William H. Carter, "Army Reformers," *The North American Review*, Vol. 208, No. 755, 1918, p. 552.

[17] U.S. Statutes at Large, An Act to More Effectually to Provide for the National Defense by Establishing a Uniform Militia Throughout the United States, Second Congress, Session I, Chapter 33, May 8, 1792 (1 Stat. 271).

[18] U.S. Statutes at Large, An Act to Promote the Efficiency of the Militia, and for Other Purposes, Fifty-Seventh Congress, Session II, Chapter 196, January 21, 1903 (32 Stat. 775).

and envisioned that it would receive substantial federal funding, since state expenditures had generally been somewhat unpredictable. They did not, however, envision the Guard's role as *only* to serve as a federal reserve. Instead, they proposed that the National Guard serve two political masters: state governors and the President of the United States. In this arrangement, the Guard would be governed by both the armies and militia clauses.[19]

At the turn of the century, strident debates on military policy appeared in professional journals and popular magazines.[20] One popular source was the *Journal of the Military Service Institution of the United States* (*JMSI*), the mouthpiece of an organization by the same name founded in New York City in 1878. This voluntary institution consisted originally of Regular Army officers, but it later extended membership to National Guard officers. Most of its members had witnessed firsthand in recent years the profound transformation in the American military profession and the art of war.[21] Reflecting its members' experience, the institution sought to contribute to the flourishing debate over modern warfare. As the *New York Times* described in coverage of the institution's inaugural meeting, the institution espoused the advancement of military science and sought to produce "professional unity and improvement by correspondence, discussion and the reading and publication of papers, the ultimate establishment of a military library and museum, and generally the promotion of the military interest of the United States."[22]

---

[19] For an elaboration on these perspectives from the viewpoint of the National Guard, see the still useful Frederick P. Todd, "Our National Guard: An Introduction to Its History," *Military Affairs*, Vol. 5, No. 3, 1941.

[20] This proliferation of writing would continue for the early part of the 20th century. Lance Betros offers great detail on this phenomenon as it relates to civil-military relations: Lance Betros, "Officer Professionalism in the Late Progressive Era," in Lloyd J. Matthews, ed., *The Future of the Army Profession*, New York: McGraw-Hill Primis Custom Publishing, 2002, pp. 271–290.

[21] On the history of this transformation, see Brian McAllister Linn, *Guardians of Empire: The U.S. Army and the Pacific, 1902–1940*, Chapel Hill, N.C.: University of North Carolina Press, 1997; Edward M. Coffman, *The Regulars: The American Army, 1898–1941*, Cambridge, Mass.: Belknap Press of Harvard University Press, 2004; Walter E. Kretchik, *U.S. Army Doctrine: From the American Revolution to the War on Terror*, Lawrence, Kans.: University Press of Kansas, 2011, pp. 104–124; Michael R. Matheny, *Carrying the War to the Enemy: American Operational Art to 1945*, Norman, Okla.: University of Oklahoma Press, 2011, pp. 17–44; Jason Patrick Clark, *The Many Faces of Reform: Military Progressivism in the U.S. Army, 1866–1916*, PhD dissertation, Durham, N.C.: Duke University, 2009, pp. 116–349; Michael A. Bonura, *Under the Shadow of Napoleon: French Influence on the American Way of Warfare from the War of 1812 to the Outbreak of WWII*, New York: New York University Press, 2012, pp. 173–212; Brian McAllister Linn, *The Echo of Battle: The Army's Way of War*, Cambridge, Mass.: Harvard University Press, 2007. For studies beyond the U.S. Army, see Manfred F. Boemeke, Roger Chickering, and Stig Förster, eds., *Anticipating Total War: The German and American Experiences, 1871–1914*, Cambridge, UK: Cambridge University Press, 1999; Isabel V. Hull, *Absolute Destruction: Military Culture and the Practices of War in Imperial Germany*, Ithaca, N.Y.: Cornell University Press, 2004; Holger H. Herwig, "The Battlefleet Revolution, 1885–1914," in MacGregor Knox and Williamson Murray, eds., *The Dynamics of Military Revolution, 1300–2050*, Cambridge, UK: Cambridge University Press, 2001, pp. 132–153.

[22] "Army Officers Uniting," *New York Times*, September 29, 1878, p. 5.

The opinions expressed in the pages of the *JMSI* exposed the gap between existing legislation and the new challenges the Army faced as it entered the 20th century.[23] With the signing of the 1898 armistice, the United States assumed new political and security commitments in Cuba, Puerto Rico, and the Philippines. The burden fell heavily on the Army. The service had enjoyed a wartime high of 210,000 men in 1898; however, the enlistment period for the temporary forces in the Philippines was winding down. War Department leadership was concerned about the prospect of a customary postwar drawdown of the Regular Army despite the country's new colonial responsibilities. Convinced that such duty required a permanent military expansion, Congress passed the February 1901 Army Reorganization Act, which specified that "the total enlisted force of the line of the Army, together with such native [Filipino] organizations shall not exceed at any one time one hundred thousand." This was a marked increase from the prewar level of 25,000 enlisted men.[24]

In this context, military thinkers picked up an ongoing debate. *JSMI*'s contributors had heatedly discussed the question of what to do with the National Guard for half a decade. An exchange between First Lieutenant W. E. Birkhimer, recently the judge advocate for the Department of Columbia, and Colonel James M. Rice, an Illinois National Guardsman, illustrates this debate.[25] Writing in 1896, Colonel Rice and Lieutenant Birkhimer argued the affirmative and negative, respectively, on the proposition of "whether or not the National Government can safely trust to State militia, temporarily called into the service of the United States, for general war purposes." Colonel

---

[23] For secondary sources covering these same themes, see James L. Abrahamson, *American Arms for a New Century: The Making of a Great Military Power*, New York: The Free Press, 1981; Cosmas, 1971a, pp. 297–327; Jerry Cooper, *The Rise of the National Guard: The Evolution of the American Militia, 1865–1920*, Lincoln, Neb.: University of Nebraska Press, 1997, pp. 106–127; Daniel R. Beaver, *Modernizing the American War Department: Change and Continuity in a Turbulent Era, 1885–1920*, Kent, Ohio: Kent State University Press, 2006, pp. 56–76.

[24] Public Law 66-242, An Act to Amend an Act Entitled "An Act for Making Further and More Effectual Provision for the National Defense, and for Other Purposes," June 4, 1920; Weigley, 1967, p. 317; Jason Patrick Clark, *Preparing for War: The Emergence of the Modern U.S. Army, 1815–1917*, Cambridge, Mass.: Harvard University Press, 2017, pp. 187–188. For enlistment end strength in the U.S. Army, see Francis B. Heitman, *Historical Register and Dictionary of the United States Army*, Vol. 2, Washington, D.C.: Government Printing Office, 1903, p. 626.

[25] Birkhimer led a remarkable professional career. He joined the Army at age 16 during the Civil War, graduated from West Point in 1870, and was commissioned as a Regular Army artillery officer. He earned a law degree in 1889 and would go on to receive the Medal of Honor for service in the Philippines in 1899, ending his career in 1906 as a brigadier general. An accomplished writer, his volume on the history of artillery in the U.S. Army was the authoritative work on the subject for over a century, and his book, *Military Government and Martial Law*, was equally impactful. (See Janice E. McKenney, *The Organizational History of Field Artillery, 1775–2003*, Washington, D.C.: United States Army Center of Military History, 2007, p. ix; Walter M. Hudson, *Army Diplomacy: American Military Occupation and Foreign Policy After World War II*, Lexington, Ky.: University Press of Kentucky, 2015, pp. 32–33; James H. Willbanks, ed., *America's Heroes: Medal of Honor Recipients from the Civil War to Afghanistan*, Santa Barbara, Calif.: ABC-CLIO, 2011, pp. 22–23. James W. Rice, "The Present Congress and the National Guard," *Journal of the Military Service Institution of the United States*, Vol. 19, 1896, pp. 452–479; William E. Birkhimer, "Congress and the National Guard," *Journal of the Military Service Institution of the United States*, Vol. 20, 1897, pp. 213–214.

Rice maintained that the Guard, if "rightly fostered and improved," could function as an "efficient and economical force to be used for almost any purpose at any place where a force may be needed by either the state or the nation."[26] Lieutenant Birkhimer, however, pointing to historical experience, suggested that one reason the state militias were regarded as an unreliable wartime force was political. A "governor, who is undeniably Commander-in-chief of the militia of his own State," he wrote, "may not respond promptly to the call of the President." This introduced the possibility, Birkhimer cautioned, that the United States might be "turned over bound hand and foot in the hour of peril and trial to such governors."[27]

Birkhimer's argument echoed a popular line of reasoning among some military thinkers at the turn of the century. Recalling the War of 1812, when the governors of Connecticut, Massachusetts, and Rhode Island declined to provide requested forces for federal use, as well as the immense casualties suffered in the Civil War, many professionalists expressed concern that state governors might not support a presidential directive to call forth the militias. Failure to do so would undermine the President's authority and potentially weaken national defenses. This concern emerged again in a January 1898 essay by First Lieutenant Stephen M. Foote of the 4th Artillery, which was awarded first place in the Military Service Institute's annual essay competition. In response to the institute's solicitation of proposals for raising, organizing, training, and mobilizing volunteer armies for future wars, Foote proposed a national system of raising volunteers according to congressional districts. He rejected the state militias as a federal force on four grounds: (1) that the militias were recognized for the explicit purposes of suppressing insurrections, repelling invasions, and executing the laws of the Union; (2) that the states, not the federal government, reserved the right to appoint militia officers; (3) that the "militia has been tried in three great wars and had been proved in every case a disastrous failure"; and (4) that governors might not obey federal requisitions.[28] Here again, the potential problem of state obstructionism was presented as justification for an alternative to the National Guards as a source for Army expansion in wartime.

Foote's essay reflected the professionalist perspective common among many Regular Army officers at the time.[29] To their thinking, the organized militias constituted an emergency force that could provide time for the United States to raise an effective force of federally trained volunteers.[30] This view mirrored Regular Army officers' skep-

---

[26] Rice, 1896, p. 453.

[27] Birkhimer, 1897, pp. 213–214.

[28] Stephen M. Foote, "Based on Present Conditions and Past Experience, How Should Our Volunteer Armies Fight?" *Journal of the Military Service Institution of the United States*, Vol. 22, 1898, pp. 1–49.

[29] Linn, 2007, pp. 118–119; Weigley, 1962, pp. 144–150.

[30] Barry M. Stentiford, *The American Home Guard: The State Militia in the Twentieth Century*, College Station, Tex.: Texas A&M University Press, 2002, p. 10.

ticism of National Guard loyalties and effectiveness. "It is with a laudable purpose . . . that the militia has taken the name 'National,'" Foote wrote:

> It is a much higher sounding title and expresses an aspiration to be something more than simple militias or State guards. The danger is that many people may imagine that the so-called "National" guard is in fact what it is in name only, and that we might depend upon it to carry on a war. Our past experiences . . . show that we cannot do so.[31]

This skepticism undergirded the intellectual debate over the organized militias' status in military policy. In an essay that took the argument a step further, Lieutenant Colonel Walter S. Frazier, Jr., the assistant adjutant general of the Illinois National Guard, analyzed the legal foundations of the National Guard itself, an organization he saw as a rarity among "civilized" nations.[32] Frazier questioned the National Guard's authority to serve as part of a federal force. His logic was straightforward: Because the Militia Act of 1792 was still in place, and because it defined the militia as consisting of all able-bodied male citizens between the ages of 18 and 45, and because it required the states to enroll eligible men into militias, "a fair interpretation would seem to be that a man is not a member of the militia until so enrolled." However, since states had ceased enrolling able-bodied male citizens—in violation of the law, as Frazier pointed out—then no truly *national* militia existed.[33]

As a solution, Frazier proposed that Congress recognize the National Guard as an "organized militia."[34] He called on it to create federally sanctioned state militias (potentially known as National Guards of the several states) and, in so doing, "creat[e] a distinction between the organized militia and the unorganized militia," thereby distinguishing between the mass of American white males who were, according to the 1792 Militia Act, all in the militia. In addition, Frazier urged Congress to mandate that states organize, equip, and maintain the new force.[35] In this new model, the Guard would be a partner with—not subordinate to—the Regular Army, and its arms and equipment would be standardized. Frazier's proposal thus marked an early expression

---

[31] Foote, 1898, p. 18.

[32] Walter S. Frazier, Jr., "The National Guard National in Name Only," *Journal of the Military Service Institution of the United States*, Vol. 20, 1897a, p. 519.

[33] Frazier, 1897a, p. 519.

[34] As discussed in Volume I and in Appendix C of this volume, *organized militia* refers to militias formed under the Constitution's Article 1, Section 8, militia clause. After the 1903 Dick Act, the term became equated with the National Guard. During these turn-of-the-century debates, however, the phrase was used to distinguish the new "organized" National Guard units from the "unorganized" militia units of the 18th and 19th centuries, which had been organized on an ad hoc basis in response to specific emergencies and through volunteer recruitment or compulsory service. The term *unorganized* could also refer to the men who were eligible for militia duty under the Constitution's militia clause but were not yet "organized" into units.

[35] Frazier, 1897a, p. 519.

of the notion of "dual obligation" service, ensconced in federal law, in which Guardsmen pledged allegiance to both the United States and their respective home states. Such a law would provide the Guard its desired federal recognition, while addressing the Regular Army's demand that the Guard's organizational structure be standardized to match federal structures.

The response to Frazier in the journal's pages was swift and spirited. The assistant adjutant general of the Iowa National Guard began a back-and-forth debate with Frazier when he highlighted that his state's military code bound them to serve the United States.[36] The argument was valid, as some, albeit far from most, state militia codes aligned with the spirit of the 1792 law. These reactions missed Frazier's larger point, however, that the state National Guards—irrespective of individual state military codes—did not constitute militias in strict accordance with the national law, since they did not comprise all able-bodied males between certain ages as defined in the 1792 Militia Act. That the states proclaimed their Guard units were obligated to serve the country when called did not establish a statutory requirement to do so.

Influenced by the responses to Frazier's and Foote's articles, the Military Service Institute posed a related question for its 1900 essay contest topic: "In what way can the national guard be modified so as to make it an effective reserve to the regular army in both war and peace?" The prize went to Edward E. Britton, a colonel in the New York National Guard, who argued that any plans for militia reorganization had to acknowledge that the state National Guard system was unlikely to go away. Britton noted differences in the quality of Guard forces among the various states, but cautioned that the creation of an entirely new force, "such as a National reserve, etc., would cause disturbance between the two bodies and would probably neutralize the efforts of each other."[37] Rather, he suggested using the existing National Guard as the basis for reorganization. To resolve lingering legal debates, Britton called for new federal legislation that would replace the 1792 act and codify an active militia, to be known as the Volunteer Militia of the United States and composed of the organized and uniformed

---

[36] He explained that Iowan Military Code explicitly stipulated that its National Guard members must obey requisition orders by the President, and that "the Governor as Commander-in-chief, by his proclamation *shall order out* for service the *active militia* or *national guard of the State*" (Lieutenant Colonel C. W. King, "The National Guard, National in Name Only," *Journal of the Military Service Institution of the United States*, Vol. 21, 1897a, p. 210; emphasis in original). For the debate between the two assistant adjutant generals, see King, 1897a; Lieutenant Colonel Walter S. Frazier, Jr., "The National Guard National in Name Only," *Journal of the Military Service Institution of the United States*, Vol. 21, 1897b, pp. 419–420; and Lieutenant Colonel C. W. King, "'The National Guard National in Name Only'—A Reply," *Journal of the Military Service Institution of the United States*, Vol. 21, 1897b, pp. 629–630.

[37] Edward E. Britton, "In What Way Can the National Guard Be Modified So as to Make It an Effective Reserve to the Regular Army in Both War and Peace?" *Journal of the Military Service Institution of the United States*, Vol. 26, 1900, p. 165.

military forces of the different States, and a reserve militia that would consist of all those aged 18–45 liable but not yet serving in the active militia.[38]

By the start of the 20th century, military reformers in both the Regular Army and the National Guard recognized that the 1792 act was obsolete. Agreement over how to fix the problem was, however, far from clear. The War Department and Regular Army opposed sole reliance on state militia units to expand the Army in times of war. Meanwhile, the National Guard sought formal recognition as part of the federal military system, a solution that would require the Guard to professionalize apace with the Regular Army. Thus, by 1900 a consensus emerged that a quality gap divided the federal Army and the state militias. At issue, however, was whether this difference could—or should—be bridged.

While the proponents of the Regular Army and National Guard debated these issues, Congress's intentions were unclear. Would Congress, with guidance from military professionals, develop a new plan to meet the country's evolving security needs? Could it balance the concerns of the Regular Army with the demands of the state National Guards? If Congress legislated a solution, how would the Regular Army and the state National Guards coordinate state units that had, due to a lack of federal oversight, effectively formed some 40 separate armies, led by politically connected officers who often lacked equal military skill or training?[39] Brigadier General William H. Carter, a Regular Army officer, summed up the challenge in 1903: "Under the most favorable legislation it will require a long time to perfect the details of the system which is intended to put the organized militia on a footing of preparedness for immediate and efficient service at the outbreak of war."[40]

Elihu Root and the 1903 Dick Act

Between 1903 and 1940, Congress enacted a series of laws aimed at overhauling U.S. military policy and clarifying the relationship between the Regular Army and the state National Guards. Spearheading the reforms in the immediate aftermath of the Spanish-American War was Alger's replacement at the head of the War Department, Elihu Root, whom President McKinley appointed in 1899. The selection reflected Root's sterling reputation as a corporate lawyer with the type of legal and administrative expertise that would be required in the governing of America's newly acquired overseas

---

[38] Britton, 1900, pp. 167–168.

[39] Russell Frank Weigley, *Towards an American Army: Military Thought from Washington to Marshall*, New York: Columbia University Press, 1962, p. 147.

[40] William H. Carter, "The Organized Militia: Its Past and Future," *The United Service*, Vol. 3, No. 3, 1903.

territories.⁴¹ The appointment was not without controversy. Future president Theodore Roosevelt—who would later choose to retain Root as his Secretary of War—mocked McKinley's choice of a lawyer, rather than a career military officer, as "simply foolish" and proposed his former colleague from the Cuban Campaign, General Francis Vinton Greene instead.⁴² Roosevelt did not sway the resolute McKinley, but his opposition reflected the opinion of those who, at least initially, viewed Root with suspicion.⁴³

Root swiftly assuaged fears about a "lawman" running the War Department. As secretary, he recruited knowledgeable and experienced advisers for his staff, including Brigadier General Carter, a staunch reformist who had fought in the Spanish-American War and who quickly emerged as Root's most trusted confidant.⁴⁴ With Carter's assistance, Root reorganized the department and lobbied Congress to authorize the creation of a general staff to support necessary contingency planning, conduct long-term planning, and direct Army modernization. The February 14, 1903, "Act to Increase the Efficiency of the Army" (commonly referred to as the General Staff Act) replaced the Army's commanding general with a chief of staff who supervised the 45-member General Staff Corps and "all troops of the line and of the Adjutant-General's, Inspector-General's, Judge-Advocate's, Quartermaster's, Subsistence, Medical, Pay, and Ordnance departments, the Corps of Engineers, and the Signal Corps."⁴⁵

Root and Carter shared similar reformist impulses that reflected many aspects of the professionalist school. They feared that the nation's military policy was incompatible with the country's growing international role, and they sought to modernize

---

⁴¹ Root served as Secretary of War from 1899 to 1905 under both the McKinley and Roosevelt administrations. In 1905, he was appointed Secretary of State, and, for his work in that office and later as a senator from New York, he was awarded the Nobel Peace Prize in 1912. Phillip Jessup, *Elihu Root*, Vol. 1, New York: Dodd Mead, 1938, p. 217; Louis Cantor, *The Creation of the Modern National Guard: The Dick Militia Act of 1903*, PhD dissertation, Durham, N.C.: Duke University, 1963, p. 128; Weigley, 1967, p. 314; Barr, 1998 pp. 49–50; Michael D. Doubler, *I Am the Guard: A History of the Army National Guard, 1636–2000*, Washington, D.C.: Army National Guard, 2001, p. 122.

⁴² Jessup, 1938, p. 217.

⁴³ Jessup, 1938, pp. 219–223.

⁴⁴ Russell Frank Weigley, "The Elihu Root Reforms and the Progressive Era," paper presented at Command and Commanders in Modern Warfare: The Proceedings of the Second Military History Symposium, U.S. Air Force Academy, 2–3 May 1968, Office of Air Force History and U.S. Air Force Academy, 1971, p. 17; Barr, 1998, p. 51. For an excellent biography of Carter, see Ronald G. Machoian, *William Harding Carter and the American Army: A Soldier's Story*, Norman, Okla.: University of Oklahoma Press, 2006.

⁴⁵ U.S. Statutes at Large, "An Act to Increase the Efficiency of the Army," Fifty-Seventh Congress, Session II, Chapter 553, February 14, 1903 (32 Stat. 830); Weigley, 1971, pp. 18–19; Paul Y. Hammond, *Organizing for Defense: The American Military Establishment in the Twentieth Century*, Princeton, N.J.: Princeton University Press, 1961, pp. 12–25; James E. Hewes, Jr., *From Root to McNamara: Army Organization and Administration, 1900–1963*, Washington, D.C.: U.S. Army Center of Military History, 1975, pp. 6–12; Samuel P. Huntington, *The Soldier and the State: The Theory and Politics of Civil-Military Relations*, Cambridge, Mass.: Harvard University Press, 1985, p. 251; Philip L. Semsch, "Elihu Root and the General Staff," *Military Affairs*, Vol. 27, No. 1, 1963, p. 18; Weigley, 1967, p. 315.

the Army and military institutions to keep pace with industrialization and the United States as an emerging global power. In search of a framework to guide his proposals, among other sources of inspiration, Root seized upon the work of Upton, whose pragmatic, history-based approach he respected. Root considered Upton's book *The Military Policy of the United States* to be his "chief reliance," and while in the War Department helped to publish one of two existing versions of the manuscript.[46] Root circulated Upton's writing widely and later credited it with giving him "the detail on which I could base recommendations and overcome my ignorance as a civilian."[47] While Root dedicated his tenure as Secretary of War to securing reforms similar to those envisioned by Upton, he was not simply a proxy of the deceased theorist. To be sure, the secretary's final agenda was of his own design.[48]

Root recognized that militia reform would be a critical step in building a more powerful and reliable Army. To this end, he revived proposals first circulated by other professionalists over a century earlier, such as George Washington, Henry Knox, and Friedrich Wilhelm von Steuben, who after the Revolutionary War sought to standardize training requirements across the state militias.[49] Two obstacles quickly emerged. First, Root recognized that Guardsmen's part-time status required that training programs be sufficiently flexible to accommodate civilian work rhythms and limitations. Not surprisingly, Guardsmen would not support proposals that might jeopardize their civilian employment. Second, Root wanted methods to compel states to build and maintain high-quality militia outfits, which would require substantial increases in federal funding.[50]

---

[46] Quoted in Benjamin Franklin Cooling, "The Missing Chapters of Emory Upton: A Note," *Military Affairs*, Vol. 37, No. 1, 1973; Emory Upton, *The Military Policy of the United States*, 4th ed., Washington, D.C.: U.S. Government Printing Office, 1903.

[47] Jessup, 1938, pp. 242–243.

[48] Elihu Root, *The Military and Colonial Policy of the United States: Addresses and Reports*, Cambridge, Mass.: Harvard University Press, 1916, p. 125; David Fitzpatrick, *Emory Upton: Misunderstood Reformer*, Norman, Okla.: University of Oklahoma Press, 2017, pp. 245–246; Stephen E. Ambrose, *Upton and the Army*, Baton Rouge: La: Louisiana University Press, 1992, pp. 155–156.

[49] *War Department Annual Reports, 1917: Reports of the Secretary of War*, Washington, D.C., United States Congress, U.S. Government Printing Office, 1918, p. 847. Note that some states did have training requirements during this time. Interstate National Guard Association, *Proceedings of the Third Annual Convention*, Washington, D.C.: National Guard Association of the United States Museum, 1900, p. 180; Interstate National Guard Association, *Proceedings of the Fifth Annual Convention*, Washington, D.C.: National Guard Association of the United States Museum, 1903, p. 317; National Guard Association of the United States, *Proceedings of the Convention of National Guards 1st & 3rd Conventions*, St. Louis, Mo.: John J. Daly & Company, 1879–1881.

[50] With the help of Root, congressional funding for the National Guard increased beginning in 1900 when appropriations went from $400,000 to $1,000,000. Jerry Cooper, *The Militia and National Guard in America Since Colonial Times: A Reference Guide*, Westport, Conn.: Greenwood Press, 1993, p. 99; Elbridge Colby, "Elihu Root and the National Guard," *Military Affairs*, Vol. 23, No. 1, Spring 1959, p. 29.

In 1903, Congress codified Root's proposals in a law titled "An Act to Promote the Efficiency of the Militia, and for Other Purposes," often referred to as the Military Act of 1903 or the Dick Act, after one its proponents, Congressman Charles Dick of Ohio.[51] The Dick Act replaced the outdated 1792 Militia Act and divided the militias into two "classes": "the organized militia—to be known as the National Guard" or by "such other designations as may be given them by the laws of the respective States or Territories," and the "remainder," to be referred to as the "Reserve Militia." This is the first time federal statutes refer to the National Guard by that name. Beyond that, the law focused on imposing on the Guard regulations intended to improve its quality and make it more like the Regular Army. The law also spelled out when and how the President might federalize the militia. Significantly, the Dick Act unambiguously tied the Guard to the Constitution's militia clauses and referred to federalization in terms of the President "calling forth" the militias for the sake of domestic duties—more specifically, quelling rebellion, repelling invasion, and enforcing federal laws. The implication with regard to deploying overseas was clear: National Guard units, when in federal service, remained militias and were thus constrained by the legal limits associated with them.

With respect to training, the Dick Act stipulated that Guardsmen had to participate annually in marches or "go into camp of instruction at least five consecutive days" and "assemble for drill and instruction . . . or for target practice not less than twenty-four times."[52] During drill, Guardsmen would train on rifle marksmanship and other military tasks. This "24-5" training regimen was influenced by the British militia system, which appealed to Americans more than the rigid systems of other European countries.[53] The British required reserve and auxiliary forces to participate in approximately 26 days of training spread throughout the year, as well as lengthier training sessions of four or more consecutive days commonly known as "Easter Training."[54]

---

[51] U.S. Statutes at Large, An Act to Promote the Efficiency of the Militia, and for Other Purposes, January 21, 1903 (32 Stat. 775). Charles Dick was not only a congressman, he was also a long-serving Guardsman from Ohio who had served in the Spanish-American War. He had risen through the ranks and, at the signing of the act that bears his name in 1903, was a major general in the Ohio National Guard and president of the National Guard Association.

[52] U.S. Statutes at Large, An Act to Promote the Efficiency of the Militia, and for Other Purposes, January 21, 1903 (32 Stat. 775), p. 778.

[53] A few years prior to the passing of the Dick Act, the War Department published a *Report on the Reserve and Auxiliary Forces of England and the Militia of Switzerland*. One of the authors of the study, William Sanger, served not only as the Assistant Secretary of the War Department, but as an adviser to Senator and [Interstate] National Guard Association President Charles Dick. Sanger concluded that, while the Swiss system was ideal, the British militia system would be more attainable in America. Elihu Root and William Cary Sanger, *Report on the Reserve and Auxiliary Forces of England and the Militia of Switzerland: Prepared in 1900 for President McKinley and the Hon. Elihu Root*, Washington, D.C.: U.S. Government Printing Office, 1903; Interstate National Guard Association, 1900, p. 180; Interstate National Guard Association, 1903, p. 317; National Guard Association of the United States, 1879–1881.

[54] William Howley Goodenough and James Cecil Dalton, *The Army Book from the British Empire: A Record of the Military Forces and Their Duties in Peace and War*, London: Harrison & Sons, 1893, p. 484.

The British also mandated that training take place locally to minimize interruption of vocational and "private interests."[55]

Root believed that the 24-5 training regimen would balance the need for professional, standardized training with concern for Guardsmen's civilian obligations. Rural Guard units posed a particular dilemma, as summer encampments might disrupt critical seasonal agricultural work necessary to prepare for the fall harvest.[56] Drill periods twice a month could fit into most schedules without creating a burden. As even the *National Guard Magazine* admitted, "there being fifty-two weeks in the year, manifestly twenty-four meetings was not an unreasonable requirement."[57]

Moreover, Root hoped that the Dick Act would improve the National Guard's accountability and ensure adequate training. The drill mandate would force Guardsmen to stay in contact with their units and train with them regularly, thereby improving unit cohesion and readiness.[58] State governors and their Guard adjutants general reinforced this aim by selecting training sites that could support large numbers of Guardsmen. Similarly, consistent drilling and mustering schedules and locations would facilitate standardization, build unit cohesion, and ensure familiarity with local terrain.[59] These objectives aligned with Root's argument that a professionalized National Guard could assume primary responsibility for domestic tasks, such as strike breaking, and free up federal Army forces for other missions. Moreover, the new training regime would prepare the Guard for reserve service to expand the Army when necessary.[60]

Despite his role in drafting the Dick Act, Root harbored significant concerns about the National Guard's effectiveness to serve as a trained and efficient reserve that could be quickly called into federal service. In case of future wartime expansion of the Army, Root sought to differentiate between the National Guard, which was the organized militias of the several states, and the volunteers, which consisted of the broader manpower pool of American men for federal service. Based on historical precedent, Root feared that governors would select officers for political reasons, without consideration of their suitability. He therefore favored the creation of a national volunteer force, made up of men selected on merit and loyal, first and foremost, to the United States. As he explained, the importance of that distinction stemmed from the fact that "while the selection of officers of militia shall continue as it must . . . from the States, . . . the

---

[55] I. F. W. Beckett, *Britain's Part-Time Soldiers: The Amateur Military Tradition, 1558–1945*, Barnsley, UK: Pen & Sword Military, 2011, pp. 78–88, 101–102.

[56] Root, 1916, pp. 142–144.

[57] "Our Washington Letter," *National Guard Magazine*, Vol. 8, 1907, p. 445.

[58] U.S. House of Representatives, *Efficiency of the Militia, H.R. 15345: Hearing Before the Committee on Military Affairs*, Washington, D.C., U.S. Government Printing Office, 1902.

[59] U.S. House of Representatives, 1902; U.S. Senate, *Efficiency of the Militia, H.R. 15345: Hearing Before the Committee on Military Affairs*, Washington, D.C.: U.S. Government Printing Office, December 4, 1902.

[60] Cantor, 1963, p. 149.

officers of the volunteer forces of the United States shall hold their commissions from the President."[61] This approach was in line with the writings of Upton, who favored separation of state and national forces. It was not, however, a viable political option. Root therefore favored giving the National Guard federal responsibilities, even though governors would continue to appoint officers and be responsible for training Guardsmen and units.

Irrespective of Root's hesitations, the Dick Act was a major advance in U.S. military policy. It set the National Guard on the path to a dual role organized under both the militia and armies clauses of the Constitution. Moreover, Root believed it represented a necessary first step to improving operational capability. In arguing for passage of the bill in December 1902, Root reflected:

> You all know that for more than one hundred years nearly every President of the United States has urged Congress to take some action to improve our militia system. The basis of our present militia is the act passed in 1792, which never worked well. . . . The result is that we have no militia system, and for a country which proceeds upon the principle of not maintaining a large standing army, but keeping a very small standing army and relying upon its citizen soldiery, to run along for a century with an unworkable, and for more than half a century, with an obsolete set of militia laws seems to be really almost absurd.[62]

In the same reflection, Root elaborated on the problem facing the National Guard and its ill-defined role. The National Guard, he noted, suffered from a lack of an established place within the U.S. military system, and, in turn, enlistment of its members created no "special duty toward the United States distinct from that of all able-bodied citizens between the ages of 18 and 48."[63] The impact of this disorganization, Root opined, had already manifested itself in the Spanish-American War, where a lack of clear roles or lines of obligation had produced confusion that undermined the Guard's mobilization.

Nonetheless, the secretary recognized the National Guard as a valuable source of citizen-soldiers and accepted its growing influence as a political reality. He hoped that the Dick Act would bring the 114,000 National Guardsmen into better relations with the Regular Army. "Instead of brushing them aside, instead of trying to get up a system which will ignore them," Root concluded in his statement to the Senate Military Affairs Committee, "the theory of this bill is that the Government of the United States shall recognize the immense value of the National Guard."[64]

---

[61] Elihu Root, "Preface," in Emory Upton, ed., *The Military Policy of the United States*, Washington, D.C.: U.S. Government Printing Office, 1903, p. v.

[62] U.S. Senate, 1902, p. 2.

[63] U.S. Senate, 1902.

[64] U.S. Senate, 1902, p. 4.

Congress heeded Root's call and passed the landmark bill. There was much for the National Guard—and its skeptics—to applaud. The legislation's significant changes included the following:

- Designation of all state organized militias, collectively, as the "National Guard."
- The requirement for all Guardsmen to attend an annual five-day drill at a state camp and 24 drills at home armories.
- Authorization for National Guard officers to attend Army service schools, a critical step toward promoting greater professionalization and standardization.
- Authorization for National Guard training camps to receive Regular Army instructors, if requested by the state governor.
- Provisions for governors to receive written reports on field training.
- Expansion of the National Guard's maximum federal active service obligations, when called, to nine months.
- Clarification that Guardsmen could be subject to court-martial for offenses made while in federal service. In these instances, National Guard officers would be part of the court-martial boards.
- Mandate that the National Guard conform to the Regular Army's organization in exchange for federal funds.[65]

The 1903 act thus marked the birth of the modern National Guard.[66] Subsequent laws would build on this legislative foundation to refine further the Guard's relationship with the Army and its role in national defense. Despite these achievements, however, the law neglected important issues. It did not, for example, resolve the problem of constitutional restrictions on the use of Guardsmen in federal service overseas. To that point, the Dick Act recognized the National Guard as the organized militia identified in the militia clauses, which explicitly limited the militia's purpose when federalized to suppressing internal insurrections, repelling invasions, and enforcing the laws of the United States.[67] Another shortcoming was the Dick Act's failure to specify *how* to integrate the various state militias into a unified Army. After all the debate on the inconsistencies among the state militias, Congress neglected to include provisions on unit consolidation, training standards, facilities, and other issues. It would take several more years for these questions to be resolved.

---

[65] U.S. Statutes at Large, An Act to Promote the Efficiency of the Militia, and for Other Purposes, January 21, 1903, pp. 67–68. Shaw offers this list among some of the most important parts of the legislation: William L. Shaw, "The Interrelationship of the United States Army and the National Guard," *Military Law Review*, Vol. 31, January 1, 1966.

[66] Louis Cantor, "Elihu Root and the National Guard: Friend or Foe?" *Military Affairs*, Vol. 33, No. 3, December 1969, pp. 370–373; Cantor, 1963; Cooper, 1993, pp. 99–100.

[67] Carter, 1903, p. 792.

Conclusion

The Dick Act was a turning point in U.S. military policy. After over a century of congressional inactivity, the legislation replaced the long-obsolete 1792 Militia Act and began a period of substantial reform. Still, it was not a panacea. Although it imposed new standards for training and coordination, it did not provide a clear path for implementation, nor did it mitigate the War Department's and Regular Army's concern that reliance on the state National Guards was not the most optimal approach for rapidly expanding the Army to fight America's wars or fulfill the nation's expanding expectations of its Army. Indeed, the continued debates between proponents of the National Guard and professionalists demonstrated how the Dick Act was an initial step. A long legislative road still lay ahead. Debates would continue for decades in response to new challenges to American security. At the dawn of the 20th century, the Army was scarcely ready for the trials awaiting it. The demands of modern warfare and the emergence of new actors would amplify voices for reform.

CHAPTER THREE
Army Reform from 1903 to 1916: The Debates Continue

Introduction

As an initial step toward Army reform, the 1903 Dick Act had at least replaced the antiquated 1792 Militia Act. Over the next 13 years, the nation would see continued strident debate over what the next steps of Army reform should be, along with new legislation governing U.S. military policy. Much of the debate, just as it had in the years leading up to the Dick Act, centered on the question of how the Army should expand in wartime: Should standing Army reserve forces be solely under federal control, or should the states maintain statutory links to their National Guard units, at least in peacetime? As part of this debate, another question related to using militias to expand the Army came to the fore between 1903 and 1916: Did the Constitution allow the organized militias of the several states—now the National Guards—to be deployed overseas for any purpose, and especially to fight foreign foes? By 1916, this issue had been largely settled. Legal scholars generally agreed that the Constitution did not allow deployment of National Guard units, in their organized militia status, beyond U.S. borders. New federal legislation would have to be passed for the National Guards to deploy as part of the Army to foreign lands.

While U.S. policymakers and legal scholars quarreled over these issues, new threats emerged abroad. The 1904–1905 Russo-Japanese war, in which each belligerent mobilized a million-man army, foreshadowed the rise of industrial warfare. Americans wondered whether the United States could—or should—be capable of harnessing commensurate forces. These debates intensified in 1914 with the outbreak of war in Europe.

After the Dick Act: The Debate Continued

Although the 1903 Dick Act gave a statutory basis for the National Guards, implementing the legislation proved difficult. Many state Guard units viewed efforts to impose consistent standards and eligibility requirements as intrusive federal intervention that undermined their autonomy.[1] Enforcing compliance across state lines therefore proved challenging. The *New York Evening Post* criticized the provision requiring state troops mustered into federal service in times of war to undergo a medical examination:

> To enforce the regular physical standard in our [New York] Guard today would be to decrease it by at least one-fifth . . . perhaps the best part of the force—young business men of slightly defective eyesight or chest measurement, perfectly capable of serving the State well.[2]

It quickly became clear that the law was more aspirational than effectual.

For Regular Army officers, the law ignored the perceived need for a vastly expanded standing Army. Regular Army Captain Alfred W. Bjornstad, 28th Infantry Regiment and a veteran of Army campaigns in the Philippines, explained this sentiment in a 1908 *JMSI* article titled "The Military Necessities of the United States, and the Best Provisions for Meeting Them."[3] Bjornstad cautioned that colonial rivalries might force the United States into a war with another great power, a scenario in which the Army, despite the nation's unequaled natural resources, would prove severely inadequate. Bjornstad placed blame on the country's political leadership:

> Our most urgent need is a military policy . . . undeviatingly pursued and designed to provide a peace organization expansible in time of war, to a trained, effective and properly balanced army of a predetermined maximum size, or any desired lesser size; a policy which, in time of peace, anticipates as much as the human mind can anticipate, and leaves to the early days of the war as little as possible undone; and, lastly, a policy which gives the Government the desired military strength with the least expenditure consistent with the absolutely indispensable qualities of preparedness and efficiency.[4]

Bjornstad promoted an expansible concept similar to Upton's. He asserted that the nation required a peacetime Regular Army half the size needed in wartime. The first line of a mobile army required 250,000 troops—half Regular Army and half Regular Army Reserves—capable of effectiveness at the moment of mobilization. The second line of the mobile army would number about 700,000 personnel who "must be chiefly organized militia, and such surplus reserves as we may have converted into

---

[1] Jason Kaufman, *For the Common Good? American Civic Life and the Golden Age of Fraternity*, Oxford, UK: Oxford University Press, 2002.

[2] *New York Evening Post*, "The New Militia Law," *Journal of the Military Service Institution of the United States*, Vol. 34, 1904, p. 329.

[3] Alfred W. Bjornstad, "The Military Necessities of the United States, and the Best Provisions for Meeting Them," *Journal of the Military Service Institution of the United States*, Vol. 42, May–June 1908.

[4] Bjornstad, 1908, pp. 336–337.

volunteer organizations and filled up with recruits."[5] During wartime these partially trained troops would be mobilized in camps until needed and then sent to augment the first line to bring it to maximum strength. Bjornstad argued that, due to present policies, three obstacles stood in the way of federal development of the organized militia for such a large second line: The federal government could not compel the formation of a proper number of units, it could not impose standardized efficiency, and there was no way to know the size of the force that would answer the call.[6] To sidestep these defects, and to avoid "a repetition of the fiasco of 1898," he proposed congressional funding of a militia reserve made up of men who were active members of the organized militia, met certain regular training requirements, and would agree to serve as federal volunteers in wartime.[7]

Military professionals such as Bjornstad viewed with disdain many Guard practices, such as the reliance upon individual states to produce fighting units, the election of officers by their men, the requirement for some militia members to pay dues to their units, and the social focus of many Guard units. According to Regular Army officers and War Department leaders, these practices often resulted in untrained and poorly led units that were not adequate for Army expansion. Bjornstad expressed an opinion common in Regular Army writing at the time, blaming public naiveté for the militia system's continued failure: "The temper of our people, ignorant and thoughtless in military affairs," he warned, "will not tolerate the patient and costly defense which is the logical alternative of unpreparedness."[8] Bjornstad's view exemplified the Regular Army's conflicted relationship with the American public. It is perhaps unsurprising that Bjornstad, a Regular Army captain who started his military service in the 13th Minnesota Infantry Regiment, should focus much of his critique of the Army on the militia system and national unpreparedness. Based on its muddled performance in 1898, Bjornstad's charge that an uninformed public and an inefficient militia system were the primary inhibitors to military effectiveness tended to disregard the Army's dire need for its own reforms.

Secretary Root's task, however, was much broader than addressing the inadequacies of state National Guard units. His charge was to reform the entire War Department in the wake of the systemic deficiencies that the Spanish-American War had laid bare. In this light, revising militia policy was only one aspect of the reform process—and perhaps not even the most important. Indeed, the Regular Army was experiencing a myriad of problems, namely in the form of a personnel crisis. Persistent shortages of officers in line units, and the continual turnover of the young and inexperienced officers who filled in, undercut training efforts. Ultimately, inconsistent training put into

---

[5] Bjornstad, 1908, p. 355.
[6] Bjornstad, 1908, p. 335.
[7] Bjornstad, 1908, pp. 358–359.
[8] Bjornstad, 1908, p. 341.

question whether the Army was conditioned suitably for entering active service quickly when needed.⁹ Morale suffered as well: Chief of Staff Major General J. Franklin Bell reported in 1907 that "nothing has contributed to a greater degree to the prevailing discontent among enlisted men in the Army than continual change of company commanders, and having so many companies commanded by inexperienced officers."[10]

Related to poor morale was a desertion problem, which in the mind of Chief of Staff Lieutenant General Adna R. Chaffee in 1904 was at least partly related to the issue of inexperienced officers who lacked "intelligent sympathy" when "counsel and admonition, rather than rigid mechanical enforcement of the Articles of War for minor faults" was the preferred method of dealing with young soldiers.[11] Desertions rose to 7.4 percent in 1906, the highest since 1889. In January, the *Chicago Daily Tribune* ran a front-page story about the Army, a service that required "radical measures" in order "to stop practices which are demoralizing and tend to cause inefficiency." According to "one of the high officers in the service," poor leadership was a principal cause of desertion and stood as "'the bane and disgrace of the army.'"[12] Desertions had become so widespread that, by 1907, the Secretary of War ordered a special investigation to diagnose the causes and recommend possible solutions. Investigators corroborated the prevalent belief that poor officering was the principal factor, but harsh treatment and bad food also contributed.[13]

Low pay also precipitated the Army's personnel issues. With the American economy experiencing a boom around this time and with unemployment at less than 1 percent in 1906, soldiers dissatisfied with comparatively meager wages looked elsewhere for employment. Without the attraction of a competitive salary, there were also persistent shortfalls in recruiting.[14] Many of those the Army managed to attract did not impress leaders like Chaffee, as he found a number of recruits to be "weaklings, and

---

[9] Coffman, 2004, pp. 107–108.

[10] *Annual Report of the Secretary of War, 1907*, Volume I, Washington, D.C.: U.S. Government Printing Office, 1907, p. 198.

[11] *Annual Report of the Secretary of War, 1904*, Volume I, Washington, D.C.: U.S. Government Printing Office, 1904, p. 227.

[12] John Callan O'Laughlin, "Uncle Sam's Eyes on Evils in Army," *Chicago Daily Tribune*, January 22, 1906, p. 1. Also see "Army Desertions and the Remedy," *Washington Post*, October 16, 1903, p. 6; "Army Gossip in Washington," *Daily Kennebec Journal*, August 12, 1904, p. 8; "Young America as a Soldier," *Washington Post*, April 4, 1905, p. 6; "Army Desertion on the Increase," *Helena Independent*, August 10, 1905, p. 5; "Worst of Army Evils," *Washington Post*, October 15, 1905, p. JJ2; "Army Desertions Increase," *Washington Post*, November 27, 1906, p. 15; "Army Desertions," *Boston Daily Globe*, October 27, 1907, p. SM5; "Army Desertion Causes," *Galveston Daily News*, October 30, 1907, p. 10; "Desertions from the Army," *Boston Daily Globe*, March 3, 1906, p. 10; "Men Stick to Army," *Washington Post*, December 5, 1908, p. 11; "Desertions Increasing," *Washington Post*, November 19, 1909, p. 6.

[13] Joseph W. A. Whitehorne, *The Inspectors General of the United States Army, 1903–1939*, Washington, D.C.: Office of the Inspector General and the United States Army Center of Military History, 1998, pp. 84–85.

[14] Coffman, 2004, p. 114.

not fitted to endure the physical hardship and exposure soldiers frequently are called upon to undergo."[15] When combined, these issues seemed to undercut the Regular Army's argument that it alone could be trusted with the nation's defense.[16]

The Military Service Institution's 1905 essay competition focused on the problem of improving preparedness and solicited essays on the question, "How Far Does Democracy Affect the Organization and Discipline of our Armies, and How Can Its Influence Be Most Effectively Utilized?" In his winning essay, Lieutenant Colonel James S. Pettit, of the Regular Army's 8th Infantry Regiment, argued that the American system of government was inimical to the maintenance of a disciplined Army.[17] In many ways, Pettit's views were a 20th century mirroring of Upton's *Military Policy*.[18] Pettit emphasized the importance of unity of command—what he described as "one man power"—but warned that the nation's political environment undermined the possibility that a single man could yield the necessary power in times of war. "It is a self-evident proposition," he maintained, "that a democracy based on the will of millions of people, expressed through devious and changing channels, cannot be as skillful or efficient in the conduct of military affairs as a monarchy headed by a wise and powerful chief."[19]

Pettit's view could hardly have been more pessimistic. He believed that a democratic government could not maintain a military on par with the organization or discipline "of little Japan," and he dismissed popular patriotism as "largely of the lip."[20] Likewise, he heaped scorn upon what he viewed as a corrupt Congress, whose legislation was "greased with the slimy oil of political spoils and party expediency unredeemed by the salt of honest, manly independence and belief as to the right and justice of the cause and needs of the country."[21] As to the executive branch, the slow and convoluted democratic system entangled the President and undermined his authority as commander-in-chief of the Army, a situation made worse by the tradition of a civilian

---

[15] *Annual Report of the Secretary of War*, 1904, p. 226.

[16] The National Guard was not immune to retention and recruiting problems. State adjutants general and the Division of Militia Affairs estimated that, around this time, the annual turnover rate was between one-third to one-half. Fearful of deterring volunteerism, essentially no states forced men to honor their enlistment contracts in full. Absenteeism at the annual inspections fluctuated between 20 and 14 percent in the first decade of the 20th century. Cooper, 1997, pp. 144–145.

[17] James S. Pettit, "How Far Does Democracy Affect the Organization and Discipline of Our Armies, and How Can Its Influence Be Most Effectively Utilized?" *Journal of the Military Service Institution of the United States*, Vol. 38, January–February 1906.

[18] Weigley, 1962, pp. 158–162.

[19] Pettit, 1906, p. 2.

[20] Pettit, 1906, p. 37.

[21] Pettit, 1906, p. 4.

Secretary of War—a man, Pettit wrote, usually "devoid of knowledge of the laws and customs governing armies in peace and in war."[22]

Pettit's criticism of the American form of government was not limited to the federal level. He argued that these failings were replicated and compounded in the states, whose undisciplined militias he viewed as "the weakest link in the chain in time of war." Like many with a professionalist mindset, Pettit feared the militias would "represent the States rather than the nation, and discipline will be feeble."[23] He had little sympathy for states' rights advocates or Americans' unwillingness to build a competent and sufficiently sized Regular Army.

Despite the constricting effects the nation's system of government and its history had on an efficient and well-organized military, Pettit believed he had hit upon "a scheme which is friendly to our Constitution and traditions, and while it may not arouse any enthusiasm among our people it will not provoke antagonisms" at home or abroad.[24] Pettit argued for a small Regular Army in peacetime—no less than 75,000 men—with a regenerating pool of officers kept young and motivated through sufficient pay and sensible promotion. This first line would expand in wartime through a Regular Army Reserve made up of discharged soldiers obligated for five years to return to uniform when called upon. Within the first eight years of the proposed system, he calculated, the reserve would maintain around 70,000 men. Pettit's proposed second line "must consist of the organized militia and its reserve," a force he supposed would benefit in size and capability if the nation and the states paid for all expenses and offered more money for time spent on duty. Such an investment would mean "there would be no difficulty in organizing 200,000 'well-regulated militia' on an expansion scheme," increasing to 300,000 in wartime.[25] Pettit ended with a warning. As it had since its founding, the country would continue to enter successive wars with a peacetime military organization built upon "the fallacious belief" that "any American, be he lawyer, doctor, or politician can command men as soon as he dons a uniform." With the nation taking a greater interest in global affairs, this mistaken belief would probably continue "until some strong foe shall teach us that a well-organized and disciplined army is the best guaranty of peace, and the cheapest insurance against the extravagance and the horrors of war."[26]

Pettit's stinging criticism of the American people and democratic governance received hearty applause from some of the *JMSI* subscribers. One lieutenant colonel suggested that Pettit deserved both the Army's gratitude and the nation's thanks "for

---

[22] Pettit, 1906, p. 6.

[23] Pettit, 1906, p. 8.

[24] Pettit, 1906, p. 33.

[25] Pettit, 1906, pp. 34–35.

[26] Pettit, 1906, p. 37.

the boldness and fidelity" with which he presented his view.[27] Another Regular Army officer, Captain Matthew F. Steele of the 6th Cavalry, wrote that Pettit was justified in placing the needs of reforming the Army over American democracy because the system's survival necessitated the recommended changes.[28] Even the *Army and Navy Journal* offered a favorable review and defended his proposal. For turn-of-the-century military professionalists, the norms of American politics were hopelessly corrupt and barriers to the modernization they believed necessary to strengthen *both* the military and civil government.[29]

Pettit's essay reflected a perception gap between professional soldiers, who emphasized the careful study of military science, and the average American, who rarely pondered such esoteric questions as the suitable arrangement of a volunteer system or the National Guard's proper role.[30] Despite Pettit's command of citizen-soldiers in the 31st Infantry, U.S. Volunteers in the Philippines, his writing also completely ignored the Army's largely positive experience with the volunteers in the Philippine War. The *New York Sun* accused Pettit of misjudging the patriotism of the American people, who would serve "when the call to duty comes, if that call be sounded from the battlefield."[31] The *New York Times* went further, cautioning its readers that Pettit's views were extreme and even dangerous:

> To wish that the President of the United States had [the power to plunge us into war whenever his personal susceptibilities seemed to him to be sufficiently involved] is to wish for a recurrence of the times when war was held to be the normal and essential, and peace the abnormal and incidental, business of a nation. Colonel Pettit's watch is at least four hundred years slow.[32]

This responses of the *Sun* and the *Times* highlighted a central problem in some professionalists' advocacy for military reform: The proposals and perspectives advanced by the professionalists at the turn of the century were increasingly out of touch with the American people and reflected a dangerous contempt for both civilian suprem-

---

[27] Charles J. Crane, "Comment and Criticism: Democracy and Our Armies," *Journal of the Military Service Institution of the United States*, Vol. 38, 1906, pp. 353–356.

[28] Matthew F. Steele, "Comment and Criticism: Democracy and Our Armies," *Journal of the Military Service Institution of the United States*, Vol. 38, 1906, pp. 358–361.

[29] Stephen Skowronek, *Building a New American State: The Expansion of National Administrative Capacities, 1877–1920*, Cambridge, UK: Cambridge University Press, 1982, pp. 118–119.

[30] Marcus Cunliffe, *Soldiers and Civilians: The Martial Spirit in America, 1775–1865*, Boston: Little, Brown, and Company, 1968.

[31] *New York Sun*, "Comment and Criticism: Democracy and Our Armies," *Journal of the Military Service Institution of the United States*, Vol. 38, 1906, pp. 363.

[32] *New York Times*, "Comment and Criticism: Democracy and Our Armies," *Journal of the Military Service Institution of the United States*, Vol. 38, 1906, pp. 364.

acy and republican government.³³ Moreover, Pettit's proposals—like many others in the *JMSI*—were in many ways politically unpalatable and tone deaf. This disconnect would hamper the Regular Army's reform efforts and would shape the legislative battles soon to come, deepening the divisions between the Department of War and Regular Army and the National Guards of the states.

1908: Amending the Dick Act and Establishing the Medical Reserve Corps

On May 27, 1908, both the Department of War and the National Guard secured major victories when Congress amended the Dick Act,³⁴ making changes that affected the organization and roles of both the Regular Army and the National Guard. The act, sometimes referred to as the 1908 Militia Act, mandated that the organization, armament, and discipline of the Guard were to be the same as that of the Regular Army. It abolished the nine-month limit on federal use of the Guard and included a provision allowing the President to specify the length of service, not to exceed terms of enlistment or commission.³⁵ In an attempt to address constitutional concerns that had arisen during the Spanish-American War, Congress stipulated that the Guard, when called to federal service, could be used "either within or without the territory of the United States."³⁶ Most important, the new legislation stipulated that National Guard units would be called up "in advance of any volunteer force which [the Federal Government] may be determined to raise."³⁷

Even with the amendment, two issues remained unresolved. The first was continued uncertainty over the National Guard's lingering dual status between state and

---

³³ For more on civil-military relations during this era, see Huntington, 1957; Russell F. Weigley, "The American Military and the Principle of Civilian Control from McClellan to Powell," *Journal of Military History*, Vol. 57, No. 5, October 1993, pp. 27–58; Russell F. Weigley, "The American Civil-Military Gap: A Historical Perspective, Colonial Times to the Present," in Peter D. Feaver and Richard H. Kohn, eds., *Soldiers and Civilians: The Civil-Military Gap and American National Security*, Cambridge, Mass.: MIT Press, 2001; Charles A. Byler, *Civil-Military Relations on the Frontier and Beyond, 1865–1917*, Westport, Conn.: Praeger, 2006; Thomas S. Langston, *Uneasy Balance: Civil-Military Relations in Peacetime America Since 1783*, Baltimore, Md.: Johns Hopkins University Press, 2003; Matthew M. Oyos, "Theodore Roosevelt, Congress, and the Military: U.S. Civil-Military Relations in the Early Twentieth Century," *Presidential Studies Quarterly*, Vol. 30, No. 2, June 2000, pp. 312–330; Clark, 2017.

³⁴ U.S. Statutes at Large, An Act to Further Amend the Act Entitled "An Act to Promote the Efficiency of the Militia, and for Other Purposes," Sixtieth Congress, Session I, Chapter 204, May 27, 1908 (35 Stat. 339).

³⁵ Weigley, 1967, p. 324; Cooper, 1993, p. 100.

³⁶ U.S. Statutes at Large, An Act to Further Amend the Act Entitled "An Act to Promote the Efficiency of the Militia, and for Other Purposes," May 27, 1908 (35 Stat. 339).

³⁷ U.S. Statutes at Large, An Act to Further Amend the Act Entitled "An Act to Promote the Efficiency of the Militia, and for Other Purposes," May 27, 1908 (35 Stat. 339), pp. 400–401.

federal authorities.[38] For the War Department, sharing authority with state governors remained a stumbling block. Second, the 1908 legislation did not address how the Army would expand in the event of war; it stipulated only that the state National Guard units were to be called into federal service before volunteer forces would be formed. Neither the Dick Act of 1903 nor its May 1908 amendment rectified these problems, which would resurface with new intensity in subsequent years.

By 1908, it had also become apparent to the War Department that the new standards for training and coordination brought about by the Dick Act required an organization within the military structure dedicated solely to coordinating militia matters. On February 12, the Division of Militia Affairs (DMA)—the precursor to the Militia Bureau, and in turn the National Guard Bureau—formed inside of the Office of the Secretary of War. As the central federal agency in charge of organized and unorganized militia issues, the DMA would potentially solve what had been a frustratingly inefficient delegation of authority; since 1903, more than half a dozen offices throughout the War Department were responsible for the various administrative duties that affected the militia. Heading the new division was a Regular Army Coast Artillery officer, Lieutenant Colonel Erasmus M. Weaver. Along with 14 Regular Army staff officers in his office, Weaver coordinated between the state militias and the Department of War during peacetime. Their administrative responsibilities also included arming, equipping, training, educating, disciplining and organizing the militias, as well as matters related to conducting camps and field exercises.[39]

Secretary Root had also proposed federally funded joint field exercises between the Regular Army and National Guard as a means of promoting training and preparation among the militias and fostering better relations and cooperation between the two groups. The first maneuvers occurred in 1902 in New England and continued every year until 1916, save for 1905, when no funds were made available by Congress. In 1908 alone, eight major joint maneuvers occurred. The results were mixed, but for inexperienced Regular officers it turned theoretical classroom study into practical instruction when they were offered their first opportunity to observe and command large bodies of soldiers in the field. There is evidence that the training operated as intended—forging strong relationships between some Guardsmen and Regular officers. Still, at times the exercises employed unrealistic scenarios that tended to emphasize only tactics while

---

[38] Eilene Marie Slack Galloway, History of United States Military Policy on Reserve Forces, 1775–1957, Washington, D.C.: U.S. Government Printing Office, 1957 p. 455.

[39] *Annual Report of the Chief, Division of Militia Affairs*, Washington, D.C.: U.S. Government Printing Office, 1908, p. 5; Cooper, 1997, pp. 112–113; Bill Boehm, *The Chiefs of the National Guard Bureau, 1908–2011*, Arlington, Va.: Historical Services Division, Office of Public Affairs, National Guard Bureau, 2011, p. 1; Jim Dan Hill, *The Minute Man in Peace and War*, Harrisburg, Pa.: The Stackpole Company, 1964, p. 209.

overlooking logistics, and despite special appropriations to modernize the National Guard, many units made do with obsolete equipment.[40]

In April 1908, Congress passed the Army Medical Department Act.[41] The new legislation established the Army Medical Department and stipulated that it include a new Army Medical Corps Reserve, all under the armies clause of the Constitution. Ironically, Root's 1902 proposal referenced the notion of an Army reserve separate from the state militias when he suggested the establishment of two types of volunteer reserves to supplement the Army during wartime. The first volunteer reserve would be composed of National Guard units that had volunteered for unlimited service during war. The second would be made up of men with prior training in the National Guard, Regular Army, or volunteer army. Legislators ultimately omitted this model from the Dick Act because even Root himself recognized that establishment of a federal reserve force would be unpopular with National Guardsmen and their supporters. However, now that Congress had directed that the Guard be called to federal service in "advance" of other volunteer forces, the notion of a specialized federal reserve became politically viable.[42] The 1908 law allowed the Army to establish a reserve corps of medical officers who could be ordered to duty by the Secretary of War during a time of emergency, and permitted the commissioning of contract physicians into either the Regular Army or the Medical Reserve Corps, depending on their age.

The creation of the Medical Reserve Corps marked a first step in the development of a federal reserve for the Army. The War Department acted quickly to recruit qualified doctors, surgeons, hygienists, and laboratory workers into the Medical Reserve Corps; by mid-1909 it had commissioned 364 of them. In addition to providing medical care for servicemen, the Medical Reserve Corps advised Army leaders on a range of military health issues, such as inoculation for typhoid fever. The Medical Reserve Corps continued to grow in size and responsibility. It numbered over 1,000 by 1910, and, by 1913, Medical Reserve doctors were routinely reporting to Army garrisons to backfill their Regular Army counterparts on operational deployments.[43]

As Root had anticipated, Guardsmen viewed the Medical Reserve Corps as a threat. Before 1908 and after 1903, National Guard units had enjoyed an effective monopoly on standing reserve manpower available in time of crisis. After the 1908

---

[40] Timothy K. Nenninger, "The Army Enters the Twentieth Century, 1904–1917," in Kenneth J. Hagan and William R. Roberts, eds., *Against All Enemies: Interpretations of American Military History from Colonial Times to the Present*, Westport, Conn.: Greenwood Press, 1986, pp. 221–222; Coffman, 2004, p. 111; Cooper, 1997, pp. 110, 140; Whitehorne, 1998, p. 70. Also see Charles Douglas McKenna, *The Forgotten Reform: Field Maneuvers in the Development of the United States Army, 1900–1920*, PhD Dissertation, Duke University, 1981.

[41] U.S. Statutes at Large, An Act to Increase the Efficiency of the Medical Department of the United States Army, Sixtieth Congress, Session I, Chapter 150, April 23, 1908 (35 Stat. 66).

[42] Richard B. Crossland and James T. Currie, *Twice the Citizen: A History of the United States Army Reserve, 1908–1983*, Washington, D.C.: Office of the Chief, Army Reserve, 1984, pp. 12–18.

[43] Crossland and Currie, 1984.

act, they would have to share this status this status with a standing federal reserve—an organization that, because it was federally controlled and trained with specialized skills, might become the preferred source of reserve manpower for the Army.[44] Determined to avoid this outcome, the National Guard redoubled its effort to secure its desired position within the military establishment.

The law amending the Dick Act and the new one establishing the Medical Reserve Corps illustrated differing visions between the War Department and the National Guard over future military policy. Even though the 1908 amendment to the Dick Act attempted to resolve the continued debate over the constitutionality of deploying the National Guard beyond U.S. borders, it did not satisfy those who maintained that such deployment was prohibited by the militia clause. The two 1908 laws reflected the competing arguments between the proponents of the Regular Army, National Guard, and reserve forces. Table 3.1 highlights the competing issues in the two laws.

Ten years after the Spanish-American War, Congress was steadily addressing the deficiencies of the nation's ground forces revealed by that short conflict. It created a nascent Medical Reserve Component and codified the National Guard, to be organized, equipped, and disciplined in line with the Regular Army. It had also increased the size of the Regular Army and established the Chief of Staff and General Staff Corps. Regardless, many still feared that these initiatives were insufficient to keep pace with increasing global dangers. Could the nation fight successfully against a European power should the need arise? This question animated members of the emerging preparedness movement—a broad-based national campaign that gained momentum in the years prior to America entering World War I.

The Preparedness Movement

The 1903 Dick Act, the 1903 General Staff Act, and the two 1908 acts marked the beginning of a statutory process that continued over the next several decades to define a new set of federal laws that would shape the Army. The associated debates reflected larger issues of federal power, the changing international system, and the role of the United States in world affairs. Also influencing the debate were such domestic issues as urban blight, industrial and economic dislocation, mass immigration, and government corruption.[45]

---

[44] With legislation in 1912, all enlistments in the Regular Army were for seven years: four in whatever organization the individual entered and the final three on furlough and attached to the Army Reserve. If an individual earned an honorable discharge and was under 45 years old, they could enlist in the Army Reserve for a three-year term (Public Law 62-338, An Act Making Appropriation for the Support of the Army for the Fiscal Year Ending June Thirtieth, Nineteen Hundred and Thirteen, and for Other Purposes, August 24, 1912).

[45] George C. Herring, Jr., *From Colony to Superpower: U.S. Foreign Relations Since 1776*, New York and London: Oxford University Press, 2008, pp. 337–377.

Table 3.1
Key Provisions of the 1908 Militia Act and Army Medical Department Act

1908 Militia Act (Amendment to the 1903 Dick Act)	1908 Army Medical Department Act
• Reaffirmed the militia as consisting of all able-bodied male citizens and those who have declared intention to become citizens between 18 and 45 years of age • Divided the militia into (1) organized militia, "otherwise known as the National Guard," and (2) the Reserve Militia, or unorganized militia. • Dictated that the organized militia's organization, armament, and discipline would be the same as those of the Regular Army • Codified the War Department's authority to control the militia's organization and outlined the structure • Empowered the President to fix the minimum number of enlisted men in each National Guard unit • Empowered the President to call forth the militia when necessary to repel invasion, suppress rebellion, or execute the laws of the Union; also empowered the President to issue orders through the governor or commanding general of the militia of the District of Columbia and specify length of service • Authorized the Secretary of War to procure service arms, equipment, uniforms, clothing, military stores, etc., as necessary to equip the organized militias to meet the act's requirements • Authorized the Secretary of War to provide for militia participation in encampments, maneuvers, and field exercises of the Regular Army • Established National Guard procedures for medical exams, courts martial, payment during federal service, and military education • Authorized the assignment of Regular Army officers and enlisted men to the militia as needed	• Established a Medical Reserve Corps and authorized the hospital corps, nurse corps, and dental surgeons • Established a Medical Department of the U.S. Army consisting of (1) the Medical Corps, (2) the Medical Reserve Corps, and (3) hospital corps, nurse corps, and dental surgeons • Appointed a Surgeon General with the rank of brigadier general as chief of the Medical Corps and set rank and number of supporting officers • Declared that all officers of the Medical Department then in active service would be recommissioned in the corresponding grades of the new Medical Corps in order of seniority and without loss of relative rank in the Army • Empowered the Secretary of War to order Medical Reserve Corps officers to active duty in the service of the United States in numbers and terms of service dictated by need at the time • Authorized officers of the Medical Reserve Corps to serve in active duty with the militia or volunteer troops, without being subject to call of duty as a Reserve Corps member • Established procedures for promotions, vacancies, examinations, retirement, advanced education, contract surgeons, eligibility, discharge, and legal obligations

A wave of reformism associated in U.S. history with the Progressive Era emerged in response to these anxieties. Progressivism sought "to rationalize and democratize American life . . . to reform the political parties, curb the power of monopoly, and humanize the cities."[46] The movement spanned economic, social, and political policies and promised to bring new order and efficiency to national life. Proponents emphasized the need to develop efficient bureaucracies, praised specialization and standardization, and pushed a trend of professionalization within occupational groups. Professionals in

---

[46] John Patrick Finnegan, *Against the Specter of a Dragon: The Campaign for American Military Preparedness, 1914–1917*, Contributions in Military History, Westport, Conn.: Greenwood Press, 1974, p. 10.

such occupations as medicine, law, education, and the military organized new professional journals and societies dedicated to institutionalizing the ethos of training and specialist authority.

An offshoot of Progressivism that informed military policy debates was the "preparedness movement." Its proponents—a coalition of educated, often northeastern lawyers, businessmen, and other elites—grew increasingly concerned about both the inefficiency of the U.S. military system and the degeneration of American society.[47] Preparedness advocates used language that echoed Progressives' simultaneous calls to reform local and national government, and these Progressive military reformers began to view the Army as an institution that was ripe for reform. "Preparedness," historian John Patrick Finnegan notes, "was a way to transform America and reshape her whole society, to homogenize a drifting mass of immigrants, rationalize her industries, and ennoble her spirits."[48]

Despite its civilian provenance, the preparedness movement advocated for reforms that aligned more with the War Department than the National Guard. For instance, many preparedness advocates favored a Regular Army supported by an organized federal reserve and an unorganized manpower pool, and they proposed initiatives to increase preparedness by training American youth. In contrast, a military policy predicated on a small, well-trained Regular Army backed by a larger, less-trained National Guard was not as appealing to preparedness advocates.

Regardless of its call for broad social reforms, the preparedness movement, like the Progressive movement in general, spread unevenly across the United States.[49] It was concentrated on the coasts, with its leadership centered in the northeast and, in particular, New York City—the nation's economic and business capital. The movement's geographic orientation was a mirror image of its greatest opposition: namely, the South and Midwest, where agrarian populations were often isolationist and wary of federal military power. Many in the South still vividly remembered the actions of federal troops brought in to enforce civil rights during Reconstruction, while Midwesterners were suspicious of the motives of eastern bankers and industrialists. These

---

[47] See Jack C. Lane, *Armed Progressive: General Leonard Wood*, Lincoln, Neb.: University of Nebraska Press, 2009, pp. 184–217; Michael David Pearlman, *To Make Democracy Safe for America: Patricians and Preparedness in the Progressive Era*, Champaign, Ill.: University of Illinois Press, 1984; Nancy Gentile Ford, *The Great War and America: Civil-Military Relations During World War I*, Westport, Conn.: Praeger Security International, 2008, pp. 1–26; George C. Herring, Jr., "James Hay and the Preparedness Controversy, 1915–1916," *Journal of Southern History*, Vol. 30, No. 4, November 1964; William H. Tinsley, *The American Preparedness Movement, 1914–1916*, PhD dissertation, Stanford University, 1939; Finnegan, 1974; John Garry Clifford, *The Citizen Soldiers: The Plattsburg Training Camp Movement, 1913–1920*, Lexington, Ky.: University Press of Kentucky, 2014.

[48] Finnegan, 1974, p. 108.

[49] Edward Brooke Lee, Jr., *Politics of our Military's National Defense: History of the Action of Political Forces Within the United States Which has Shaped Our Military National Defense Policies from 1783 to 1940 Together with the Defense Acts of 1916 and 1920 as Case Studies*, Washington, D.C.: U.S. Government Printing Office, 1940, p. 274.

geographic divisions reflected disparities in education, urbanization, and diversity and, perhaps most critically, a disregard for preparation for war. As the preparedness advocates agitated for a stronger military, opponents questioned the centralized role of the government in state and militia affairs. Although the movement would spread rapidly between 1914 and 1917, it never bridged these sectional divisions.

Major General Leonard Wood—who had been awarded the Medal of Honor, served as President McKinley's physician, commanded the Rough Riders, and served as the imperial proconsul in Cuba and the Philippines and subsequently as the Army Chief of Staff—was the preparedness movement's greatest champion.[50] A political schemer and self-taught soldier, his rapid advancement was an outrage to Regular Army professionalists.[51]

Following four years as Army Chief of Staff (1910–1914), Wood took command of the Department of the East, headquartered in New York. With a progressive's faith in organization and planning, he turned his attention to national defense, focusing on reforms that might arrest a supposed decline in America's martial spirit.[52] Wood's calls for reform reverberated among other advocates in the Northeast who sought to improve popular understanding of the military and bolster readiness. The Progressive movement's emphasis on physical fitness and virility inspired the creation of new youth and men's organizations, including summer camps designed to instruct qualified college students in military arts and culture. In 1913, Henry T. Bull, a Cornell University professor of military science, suggested to Wood that the Army consider funding specialized camps. With little time available, only two camps would be formed that summer to train 222 students alongside Regular Army units for five weeks.

After securing the Secretary of War's support, Wood sent out a letter on May 10, 1913, to the nation's university and college presidents. He notified them of the upcoming summer program and solicited applications for four "experimental military camps of instruction" spread across the country and held annually if the trial proved successful.[53] The goal was to increase the number of college-educated men trained in military

---

[50] For additional sources on Wood, see Hermann Hagedorn, *Leonard Wood: A Biography*, Vols. 1 and 2, New York: Harper and Brothers Publishers, 1931; Isaac F. Marcosson, *Leonard Wood: Prophet of Preparedness*, New York: John Lane Company, 1917; Joseph H. Sears, *The Career of Leonard Wood*, New York: D. Appleton and Company, 1920; William H. Hobbs, *Leonard Wood: Administrator, Soldier, and Citizen*, New York: C. P. Putnam's Sons, 1920; James Herman Pruitt, II, *Leonard Wood and the American Empire*, PhD dissertation, Texas A&M University, 2011; John G. Holme, *The Life of Leonard Wood*, New York: Doubleday, Page, and Company, 1920; Jack C. Lane, *Leonard Wood and the Shaping of American Defense Policy, 1900–1920*, PhD dissertation, University of Georgia, 1963; Lane, 2009.

[51] Lane, 2009, pp. 125–126, 150, 228; James H. Hitchman, *Leonard Wood and Cuban Independence, 1898–1902*, The Hague: Martinus Nijhoff, 1971, p. 21; Jack McCallum, *Leonard Wood: Rough Rider, Surgeon, Architect of American Imperialism*, New York: New York University Press, 2006, pp. 139, 207–210.

[52] Clark, 2017, pp. 248–249.

[53] Preston Brown, "The Genesis of the Military Training Camp," *Infantry Journal*, December 1930, p. 609; Clark, 2017, p. 249, Clifford, 2014, pp. 11–12.

affairs who could serve as officers when a national crisis arose and when needed to expand the Army. Preempting accusations of warmongering, Wood assured his academic audience that "The object sought is not in any way one of military aggrandizement, but a means of meeting a vital need confronting a peaceful, unmilitary, though warlike nation, to preserve that desired peace and prosperity by the best known precaution . . . more thorough preparation."[54]

Not only might the camps bring in a better quality of recruit for the U.S. Army, but they would make military service a place where young men could learn civic and technical skills that would benefit the nation and provide a strong national defense in the process. Progressive college and university presidents welcomed Wood's proposals warmly.[55] Wood gauged the experimental program in summer of 1913 to be a success, spurring him to implement the program on a wider scale. College students impressed Wood with their dedication and speed of adaption, and he quickly embraced the camp model as a tool for public education.[56] He established the precedent for a new form of public-private partnership, in which the War Department would support civilian-sponsored training camps and work alongside colleges and universities.[57] These efforts laid the groundwork for the Reserve Officers' Training Corps (ROTC) program, established by law in the 1916 National Defense Act (NDA).

Wood's plans would not have succeeded but for the existence of willing civilians who, fearful of growing civil-military divisions, eagerly funded, promoted, and joined the student training camps. The most important assistance came from a group of northeastern businessmen and lawyers led by rising Wall Street lawyer Grenville Clark, a colleague of former Secretary of War Elihu Root and a family friend of Theodore Roosevelt.

---

[54] Quoted in Ralph Barton Perry, *The Plattsburg Movement: A Chapter of America's Participation in the World War*, New York: E. P. Dutton & Company, 1921, p. 2.

[55] A 1915 editorial in the *Army and Navy Journal* happily recounted that 18 of 27 college and university heads who wrote to the *New York Times* on the subject of students' military training favored martial education ("Editorial," *The Army and Navy Journal*, Vol. 52, January 30, 1915, p. 681; Marcosson, 1917, p. 68).

[56] Clifford, 2014, p. 12; Lane, 2009, pp. 193–194.

[57] Finnegan, 1974, p. 20. These forms of public-private partnerships were common in the early 20th century, when pro-imperial bureaucrats, constrained by tepid popular and congressional support for further American expansion abroad, began to look to the private sphere for resources, manpower, and (in keeping with the Progressivist ethos) specialized knowledge and skill (Colin D. Moore, "State Building Through Partnership: Delegation, Public-Private Partnerships, and the Political Development of American Imperialism, 1898–1916," *Studies in American Political Development*, Vol. 25, April 2011). Some historians have linked these early efforts to build ties between higher education institutions and the War Department to the post-1945 military-intellectual complex (Christopher Loss, *Between Citizens and State: The Politics of American Higher Education in the Twentieth Century*, Princeton, N.J.: Princeton University Press, 2012).

Clark had been struck by Wood's public statements about the Army's military weakness.[58] In Clark's mind, the 1915 *Lusitania* crisis underscored the need for dramatic action and led him to found a private advocacy organization, the Committee of Hundred, in order to explore new preparedness initiatives and implement his idea for a network of civilian camps.[59] Through shared acquaintances, Clark and the Committee of Hundred approached Wood to join forces.[60] With private funding, Wood, Clark, and like-minded prominent businessmen and military officers campaigned to enroll college students and interested businessmen in an expanded student summer camp.

In June 1915, ten months after Germany invaded Belgium, Wood secured War Department authorization to host the first Business Men's Camp. The maiden encampment started soon after, from August 8 to September 6, in Plattsburg, New York.[61] The camp's principal impact was that it introduced a new segment of the population to military life. To the businessmen who participated, "preparedness meant more than armaments and patriotic propaganda . . . it became a kind of moral reawakening, a demonstration of national service."[62] Upon graduation, the first cohort pledged to support and encourage a national system of universal military training camps and organized a new alumni lobby organization. Additional camps were established across the Northeast, Midwest, and California. In early 1916, Clark spearheaded the creation of a unified Military Training Camps Association (MTCA).[63] Wood's plan was bearing fruit.

The 1915 Plattsburg Camp's success, coupled with the worsening war in Europe, ignited a broader national movement for civilian training and education in military skills. Membership in organizations such as the National Security League, a patriotic, nonprofit organization dedicated to national preparedness and universal service, grew quickly. By 1915, the league had established 70 branches across the country, and its Preparedness Day Parade attracted an estimated half-million participants to New York City.[64] The cause would gain new members in 1917, when a border crisis with Mexico heightened public awareness of the United States' vulnerabilities.

---

[58] Nancy Peterson Hill, *A Very Private Public Citizen: The Life of Grenville Clark*, St. Louis, Mo.: University of Missouri Press, 2014, pp. 45–46.

[59] Hill, 2014, p. 46.

[60] Leonard Wood, "The Plattsburg Idea," *National Service*, February 1917, pp. 12–14; Hill, 2014, pp. 46–47.

[61] "General Order 38: June 22, 1915," *General Orders and Bulletins*, Washington, D.C.: U.S. Government Printing Office, 1915.

[62] Clifford, 2014, p. 58.

[63] Finnegan, 1974, p. 70.

[64] Robert D. Ward, "The Origin and Activities of the National Security League, 1914–1919," *Mississippi Valley Historical Review*, Vol. 47, No. 1, June 1960; John Carver Edwards, *Patriots in Pinstripes: Men of the National Security League*, Washington, D.C.: University Press of America, 1982; Clifford, 2014, p. 143.

Plattsburg's success afforded Wood an opportunity to demonstrate that martial education could occur on a large scale. Both Roosevelt and Wood understood that such abbreviated training might not immediately produce a proficient military force, but more fundamentally, weeks of training promoted civic virtue and patriotism.[65] Wood began a flurry of public speaking engagements to spread his preparedness plans from 1915 into 1916—nearly 160 in a seven month period.[66] He penned *The Military Obligation of Citizenship* and *Our Military History*, in which Wood admitted that, while only 50 percent of men turning 18 each year were fit for military service, and far less than that were fit for the Regular Army, "the minor defects rejecting them for the regular army would not reject them for general military service." That equated to upward of 500,000 new men each year. About 3.5 million would then be available at any given time at their peak physical years "and of minimum dependent and business responsibility."[67] As for officers, Wood called for five weeks of training in U.S. Military Training Camps for two consecutive years. The nation had "the material and the machinery for turning out an excellent corps of reserve officers," he wrote. "All that is needed is to take hold of it and shape it."[68]

Sympathetic journalists, editors, and owners of major American newspapers published articles and editorials preaching "preparedness consciousness" and providing information on upcoming training camps. In 1917, preparedness advocates founded the *National Service Magazine*, "devoted to the cause of universal military training."[69] The magazine published essays by military and political leaders, including Secretary of War Newton D. Baker, former President of Harvard University Charles W. Elliot, and former President Theodore Roosevelt, who wrote on the need for the "revival" of Americans' sense of patriotism and national duty. *National Service* sought to rectify civilians' general ignorance of military affairs. In addition, it advocated "the belief of the younger generation that a revival or readiness to sacrifice personal interests in

---

[65] Roosevelt's speeches after the sinking of the *Lusitania* often appealed to notions of civic duty and bravery. In San Francisco in July 1915 he averred that "A mother who is not willing to raise her boy to be a soldier is not fit for citizenship." At a speech in Plattsburg in August he argued that "Camps like this are schools of civic virtue, as well as of military efficiency. They should be universal and obligatory for all our young men." Pacifists were supposedly "as much out of place in a democracy as the poltroon himself; and he is no better citizen than the poltroon." "Roosevelt Urges Nation to Prepare," *New York Times*, July 22, 1915, p. 1; "Fit All for War—T.R.," *Washington Post*, August 26, 1915, pp. 1–2.

[66] Clark, 2017, p. 251.

[67] Leonard Wood, *The Military Obligation of Citizenship*, Princeton: Princeton University Press, 1915; Leonard Wood, *Our Military History: Its Facts and Fallacies*, Chicago, Il.: The Reilly & Britton, Co., 1916, pp. 200–202.

[68] Wood, 1916, pp. 210–212.

[69] I. B. Holley, *General John M. Palmer, Citizen Soldiers, and the Army of a Democracy*, Westport, Conn.: Greenwood Press, 1982, p. 252.

some degree to the common welfare is desirable and necessary for the security and best development of American institutions."[70]

The relationship between National Guard and preparedness advocates was tenuous. Many preparedness advocates doubted National Guard unit effectiveness as a reserve fighting force. They expressed concern about the lack of interstate coordination and the nonstandardized training and equipment that hampered the readiness of National Guard personnel and units. They were skeptical that these units of the National Guard could overcome these problems quickly in the event of a national emergency, since they had not done so in previous mobilizations. Meanwhile, the National Guard eyed the preparedness movement warily. Southern Guardsmen, historically wary of federal power, were generally opposed to the movement's call for universal military training; in contrast, midwestern and northeastern Guardsmen recognized the potential benefits of receiving federal funding. Overall, most Guardsmen viewed universal military training with skepticism. They feared it might result in a large, federal manpower pool that would supplant the National Guard as part of the nation's first-line defense, a role that the Division of Militia Affairs (DMA) argued Congress "undoubtedly intended" in the 1903 and 1908 acts for the Regular Army and the Organized Militia to fill together.[71] Preparedness advocates, for their part, acknowledged that any effort to reform military policy would need to gain the National Guard's political support. The National Guard and the preparedness advocates thus reached a tenuous truce; so long as calls for universal training were focused on Army issues and did not interfere with the Guard's claim to be a first line of defense, the National Guard would not openly oppose the movement. This arrangement, which was not bounded by any legislation, could not last, and in the coming legislative battles over military policy, the National Guard would forcefully oppose legislation promoting universal military training.[72]

---

[70] Wood, 1917.

[71] *Annual Report of the Chief, Division of Militia Affairs*, Washington, D.C.: U.S. Government Printing Office, 1911, p. 162.

[72] The evolution of U.S. military policy shows the term *first-line defenses* along with a related term *second-line defenses* used often. The general meaning of *first-line defenses* includes U.S. ground and naval forces that will first meet an enemy of the U.S. in combat. *Second-line defenses* refers to the follow-on forces that will take longer to mobilize and prepare for battle. But within the various historical contexts that this four-volume history covers, the specific types of ground force units that have constituted the first and second-line defenses varied. For example, in the 19th century, the first line of ground defenses against an invasion from a foreign power was the small Regular Army scattered throughout the country alongside the state militias. The second line in this context would have been a larger volunteer army that would be mobilized by the several states and provided for federal service. In the 20th century, the terms became caught up in the debates between the War Department, Regular Army, and National Guard as to which ground forces were in the first- and second-line defense. Guardsmen saw their organized state militia units as being a part of the first-line defense with the Regular Army. In their view, the Regular Army would respond first but be joined by ready National Guard units. In this view, the second line would have potentially been the larger volunteer army. However, this view was contested by Regular Army officers who believed that the first-line defenses ought to be made up of the Regular Army and a federal-only reserve force. The

John McAuley Palmer and the 1912 Plan for Army Reorganization

Overall, the 1903 Dick Act, its 1908 and 1910 amendments, and the 1908 Army Medical Department Act, and the aspirations of the preparedness movement represented significant steps toward greater efficiency. Still, while the War Department sought to transform the Regular Army from a frontier constabulary to a warfighting force equivalent to the armies of great European powers, the National Guard fought back against some of these efforts to promote efficiency and modernization. For example, the National Guard opposed some provisions that called for states to create specialized units, such as cavalry and artillery, on the grounds that training and equipping such units was prohibitively expensive, since states were paying much of the Guard's equipping and training costs in those days.[73] Regular Army Brigadier General Robert K. Evans—who replaced Colonel Erasmus Weaver as the Chief of Militia Affairs in 1911 after organizational reforms moved the Division of Militia Affairs from the Secretary of War's office to the Army Chief of Staff's office and Congress elevated the DMA Chief's rank to General Officer—acknowledged that financial problems hampered the effectiveness of specialized militia units, but highlighted the fact that many states maintained the units on paper.[74] He concluded in his 1911 annual report that nearly all

---

second line of defense for the Regular Army officers would have been the larger volunteer army that would take time to mobilize and train. In this view, Regular Army officers believed the National Guard should be principally used in state missions, and not part of the larger war army, which they believed must be under only one political master, namely the President, and not subordinate to state governors, as was the National Guard. For contemporary mentions of what did, or should, constitute the first- and second-line defenses, see General Charles Dick, "Our Second Line of Defense," *Journal of the Military Service Institution of the United States*, Vol. 31, 1902, pp. 747–751; Lieutenant Colonel Edwin F. Glenn, "The Militia Law and Some Remarks About the Maneuver Camp at Pine Planes, N.Y.," *Journal of the Military Service Institution of the United States*, Vol. 43, July–December 1908, pp. 359–360; Major Daniel M. Taylor, "In What Way Can the National Guard be Modified So as to Make It an Effective Reserve to the Regular Army in Both War and Peace?" *Journal of the Military Service Institution of the United States*, Vol. 26, 1900, pp. 239–240; Brigadier General Tasker H. Bliss, "Mobilization and Maneuvers," *Journal of the Military Service Institution of the United States*, Vol. 50, January–June 1912, pp. 180–182; *Annual Report of the Chief, Division of Militia Affairs*, Washington, D.C.: U.S. Government Printing Office, 1909, p. 20; *Annual Report of the Chief, Division of Militia Affairs*, 1911, p. 162; *Annual Report of the Chief, Division of Militia Affairs*, Washington, D.C.: U.S. Government Printing Office, 1913, pp. 14–15.

[73] The Annual Report of the Secretary of War details joint maneuver camps held in the summer of 1908, describing the War Department's policy "to have joint maneuvers between the regular and militia field troops only on alternate years" (*Annual Report of the Secretary of War*, Washington, D.C.: U.S. Government Printing Office, 1908).

[74] A year after the DMA moved into the Office of the Chief of Staff, an act of Congress decreed that, thereafter, general officers would head the DMA, and he would become an additional member of the General Staff Corps. *Annual Report of the Chief, Division of Militia Affairs*, 1911, pp. 179–180; Barr, 1998, p. 183; Boehm, 2011, pp. 2–3; Hill, 1964, pp. 209–210.

of the National Guard's cavalry units were "untrained in the use of its most important weapon—the horse."[75]

The continuing debate over Army organization prompted Regular Army captain and 1892 West Point graduate John McAuley Palmer to pen his influential *Report on the Organization of the Land Forces of the United States* for Secretary of War Henry Stimson in 1912.[76] In his younger years, fresh out of West Point, Palmer had been a strong advocate for the professionalist school. However, he came to appreciate the necessity of military policies that recognized the importance of political feasibility and acceptance. The best military approach that could not gain congressional support was of no value. He therefore became a strong advocate of a civilian-based reserve component for the Army, and the 1912 report represented his first major venture into the issue.[77] The report addressed Army organization in peacetime to facilitate its rapid transition to war, including a Regular Army Reserve and a National Guard reserve. In an overture to the National Guard (and despite skepticism from Regular Army officers), he proposed incorporating elements of the National Guard into a federal force.

Palmer proposed the mobile land forces comprise (1) the Regular Army, augmented by its Regular Army Reserve, as the first line of defense; (2) an "army of national citizen soldiers," who would organize their own units to conduct peacetime training, as the second line of defense; and (3) an "army of volunteers to be organized under prearranged plans when greater forces are required than can be furnished by the Regular Army and the organized citizen soldiery," who would be trained once war began as the "great third line of national defense."[78] In keeping with American tradition, the Regular Army would remain small and, in an echo of Upton's expansible army, would serve as the "peace nucleus of a greater war Army, fulfilling a variety of roles until the citizen soldiery could be mobilized and trained for war."[79]

In peacetime, it would form into mobile units organized to prevent naval raids, fortify harbors, protect U.S. overseas territories, and furnish expeditionary forces as needed. These Regular Army forces would be the first to respond and would "seize important strategic positions before they can be occupied or adequately defended by

---

[75] *Relative to the Organized Militia of the United States*, Washington, D.C.: War Department, Division of Military Affairs in the Office of the Chief of Staff, U.S. Government Printing Office, 1911, pp. 22–23.

[76] John McAuley Palmer, *Report on the Organization of the Land Forces of the United States*, Washington, D.C.: U.S. Department of War, 1912. The War Department report was originally published under Secretary Stimson's name. Palmer was promoted several times during the period under review in this chapter. In 1914, he was promoted to the rank of major after service in China. He was promoted to colonel during World War I and retired as a brigadier general in 1923. For recollections of his time in the War Department, see Holley, 1982, pp. 200–213.

[77] Jonathan M. House, "John McAuley Palmer and the Reserve Components," *Parameters*, Vol. 12, No. 3, September 1982, pp. 12–13.

[78] Palmer, 1912, p. 61.

[79] Palmer, 1912, p. 12.

the enemy and before the concentration of the Army of citizen soldiers is complete."[80] Palmer called for the National Guard to be organized in peacetime into tactical units that would make it a well-balanced force. Upon mobilization and completion of their predeployment training, the "army of national citizen soldiers" would "reenforce the Regular Army," while volunteer forces were raised, organized, and trained.[81] While Palmer respected the militia clause, he did believe there was a way for the federal government to ensure greater readiness of parts of the National Guard. Under a recent congressional proposal, militia organizations that willingly conformed to certain efficiency standards would be entitled to federal pay. According to Palmer, enactment of the bill would effectively permit federal influence over the organization, training, and discipline of parts of the organized militia that voluntarily "engages to form a part of the national war army of citizen soldiery." Even for the portion that willingly met federal standards, federal influence "would be indirect and without encroachment upon the powers reserved to the States by the Constitution," but it would still act as a way for the federal government to incorporate parts of the organized militia into the national Army during peacetime under the armies clause of the Constitution.[82]

Palmer proposed an Army of 460,000 mobile troops, not including those assigned to Coastal Artillery or garrisoned overseas. The "regular contingent of mobile troops within the United States proper when raised to war strength, would comprise about 112,000 men. The remaining 348,000 mobile troops would be made up of citizen soldiers."[83] Palmer went on to note that "the detailed organization of the citizen soldiery will depend upon the extent to which the present organized militia can be utilized for general military purposes."[84] The National Guard in 1912 was just under 122,000 men, meaning that Palmer envisioned a federal volunteer force of between 226,000 and 348,000 men, depending upon access to the organized militia forces, or some combination of a federal volunteer force and an expanded organized militia. Palmer's proposal would have made an undetermined portion of the National Guard in each state and territory available to the War Department under the armies clause. When mobilized and severed from the militia clause, the Guard would lose its relationship with the states and would no longer be commanded by the governors. Palmer called for new programs to train prospective volunteers. "Our history is full of the success of the volunteer soldier after he has been trained for war," Palmer wrote, "but it contains no record of the successful employment of raw levies. . . . It is therefore our

---

[80] Palmer, 1912, p. 15.
[81] Palmer, 1912, pp. 60–61.
[82] Palmer, 1912, pp. 57–59.
[83] Palmer, 1912, p. 63.
[84] Palmer, 1912, p. 63.

most important military problem to devise means for preparing great armies of citizen soldiers."[85]

Palmer also proposed a Regular Army reserve that would be trained prior to the need for its use. Its main role would be to bring the Regular Army to war strength and maintain it during the interval between the outbreak of fighting and when recruits were finally prepared to enter the war. Reservists would consist of soldiers who were completing their Regular Army service, but Palmer suggested also allowing them to reenlist if they met physical and training qualifications. For the large pool of able and qualified men who had been discharged before the start of the new system, there would also be provisions for them to enlist in the Regular Army reserve.[86]

Palmer's proposal was not in lockstep with the conventional thinking of Regular Army officers of the time; most viewed volunteers as a useful resource to fill out Regular Army units, but emphasized the importance of professional leadership and years of training. Palmer, in contrast, felt that the United States would be better served in peacetime by a small, combat-ready Regular Army that could garrison overseas possessions and coastal defenses, respond immediately to contingencies as necessary, and serve as a training and leadership cadre in wartime for a mass citizen-soldier force comprising both the organized militia and federal volunteers. Palmer believed that civilians, once trained, would make good soldiers and leaders for the volunteer force. In Palmer's view, the Regular Army would be highly professionalized and provide a model for emulation by the National Guard and the volunteer army.

Aspects of Palmer's proposal mirrored the National Guard's preferred policy solutions. On the one hand, Palmer's assertion that "the traditional policy of the United States . . . is to be a small Regular Army and that the ultimate war force of the Nation is to be a great army of citizen soldiers" confirmed what the Guard had been claiming since the late 19th century. Guardsmen shared his belief that "this fundamental theory of military organization is sound economically and politically."[87] The Guard's affiliation with the states and its status as a militia were core elements of its institutional identity, and Palmer shared the Guardsmen view of that relationship as sacrosanct.

In the end, Palmer's report failed to spur new legislation or reorganization. Two factors limited its effect. First, the National Guard's ambivalence was a formidable obstacle to new legislation. The close relationship between the National Guard and some members of Congress compounded this challenge. Second, many in the War Department's General Staff continued to question the Guard's usefulness on constitutional grounds: The 1903 Dick Act clearly linked the Guard to the militia clause, which explicitly limited the Guard's use outside the United States' borders; even though the 1908 amendment attempted to permit Guard service abroad, constitutional critics,

---

[85] Palmer, 1912, pp. 12–14.

[86] Palmer, 1912, p. 34.

[87] Palmer, 1912, p. 12.

including the United States Attorney General, were still not satisfied.[88] In 1912, Attorney General George Wickersham issued a legal opinion reinforcing the constitutional limitations on National Guard service abroad. In a strict interpretation of the Constitution, Wickersham ruled that the federal government could employ the militia only to suppress insurrection, repel invasion, and execute the laws of the Union under the militia clause of the Constitution. According to Wickersham, the federal government could not use the National Guard—which was organized per the Dick Act under the militia clause—for service outside the borders of the United States.[89] The decision was a major setback to those National Guardsmen who sought an expanded role in the military establishment.

The 1915 General Staff Plan

By the end of 1912, the debate over the proper military policy for the U.S. had become pronounced and public. Both sides of the debate recognized that systemic changes were necessary: As Chief of Staff Wood explained, "it is the system under which we are serving which is at fault."[90] Secretary of War Stimson shared this sentiment, concluding that the "trouble with the Army comes down . . . to our own lack of an intelligent policy."[91] Some from the professionalist school advocated for a peacetime establishment that could be rapidly expanded for war and that did not violate the constitutional limitations on the federal use of the militia. As one officer wrote in *The North American Review*, the time had come for the "organization and maintenance during peace of a considerable body of United States volunteers separate and distinct from the State militia and with officers appointed by the President."[92]

The Guard vigorously resisted efforts to expand the military establishment through the adoption of federal reserves, increased volunteers, or universal military training. Major General John F. O'Ryan, commander of the New York National Guard and its 27th Division, denounced calls for conscription-based universal military service on the grounds that such a system would not be universal, and would therefore encourage favoritism and other abuses. He argued that, other than Great Britain, the United

---

[88] See House, 1982; Alan Hirsch, "The Militia Clause of the Constitution and the National Guard," *University of Cincinnati Law Review*, No. 59, 1988, pp. 944–946.

[89] Cooper, 1997, p. 114.

[90] Leonard Wood, "What Is the Matter with Our Army? It Lacks Concentration," *The Independent*, February 8, 1912a; Leonard Wood, "What Is the Matter with Our Army? The National Failure to Realize Its Purpose," *The Independent*, April 11, 1912b; Kreidberg and Henry, 1955, p. 183; Henry L. Stimson, "What Is the Matter with Our Army?" *The Independent*, April 4, 1912.

[91] Stimson, 1912.

[92] William H. Carter, "The Militia Is Not a National Force," *The North American Review*, Vol. 196, No. 680, 1912, p. 135.

States was the only great power that utilized "mercenary armies supplemented by volunteer forces" rather than the "European system of universal military service in time of peace."[93] This continental Europe model was not compatible with American democracy or traditions, O'Ryan believed. If adopted on a similar scale, based on population size in the United States universal military service would also create a needlessly large standing army in peacetime of more than 1.5 million men; all experts, he assured, agreed that it would take a force of only 500,000 men to repel any invasion imaginable.

Rather than turning to universal military service to solve the manpower needs, O'Ryan advocated for new legislation that built a larger and more efficient National Guard. He describes the Organized Militia contemporary to his time as "a vastly different force in its efficiency from the militia of the Constitution" due to improved peacetime standards. It needed to be federal at all times, however, and O'Ryan believed that the "present force known as the 'Organized Militia' is not in time of peace a real federal force, but a force composed of forty-eight little armies each with its own ideals and standards of efficiency, and each periodically affected, favorably or adversely as the case may be, by the appointment and activities of a new Adjutant General."[94] O'Ryan viewed the National Guard as a more cost-effective option than universal military service, asserting that "Pay would soon be demanded by those who serve." He further opined that "The force, if paid, would become a mercenary professional army, and the cost of such an institution would stagger even a Government as rich as ours."[95] Instead, Ryan proposed new legislation "to provide for a new force not to exceed 300,000 men in time of peace, and to do this not under the militia provision of the Federal Constitution, but under the provision with gives to Congress the power to raise and support armies."[96] O'Ryan accepted the argument that the Guard, as currently organized under the militia clause, could not be used overseas, and that state governors' authority over the Guard would prevent the unity of command he believed necessary to train, equip, and organize the Guard adequately. His solution, which he would argue again a number of years later, was for Congress to pass a new law that organized the Guard under the armies clause, with the stipulation that the governor of state, when deemed necessary, "might call upon the commanding officer of any or all the federal National Guard troops stationed therein to suppress riot and disorder."[97]

The outbreak of war in Europe in 1914 added new urgency to the debates over U.S. military policy. Military and civilian leaders were under pressure to improve the

---

[93] John F. O'Ryan, "The Role of the National Guard," *The North American Review*, Vol. 202, No. 718, 1915, p. 364.

[94] O'Ryan, 1915, pp. 369–370.

[95] O'Ryan, 1915, p. 366. O'Ryan makes early claims as to the cost-effectiveness of the National Guard—a theme the Guard would later promote.

[96] O'Ryan, 1915, p. 371.

[97] O'Ryan, 1915, p. 372.

Army's efficiency, as preparedness organizations such as the Army League, Navy League, National Security League, and the Military Training Camps Association, called for action.[98] Motivated by events in Europe and the potential risk of U.S. involvement, Secretary of War Lindley M. Garrison commissioned the General Staff to propose an Army restructuring plan in 1915.

At the direction of Secretary Garrison, the General Staff used Palmer's 1912 report as a starting point. The 1915 analysis, however, arrived at largely different conclusions.[99] The 1915 General Staff Plan drew on European models of military organization (as did Palmer's 1912 report). In part, this emulation reflected U.S. strategists' deference to European states' preponderant military power. It also reflected the War Department's gradual recognition of the character of the "modern warfare" that had emerged in Europe.[100] But the plan proved to be highly unpopular with the National Guard, since it highlighted the limitations of the Constitution's militia clause as a starting point for Army planning. Whereas O'Ryan, whose article was published at almost the same time as the General Staff Plan, sought a new legislative approach. The General Staff Plan called for the creation of a "Continental Army," commanded, organized, and trained by the Regular Army. The final report, *Statement of a Proper Military Policy for the United States*, set the stage for continued controversy in the coming year.[101]

The General Staff Plan began by identifying the capacity of overseas great powers to invade the U.S. homeland. It went on to catalogue the strength of the European and Japanese armies, finding that each ranged in size from 2 to 5 million men—a staggering size that dwarfed the tiny U.S. Regular Army. The report, therefore, argued that the United States' survival would be in serious peril should it have to defend itself from an invasion with the current force. Having outlined the potential danger of attack by a great power and the country's current inadequacy to deal with it, the report provided a plan for organizing the peacetime Army and its wartime expansion without violating the Constitution's limitations on the federal use of the militia.

The General Staff argued that "our system should be able to furnish 500,000 trained and organized mobile troops at the outbreak of the war and to have at least 500,000 more available within 90 days thereafter." The manpower plan did not stop at 1 million men. "Here, however, it must be pointed out," the report continued,

---

[98] For a summary and review of these organizations, see Tinsley, 1939, p. 33.

[99] At the time, the War College acted as the General Staff's analytical research body. For a history of the War College, see Judith Hicks Stiehm, *U.S. Army War College: Military Education in a Democracy*, Philadelphia, Pa.: Temple University Press, 2010.

[100] General Staff Corps, War College Division, *Statement of a Proper Military Policy for the United States*, Washington, D.C., 1915, pp. 4–5, 8–9, 14–15. Academics have used multiple names to refer to the 1915 report. We refer to it in this report as the General Staff Plan, but it is also commonly known as the 1915 War College Proposal, the War College Plan, and the Continental Army proposal.

[101] Weigley, 1967, pp. 344–346; Beaver, 2006, pp. 70–72.

that two [foreign] expeditions alone will provide a force large enough to cope with our 1,000,000 mobile troops, and consequently we must at the outbreak of hostilities provide the system to raise and train, in addition, at least 500,000 troops to replace the losses and wastage in personnel incident to war.[102]

The plan suggested that, of the 500,000 troops to be available immediately, just 121,000 of them would be Regular Army. The remaining 379,000 would be Regular Army Reserve (i.e., soldiers who had completed their initial service obligation "with the colors," but were now in a "furlough" status without pay, but subject to immediate recall). Another 74,500 Regular Army troops would be required to garrison overseas territories, and 34,500 Regular Army troops would be required for the Coastal Artillery at home and overseas, for a total of 230,000 Regular Army troops. To this, the General Staff added 30,000 troops for the Sanitary, Quartermaster, and Ordnance Departments and 21,000 for the Philippine Scouts, bringing the grand total to 281,000 troops for the Regular Army. Even excluding the Philippine Scouts, this would more than double the nearly 108,000 Regular Army troops authorized by Congress in 1915. The War Department's plan utilized the National Guards of the states in roles consistent with the Constitution's militia clause, but did not envision employing them overseas.

That the document would inflame National Guard proponents is not surprising. The 1915 report was based on the assumption that the militia could only be used in a federal role for the three purposes outlined in the Constitution and as specified by the Attorney General in his 1912 opinion. However, it was critical of unpreparedness and averse to crash mobilizations to build an effective Army, as well as wary of the limited role of the federal government in the organization and training of citizen-soldiers. Whereas Palmer had insisted that any U.S. military policy proposal should both fulfill military needs and reflect political realities, the General Staff Plan proposed an approach that was knowingly unlikely to garner strong National Guard support, and therefore fail the political realities litmus test. The General Staff Plan also claimed that the American people had drawn an erroneous conclusion from the country's military history; that is, whatever approaches were sufficient for the nation's defense in the past would be equally sufficient for future needs.[103] This sentiment was in line with other professionalist voices of the time. That same year, Wood, now commanding the Army's Eastern Department, had expressed this opinion explicitly during an address at Princeton University. With little sympathy for his civilian audience, he proclaimed that "the people of the United States are singularly lacking in information concerning both the military history of their country and its military policy."[104]

---

[102] General Staff Corps, War College Division, 1915, p. 5.

[103] General Staff Corps, War College Division, 1915, p. 8.

[104] Wood, 1915. See Chapter 1, "The Policy of the United States In Raising and Maintaining Armies," pp. 1–3.

The atmosphere that year in America was anxious due to the growing World War. Despite Woodrow Wilson running on a platform of neutrality for the 1916 election, the General Staff's call for a dramatic expansion of the Army might have survived Congress had it not circumscribed the National Guard's role, albeit consistent with the U.S. Attorney General's 1912 legal opinion. The General Staff recommended the National Guard be used in a federal role to support Coastal Artillery and defend critical infrastructure and communication lines in the homeland, roles consistent with the Constitution. The planners questioned the National Guard units' organization, equipment, and training, and argued that any portion of the nation's first line of defense had to "be maintained, fully organized, and equipped in peace at practically war strength. This would exclude Organized Militia from consideration for service."[105]

If National Guard units were ill-suited legally and in terms of preparedness, and if the Regular Army was too small to defend against invasion, then another source of manpower was necessary. The General Staff concluded that the use of federal volunteers and conscription was inevitable. It highlighted aspects of the 1903 Dick Act and its 1908 amendment as potentially problematic in modern war when trying to raise a volunteer force, particularly the portion of the law that states

> when the military needs of the Federal Government arising from the necessity to execute the laws of the Union, suppress insurrection, or repel invasion, can not be met by the regular forces, the organized militia shall be called into the service of the United States in advance of any volunteer force which it may be determined to raise.[106]

As the Organized Militia could be employed only for certain purposes, it could not "therefore, become in all respects a national force, available for all purposes for which an army may properly be employed." It would be difficult to know how many officers and men from the Organized militia would respond to a call from the President, but the "transfer from the status of militia to that of volunteer must be a voluntary act" during the time of war in question, not in peace, when such intentions were not legally binding.[107] Lest they be misunderstood as advocating for abandoning this portion of the 1908 Act, the General Staff assured that "No legislation affecting the Organized Militia is recommended beyond the repeal of all provisions of laws now in effect whereby militia or militia organizations may or must be received into the Federal service *in advance* of any other forces."[108]

---

[105] General Staff Corps, War College Division, 1915, p. 22.

[106] U.S. Statutes at Large, An Act to Further Amend the Act Entitled "An Act to Promote the Efficiency of the Militia, and for Other Purposes," May 27, 1908 (35 Stat. 339), pp. 400–401.

[107] General Staff Corps, War College Division, 1915, pp. 7–8.

[108] General Staff Corps, War College Division, 1915, p. 23.

Not surprisingly, the General Staff Plan provoked emotional resistance. Palmer, although still a serving officer of the Regular Army and a member of the General Staff himself at the time, criticized the General Staff Plan as demonstrating an "absence of tact." He acknowledged that uncertainty about the militia clause complicated efforts to use the National Guard as a federal force, but claimed that the General Staff "instead of trying to adjust the constitutional harness . . . set out to kill the horse."[109] In the House of Representatives, fiscal conservatives, such as Democratic House Majority Leader Claude Kitchin, attacked the plan on the grounds that its preparedness measures would overburden the American taxpayer.[110] A two-reserve system, he asserted, was not the economical approach. Moreover, congressional leaders were skeptical of radical change. When facing a choice, most politicians were likely to favor the National Guard—an organization whose units already existed and whose members could vote.[111]

Some Guardsmen were outraged, especially the National Guard Association and State Adjutants General. They viewed the General Staff Plan as an attempt to roll back their recent legislative victories and end their status as a part of the first-line defense with loyalty to state governors and the U.S. President. Having sought greater federal recognition and funding for years, Guardsmen were not willing to be absorbed into the mass army envisioned by the General Staff. They valued their legislative victories of 1903, 1908, and 1910, and were determined to remain, in their view, as part of the nation's first line of defense.[112]

In contrast to their opposition to the General Staff Plan, Guardsmen rallied behind new legislation sponsored by Virginia Democratic Congressman James Hay, chairman of the House Committee on Military Affairs, and who had initially supported the Continental Army plan. Hay served on the committee for 18 years, retiring after President Wilson appointed him to the U.S. Court of Claims in 1916, shortly before the national elections. At that time, the preparedness movement was largely supported by Republicans, while Democrats, to a great extent, opposed increased military spending or preparations "against" war. As such, Hay was notoriously unsympathetic to the General Staff. He was also dismissive of the notion that European powers threatened the continental United States or that the United States may be drawn into

---

[109] Quoted in Holley, 1982, p. 245.

[110] "Fails to Win Kitchin," *New York Times*, November 9, 1915, p. 4; "Sees Militarism in Wilson's Plan," *New York Times*, November 19, 1915, p. 4; Finnegan, 1974, p. 80. Also see Alex Mathews Arnett, *Claude Kitchin and the Wilson War Policies*, New York: Russell & Russell, 1971.

[111] Clifford, 2014, p. 126.

[112] Finnegan, 1974, p. 78; U.S. Statutes at Large, An Act to Promote the Efficiency of the Militia, and for Other Purposes, January 21, 1903 (32 Stat. 775); U.S. Statutes at Large, An Act to Further Amend the Act Entitled "An Act to Promote the Efficiency of the Militia, and for Other Purposes," May 27, 1908 (35 Stat. 339); U.S. Statutes at Large, An Act to Further Amend the Act Entitled "An Act to Promote the Efficiency of the Militia, and for Other Purposes," Approved January Twenty-First, Nineteen Hundred and Three," Sixty-First Congress, Session II, Chapter 185, April 21, 1910 (36 Stat. 329).

the ongoing war in Europe, and opposed to any scheme for modernizing or increasing the size of the Regular Army. He quickly emerged as the General Staff's most influential opponent.[113] Where the General Staff had sought to narrow the role of the National Guard, Hay now insisted on legislation that would unify the disjointed Democratic party behind the President in an election year and that only modestly increased military spending. He was skeptical of the General Staff's warnings about inadequate manpower and expressed confidence that the combination of organized militia, Regular Army veterans, and graduates of college military training programs could meet wartime demands.[114] Hay therefore rejected the General Staff's proposal. Instead, he proposed legislation to reform and strengthen the National Guard by allocating federal funds for equipment and drill pay, provided it met certain training standards established by the War Department.[115] The Hay Bill also called for officers and enlisted men to take oaths binding them into national service whenever federalized in times of national emergency. This provision would, in theory, give the federal government greater control than before over the National Guard and improve the mobilization process. The Hay Bill also reflected the friction between the General Staff and some congressional members by reducing the size of the General Staff to just the chief of staff with two general officer assistants and 52 officers.

In contrast to the General Staff Plan, the Hay Bill appealed to the National Guard, fiscal conservatives, and Southern opponents of federal power.[116] Ultimately, the General Staff Plan was defeated in the House Committee on Military Affairs, although it was strongly supported by its Senate counterpart. Now in an election year in 1916, Wilson expressed his intent to work with Congress to find a reasonable compromise. Hay assured the President that his bill would be supported by "nine Congressmen in ten" when it came to the House floor for vote.[117] In protest and facing humiliation, Secretary of War Garrison submitted his letter of resignation, noting that "there can be no honest or worthwhile solution which does not result in national forces under the *exclusive* control and authority of the national government."[118] Wilson accepted Garrison's resignation on February 10, 1916.

The Hay Bill overwhelmingly passed the House, as he had predicted, but failed in the Senate after lacking the President's full backing and enough senatorial support. The Senate soon developed its own bill more along the lines of the General Staff Plan.

---

[113] Finnegan, 1974, p. 74.

[114] Herring, Jr., p. 386.

[115] Weigley, 1967, p. 345.

[116] Herring, Jr., p. 386.

[117] Skowronek, 1982, p. 231.

[118] Herring, Jr., p. 386.

Over the ensuring weeks, negotiators from both chambers pounded out a compromise in conference, retaining aspects of both the House and Senate plans.

The 1916 National Defense Act

In June 1916, Congress passed the landmark National Defense Act (NDA), one of the most comprehensive pieces of defense legislation in American history. Like the 1903 Dick Act and its 1908 and 1910 amendments, the NDA of 1916 sought to improve the nation's ability to mobilize a mass army and meet the demands of modern industrial warfare. The law represented a compromise among professionalists, preparedness advocates, pacifists, fiscal conservatives, anti-federalists, and the National Guard; like most compromises, it left none of the parties completely satisfied, and did little to prepare the nation for its forthcoming role in the ongoing war in Europe. As Hay stated during congressional debate, "This is a military policy which we are laying down for a time of peace and not for war." Nonetheless, the NDA deserves credit for creating a path for federalization of the National Guard and providing the authorities for increasing the standards, discipline, and readiness of the National Guard when called into federal service. The act authorized additional units for the Regular Army, but capped "the total enlisted force of the line of the Regular Army" at 175,000 men, not including the Philippine Scouts, unassigned recruits, and the enlisted men of the Medical Department, Quartermaster Corps, or Signal Corps. Lack of appropriated funds ensured the Regular Army would not grow to its authorized level. The 1916 act also provided for expanding the size of the National Guard in each state and territory until each such National Guard force comprised 800 enlisted men for each state/territorial member of Congress (both houses). Interestingly, the act also authorized a Regular Army Reserve and a National Guard Reserve, as recommended by Palmer in his 1912 report.[119]

The sweeping legislation (see Table 3.2) defined the Army of the United States as consisting of the "Regular Army, the Volunteer Army, the Officers' Reserve Corps, the Enlisted Reserve Corps, the National Guard while in the service of the United States, and such other land forces as are now or may hereafter be authorized by law."[120] The law mandated that Guard units be organized on the model of the Regular Army. It capped the "total enlisted force of the line of the Regular Army" at 175,000 men. The standing force would be supplemented by the newly created Enlisted Reserve Corps

---

[119] Public Law 64-85, An Act for Making Further and More Effectual Provision for the National Defense, and for Other Purposes, June 3, 1916; Martha Derthick, *The National Guard in Politics*, Cambridge, Mass.: Harvard University Press, 1965; George S. Pappas, *Prudens Futuri: The U.S. Army War College, 1901–1967*, Carlisle Barracks, Pa.: Alumni Association of the U.S. Army War College, 1967; Hewes, 1975. See also George W. Baer, *One Hundred Years of Sea Power: The U.S. Navy, 1890–1990*, Stanford, Calif..: Stanford University Press, 1994, pp. 60–61.

[120] Public Law 64-85, 1916. See Section 1.

Table 3.2
Key Provisions of the National Defense Act of 1916 (Public Law 64-85)

- Premised federal use of the National Guard on the armies clause. Guardsmen would be "drafted" as individuals into federal service. "All persons so drafted shall, from the date of their draft, stand discharged from the militia."
- Circumvented constitutional limits on foreign service by mandating that Guardsmen would be drafted into federal service as individuals, based on the federal oath.
- Established the Officers' Reserve Corps and Enlisted Reserve Corps, which would provide the cadre of a citizen army in times of war.
- Authorized the President to establish and maintain the ROTC.
- Defined the composition of the Army of the United States, which "shall consist of the Regular Army, the Volunteer Army, the Officers' Reserve Corps, the Enlisted Reserve Corps, the National Guard while in the service of the United States, and such other land forces as are now or may hereafter be authorized by law."
- Required the National Guard to model itself on the Regular Army and follow federal training standards.
- Designated the Division of Militia Affairs as the Militia Bureau, reporting directly to the Secretary of War.
- Authorized federal funding to compensate members of the National Guard for weekly drills, assuming minimum attendance levels were achieved and each drill period lasted at least one and one-half hours.
- Authorized additional Regular Army units, but capped "the total enlisted force of the line of the Regular Army" at 175,000 men.
- Authorized a multiyear expansion of the National Guard to about 450,000 officers and enlisted men.[a]
- Authorized approximately $17 million for the Army's acquisition of 375 aircraft and established the Air Division to administer the Signal Corps' Aviation Section.
- Authorized President Wilson to establish the Council of National Defense, composed of the Secretaries of War, Navy, Labor, Agriculture, Interior, and Commerce and tasked with advising the President and executive departments on the mobilization of industrial goods and services in time of war.

[a] The 1916 NDA did not set a specific end strength number, but instead required each state to increase its number of National Guardsmen until a ratio of 800 men per congressional representative was reached. It did not set a specific deadline for this achievement, but historians have estimated that the number, given contemporary congressional districting, would be approximately 400,000 men.

and Officers' Reserve Corps. The act also authorized the President to establish and maintain a new training organization at civil education institutions. Known as the Reserve Officers' Training Corps (ROTC), the training organization was modeled after the university training programs Clark and Wood had established and consisted of individual citizens who participated in Regular Army instructional camps organized by the Military Training Camps Association (MTCA) and the War Department.[121]

---

[121] Section 54 of the 1916 NDA (Public Law 64-85) stipulated that "The Secretary of War is hereby authorized to maintain . . . camps for the military instruction and training of such citizens as may be selected for such instruction and training, upon their application and under such terms of enlistment and regulations as may be prescribed by the Secretary of War." See also Crossland and Currie, 1984. Section 37 defined the Officers' Reserve Corps: "there shall be organized, under such rules and regulations as the President may prescribe not inconsistent with the provisions of this Act, an Officers' Reserve Corps of the Regular Army." It also defined the Enlisted Reserve Corps: "For the purpose of securing an additional reserve of enlisted men for military service with the Engineer, Signal, and Quartermaster Corps and the Ordinance and Medical Departments of the Regular Army, an Enlisted Reserve Corps, to consist of such number of enlisted men of such grade or grades as may be designated by the President from time to time, is hereby authorized, such authorization to be effective on and after the first day of July, nineteen hundred and sixteen."

These provisions fell far short of the General Staff's preparedness proposal, reflecting a political compromise in a presidential election year; but they marked a significant improvement in military policy and reflected the emerging consensus that the war in Europe might soon require the United States to mobilize a mass army. The NDA directed the organization, training, discipline, uniforms, and equipment of the National Guard to be modeled after the Regular Army. It defined the National Guard as the Organized Militia, consisting "of the regularly enlisted militia between the ages of eighteen and forty-five years organized, armed, and equipped as hereinafter provided, and of commissioned officers between the ages of twenty-one and sixty-four years."[122] It authorized the National Guards of the states and territories to increase incrementally over a number of years until the size of each force comprised not less than 800 enlisted men per member of Congress. The law directed Guard units to assemble at least 48 times per year for drill and instruction and "shall, in addition thereto, participate in encampments, maneuvers, or other exercises, including outdoor target practice, at least fifteen days in training each year."[123] Similarly, it increased federal funding for Guard equipment and uniforms, and empowered the War Department to establish enlistment standards and organization for Guard units.

The 1916 NDA represented two important victories for the National Guard. First, it recognized the Guard's status as a part of the Army when federalized and streamlined the procedures for federalizing the National Guard during war. Second, it circumvented lingering constitutional proscriptions by allowing Guardsmen to be drafted into the Army as individuals, and simultaneously discharged from the militia. By using the armies clause and the term *drafted*, rather than *called*, the act resolved the issue of overseas service.

Guardsmen celebrated the 1916 NDA as an affirmation of their perceived role as part of the nation's first line of defense alongside the Regular Army. Implementation of the law, however, introduced new challenges for the National Guard. To bring National Guard units into federal service, the law stipulated that Guardsmen were to be drafted as individuals for federal service, thereby discharging them from the militia. This stipulation, however, did not quell uncertainties over whether or not the Guard as the organized militia could be sent overseas to fight foreign wars, since that was not one of the Constitution's three sanctioned purposes for the militia.

The 1916 NDA favored the bureau chiefs at the expense of the General Staff. It renamed the Militia Affairs Division as the Militia Bureau, directly supervised by the Secretary of War (versus its previous alignment under the Chief of Staff), and

---

[122] Public Law 64-85, 1916.

[123] Guardsmen were to participate in at least 90 minutes of training per week, usually on a weeknight. After World War II, this weekly requirement was converted to one weekend a month.

authorized up to two Guard officers to serve in the office for the first time.[124] While it increased the number of General Staff officers to 54, no more than half of them could serve in Washington, and the General Staff officers were prohibited from duplicating the administrative work of the bureaus. Finally, it eliminated the General Staff's Mobile Army Division and assigned its functions to the Office of the Adjutant General, the Army's chief administrative officer. The bureau chiefs praised the act as the "Magna Carta" because it restored their independence and weakened the General Staff.[125] For the National Guard, which had long pushed for similar reforms, the changes seemed to institutionalize its independence within the War Department.

The 1916 NDA also benefited the National Guard by forestalling the debate on universal military training, a tenet of the strengthening preparedness movement.[126] As previously noted, the National Guard eyed the MTCA—a vocal proponent of universal military training—with suspicion. It feared that the MTCA's proposals might allow the War Department and the Regular Army to bypass the National Guard and form an alternate federal reserve. For their part, the MTCA's leadership worked hard to avoid estranging the powerful National Guard lobby by insisting that military training camps and the ROTC were based on volunteerism.[127]

The 1916 NDA thus made significant strides in clarifying the mass mobilization process, including the drafting of individual Guardsmen into federal service. Still, the progress of recruiting and training raw recruits was halting. Recruitment efforts expanded over the year, as international events made the possibility of the United States' entry into World War I more and more likely.

A Test of the 1916 Act: The Mexican Border Crisis

Despite the positive features of the 1916 NDA, many preparedness advocates were unsatisfied. The 1916 NDA did not resolve the tension between the War Department, which generally reflected the views of the professionalist elements of the Regular Army, and the National Guard and the National Guard Association, which enjoyed the backing of Congress. Palmer later derided the law as "a hodgepodge of two mutually antagonistic systems" and questioned its long-term sustainability.[128] Similarly, Secretary of War Baker's endorsement of the bill was tempered by his description of it as "more or

---

[124] In 1916, the Militia Bureau's chief was authorized to be a Regular Army officer. The 1920 amendment to the NDA (Public Law 66-242) would change this provision. In 1933, the Militia Bureau was redesignated as the National Guard Bureau.

[125] Nenninger, 1986, p. 226.

[126] General John Palmer discusses the Plattsburg movement at length in Holley, 1982, pp. 248–259.

[127] Clifford, 2014, p. 203.

[128] Holley, 1982, p. 247.

less experimental."[129] Detractors, such as Wood and former Secretary of War Root, who predicted U.S. entry into the European war, called for more dramatic reforms of the Army, including the imposition of universal military training. Root's position signaled a significant change of heart toward the National Guard. In September, only three months after the NDA's passage, Root criticized its reliance on the National Guard as the primary reserve. As he explained in a letter to a colleague:

> The National Guard system is not adequate and cannot be made adequate to meet the needs of the national defense . . . it is impossible to have an effective body of soldiers who serve two masters [state governors and the President] and are raised and organized to accomplish two different purposes.[130]

Root's remarks presaged the debate that would emerge after World War I. In the near term, the 1916 NDA's insufficiency for mobilizing a mass citizen army was clear. Although the NDA stipulated a maximum enlisted strength four times the Regular Army's size in 1897, it did not provide a clear time frame to meet this goal. Moreover, Wilson's prohibition against planning for American entry into the war restricted recruitment and expansion efforts by introducing a political disincentive to act.[131] Similarly, it remained unclear when or how the National Guards of the states would reach the manpower levels authorized by the 1916 NDA.

Fifteen days after President Wilson signed the NDA into law, it received its first test, when a simmering conflict on the U.S.-Mexican border prompted the President to federalize National Guard units from many states, some as far away as Connecticut. American forces had engaged in periodic border skirmishes with the Mexicans for decades, but the 1910 Mexican Revolution heightened tensions. The conflict drove revolutionaries, criminals, and arms smugglers to border towns, where Mexico's central government lacked the ability to maintain order. The violence often spilled into the southern U.S. border states. The administration of William Howard Taft had imposed an arms embargo in 1912, but the policy backfired, and illicit activity along the border increased, heightening tensions between residents on both sides of the border. In response, Wilson ordered the Army to patrol the border and enforce U.S. neutrality; by November 1915, almost half of the Regular Army was committed to border patrol in southern Texas. Its thin presence did little to stem the escalating violence, and Mexican rebels and criminals began conducting smuggling, kidnapping, and robbery raids into the Rio Grande Valley.[132] These events culminated in Francisco "Pancho" Villa's

---

[129] Lee, 1940, p. 28.

[130] Elihu Root to Lieutenant General S. B. M. Young, September 17, 1916, in Root, 1916, p. 488.

[131] Clark, 2017.

[132] For more on this, see David K. Work, "The Tenth U.S. Cavalry on the Mexican Border, 1913–1919," *The Western Historical Quarterly*, Vol. 40, No. 2, Summer 2009; Friedrich Katz, "Pancho Villa and the Attack on Columbus, New Mexico," *The American Historical Review*, Vol. 83, No. 1, February 1978; James A. Sandos, "Pancho

March 9, 1916 raid into Columbus, New Mexico, and the death of 17 Americans. In response, Wilson ordered an Army expedition into Mexico to pursue Pancho Villa. Two months later, he federalized over 5,000 men from the Texas, New Mexico, and Arizona National Guards, but their numbers proved insufficient, leading to a June 18 call for nearly the entire National Guard to duty on the border.[133]

The crisis revealed continued shortcomings in National Guard units' mobilization process.[134] While most Guardsmen responded to orders to organize and deploy to the border, Regular Army inspectors found many Guardsmen unfit for duty. More than 10,000 were discharged for failing physical evaluations, and 10 percent failed to report for service.[135] The states handed out hardship discharges until the War Department intervened. The Guard's force structure was weighted heavily toward infantry units, when horse-mounted cavalry units were in high demand. States also lacked sufficient support units to sustain military operations. Moreover, mobilization suffered from a lack of coordination between the Department of War and the states. Because many states did not have adequate mobilization sites, some Guard units bypassed mobilization camps and, under direct orders from the War Department, reported to the border. Equipment shortages and inadequate installations for mobilized forces there reduced their effectiveness and caused hard feelings.[136]

Despite 15 years of reforms, the Guard's mobilization in 1916 was not an improvement over its performance during the Spanish-American War, as the states experienced significant logistical difficulties associated with mass mobilization.[137] The Mexican border crisis also gave reason for professionalists within the Regular Army to hold on to concerns over the readiness of National Guard members and units.

Although the 1916 NDA had ostensibly clarified the Guard's statutory authority to serve on foreign soil (i.e., via the armies clause of the Constitution), the War Department lacked confidence in the Guard's capability to fight effectively. Inspectors identified readiness shortfalls in most infantry, cavalry, and field artillery units. Inspectors typically determined that infantry regiments "might be made efficient for field service

---

Villa and American Security: Woodrow Wilson's Mexican Diplomacy Reconsidered," *Journal of Latin American Studies*, Vol. 13, No. 2, November 1981.

[133] *Report on the Mobilization of the Organized Militia and National Guard of the United States, 1916*, Washington, D.C.: U.S. Government Printing Office, 1916, pp. 9–21; *War Department Annual Reports, 1916*, Vol. I, Washington, D.C.: U.S. Government Printing Office, 1916, pp. 7–12.

[134] Galloway, 1957; Kreidberg and Henry, 1955, pp. 199–201.

[135] Doubler, 2001, p. 142.

[136] "Report to the Adjutant General of the Commonwealth of Virginia for the Year Ending December 31, 1917," *Annual Reports of Officers, Boards and Institutions of the Commonwealth of Virginia for the Year Ending September 30, 1917*, Richmond, Va.: Superintendent of Public Printing, 1918, pp. 3–4; Charles H. Harris and Louis R. Sadler, *The Great Call-Up: The Guard, the Border, and the Mexican Revolution*, Norman, Okla.: University of Oklahoma Press, 2015.

[137] Cooper, 1997, pp. 156–166.

against an inferior enemy in six months; against trained troops, it will require two years" with the assistance of regular officers.[138] Fourteen years later, Guardsmen testifying before the House Committee on Military Affairs recounted their irritation and cited the Mexican crisis as evidence, from their point of view, of the Guard's unfair treatment by the War Department and Regular Army.[139] As a report included in the 1916 Militia Bureau study on the mobilization revealed, much of the discontent of National Guardsmen on the Mexican border appears to have been self-inflicted. The report highlighted the ignorance of many National Guard officers "of the proper methods for taking care of their men" and "a lack of proper home training such that the performance of duty comes above personal interest or enjoyment." The report found that "On the whole the militia expect everything to be shown them and everything to be done for them."[140] Despite the National Guard's discontent, and regardless of their mobilization shortcomings, the border crisis was, in many ways, a valuable dress rehearsal for the larger effort to come.

Conclusion

The period 1903–1916 brought the most sweeping changes in U.S. military policy since the 1792 Militia Act. Key legislation defined the composition of the Army and established necessary mobilization policies. It was a contentious period, in which the debate over legislation that would govern U.S. military policy centered on how the Army could best transition from a peacetime footing to the mass army required for modern warfare. National Guard proponents fought to be identified as part of the nation's first-line defenses. The 1908 amendment to the Dick Act established in law that the Guard would be called in advance of any volunteer forces needed to expand the Army. As a result, advocates for a federal reserve to the Army continued to make their case. These federal reserve advocates accepted the standing legal opinion offered by the U.S. Attorney General in 1912 that the Constitution explicitly limited the federal use of the militia. In a sense, their argument won the day in the 1916 NDA, which provided for the simultaneous drafting of individuals from the National Guard under the Constitution's armies clause and their discharge from the Organized Militia. This legislative approach, very similar to that previously recommended by Major General John O'Ryan from the New York National Guard, provided the legal framework for

---

[138] *Report on the Mobilization of the Organized Militia and National Guard of the United States, 1916*, 1916, pp. 92–93.

[139] U.S. House of Representatives, *Officers' Reserve Corps–National Guard (Proposed Amendments to the National Defense Act), H.R. 10478: Hearing Before the Committee on Military Affairs*, Washington, D.C.: U.S. Government Printing Office, April 14, May 15, May 16, 1930, p. 20.

[140] *Report of the Mobilization of the Organized Militia and National Guard of the United States*, 1916, p. 152.

employment of the National Guards of the states in the nation's defense at home and abroad, without violating the limitations imposed by the Constitution's militia clause.

The following chapter will show that the 1916 NDA at least provided a basic force structure for the Army to expand in the case of national emergency or war, but that the experience of preparation and mobilization during late 1916 and early 1917 brought into sharp relief the limitations of recent reforms. U.S. military policy had certainly evolved, but not enough to deal with the complex task of mobilizing and deploying a mass, civilian-based Army to fight a world war against a major industrial power abroad.

CHAPTER FOUR

Preparedness, World War I, and the 1920 Amendment to the 1916 National Defense Act

Introduction

Preparedness advocates were influential in debates on U.S. military policy just prior to U.S. entry into World War I. Building on a foundation established by the 1916 NDA, they pushed for new reforms to transform the Army into a fighting force capable of defeating a European army. The U.S. declaration of war in April 1917 confirmed professionalists' warnings about the state of the military, and it soon became clear that the nation needed an Army of millions, not the 286,000 men authorized by the 1916 NDA. Volunteerism failed to meet political expectations (consistent with the General Staff's earlier concerns and observations during the 1916 mobilizations for duty on the Mexican border) or the Army's needs. In response, Congress authorized mass conscription via the Selective Service Act on May 18, 1917, on a level that provided a short-term solution to the Army's manpower problem, but exposed long-term problems in military policy. As a result, the postwar period would be defined by a reemergence of political debate over the United States' military policy, resulting in another significant piece of legislation—the 1920 amendment to the 1916 NDA.

The Road to War

When war broke out in 1914, President Wilson proclaimed a policy of neutrality and counseled the American people against intervention. "Every man who really loves America," he cautioned, "will act and speak in the true spirit of neutrality. . . . We must be impartial in thought, as well as action."[1] Wilson recognized that large numbers of Americans were of German and British descent, and he feared that the war might bring domestic unrest. Most Americans, confident in the security provided by their geographic isolation, opposed intervention and embraced the President's stance.

---

[1] Woodrow Wilson, *Message to Congress*, Washington, D.C.: U.S. Government Printing Office, Senate Document No. 566, 1914.

As the war dragged on, however, Americans increasingly debated their role in world affairs. Should the President punish Germany for its refusal to recognize neutral shipping rights? Should it intervene in defense of Western Europe, even if the country's interests were not directly threatened?

Most Americans who opposed U.S. entry into the war rejected reformers' calls for military investment and planning. They were confident that the United States' geographic isolation would allow the nation to weather the storm in Europe, and they opposed any action that might be perceived by the belligerents as intervention. Thousands joined such antiwar societies as the American Union Against Militarism and the Henry Street Peace Committee, and applauded the President's call for neutrality in law, policy, and official statements.[2] The war in Europe, they argued, was another chapter in the history of old-world follies, where entangling alliances, monarchical squabbles, and false pride would continue to ensure violence.[3] The United States need not stoop to Europe's level, they surmised. "There is such a thing as a man being too proud to fight," Wilson noted in 1915. "There is such a thing as a nation being so right that it does not need to convince others by force that it is right."[4]

Preparedness advocates initially shared the belief that the United States would remain neutral, but they sought to leverage public anxiety about the war to achieve long-term reforms in U.S. military policy.[5] In particular, they argued that a larger military would provide the best insurance "against" war, because it would deter aggressive action against the United States or its interests.[6]

As the war in Europe dragged on, preparedness advocates began to view the burgeoning pacifist movements with incredulity and then alarm. Americans remained steadfastly committed to neutrality even as U.S. interests began to come under foreign attack. In 1915, Germany began to attack American and British shipping in the Atlantic. Despite Wilson's calls for Germany to recognize U.S. neutrality, German aggression continued unabated. Disaster struck on May 7, 1915, when a German U-boat attack on the *Lusitania*, a British passenger ship, resulted in the death of 1,200 pas-

---

[2] C. Roland Marchand, *The American Peace Movement and Social Reform: 1898–1918*, Princeton, N.J.: Princeton University Press, 1972; John Whiteclay Chambers, *The Eagle and the Dove: The American Peace Movement and United States Foreign Policy, 1900–1922*, Syracuse, N.Y.: Syracuse University Press, 1991; David M. Kennedy, *Over Here: The First World War and American Society*, Oxford, UK: Oxford University Press, 1980, pp. 14–28, 30–49.

[3] "The 'Preparedness' Flurry," *The Nation*, Vol. 99, No. 2579, December 3, 1914.

[4] Woodrow Wilson, "Address to Naturalized Citizens at Convention Hall, Philadelphia," edited by Gerhard Peters and John T. Woolley, American Presidency Project, 1915.

[5] Kennedy, 1980, p. 30.

[6] David R. Woodward, *The American Army and the First World War*, Cambridge, UK: Cambridge University Press, 2014, pp. 21–22; "Proposes an Army of 1,000,000 Boys," *New York Times*, August 15, 1915, p. 3.

sengers, including 128 Americans.⁷ Germany defended the attack by claiming the ship was transporting small arms ammunition to Britain and had thus abdicated its rights as a neutral civilian vessel.⁸ Americans responded in outrage, and pressure mounted on the President to request a formal declaration of war. Wilson counseled caution. Through direct negotiations, he secured from Germany an informal agreement to halt its employment of unrestricted submarine warfare.

Despite the agreement, tensions with Germany worsened through 1916, a presidential election year. Contributing to the tension was Wilson's refusal to impose a trade embargo on the belligerents, an action that would have hurt the Allies more than Germany, as well as the American economy. Private industry continued to support the British and French wartime economies, and, in October 1915, Wilson permitted loans to the cash-strapped Allies. Although German-Americans could, and did, contribute to the Central Powers, the volume of trade and assistance clearly favored the Allies. Then, in January 1917, Germany announced the resumption of unrestricted submarine warfare, part of a final offensive to reclaim momentum and quickly end the war. The plan backfired, however, as German forces became bogged down on the Western Front and Wilson reconsidered the wisdom of neutrality. In March 1917, American newspapers published the text of an intercepted telegram from the German Foreign Secretary Arthur Zimmerman to the German Ambassador in Mexico. The telegram proposed a Mexico-Germany alliance in exchange for Mexican entry into the war against the United States and German assistance recovering territory lost in the 1840s. It was the final straw. On April 6, 1917, the U.S. Congress, with Wilson's recommendation, declared war on Germany.⁹

Wilson's decision to delay U.S. entry into the war caused a corresponding delay in military planning. The gradual expansion of the Army then under way was hopelessly insufficient for the fight at hand. Military planners determined that the Army needed to grow to at least 1.5 million men, consistent with the General Staff's 1915 proposal. The President hoped to rely upon volunteerism to meet the personnel goals, but this proved unrealistic and required that the nation adopt conscription. As a result, on May 18, 1917, Congress passed the Selective Service Act, authorizing the nation's

---

7   Howard Jones, *Crucible of Power: A History of U.S. Foreign Relations Since 1897*, Lanham, Md.: SR Books, 2001, p. 73.

8   The *Lusitania* had, in fact, been carrying a large quantity of ammunition intended for British buyers. German-American press in the United States soon published evidence of this fact. The British government sought to downplay the significance of the cargo, but the Mersey Investigation Committee and Mayer Liability Trial ultimately concluded similarly. Douglas Carl Pier, *Choosing War: Presidential Decisions in the Maine, Lusitania, and Panay Incidents*, Oxford, UK: Oxford University Press, 2016, pp. 84–86.

9   Arthur Link, *Woodrow Wilson: Revolution, War, and Peace*, Arlington Heights, Ill.: AHM Publishing, 1979; Herring, 2008, pp. 378–435.

first national draft premised on the armies clause of the Constitution.[10] Nearly all men between the ages of 21 and 30 were liable for conscription; by the war's end, approximately 2.8 million men were drafted.[11]

The 1917 Selective Service Act

The Selective Service Act's passage was not inevitable, and historians have suggested that President Wilson's sudden support for conscription was perhaps driven at least partly by political factors.[12] Over the course of early 1917, former President Theodore Roosevelt—Wilson's progressive political opponent—repeatedly petitioned the White House for permission to organize a volunteer division under his command to fight in France. It seems possible that Wilson did not wish Roosevelt to gain in political standing with such a prominent role. Wilson's more fundamental concerns, however, were that volunteer units could undercut manpower pools within critical war production industries. Additionally, volunteer units, especially one led by Theodore Roosevelt, might siphon off some of the more competent officers who were in search of glory in combat.[13] As a result, Wilson rejected Roosevelt's petitions. Undeterred by the rebuffs, Roosevelt wrote to Secretary of War Baker that, as "a retired Commander in Chief of the United States Army," he was "eligible to any position of command over American troops to which I may be appointed."[14] Baker forwarded the cable to Wilson on March 26; the following day, Wilson returned it without action.

In the War Department, the majority sentiment had been that conscription was politically infeasible and antithetical to American cultural norms, likely only to instigate anger similar to the New York draft riots during the Civil War. For the Army's

---

[10] Public Law 65-12, An Act to Authorize the President to Increase Temporarily the Military Establishment of the United States, May 18, 1917. Some challenged the Selective Service Act on the legal grounds that a man could not be drafted into the federal army because the 1903 Dick Act had already committed him as part of the unorganized militia. However, the Supreme Court held that the federal government's unbridled, plenary power to raise armies was "not qualified or restricted by the provisions of the militia clause." *Selective Draft Law Cases*, 245 U.S. 366, 1918; Stephen I. Vladek, *The Calling Forth Clause and the Domestic Commander-in-Chief*, Washington, D.C.: American University Washington College of Law, 2008; S. T. Ansell, "Status of State Militia Under the Hay Bill," *Harvard Law Review*, Vol. 30, No. 7, 1917.

[11] Kreidberg and Henry, 1955, pp. 235–240; Weigley, 1967, p. 354. At the start of April 1917, the Regular Army consisted of only 5,791 officers and 121,797 enlisted men. National Guard members in federal service numbered 80,446 officers and men, while an additional 101,174 remained under state control. Edward M. Coffman, *The War to End All Wars: The American Military Experience in World War I*, Lexington, Ky.: University Press of Kentucky, 1998, p. 18.

[12] John Whiteclay Chambers, *To Raise an Army: The Draft Comes to Modern America*, New York: The Free Press, 1987, p. 136.

[13] John Milton Cooper, Jr., *Woodrow Wilson: A Biography*, New York: Vintage Books, 2009, pp.393–394.

[14] Chambers, 1987, p. 137.

part, Chief of Staff Hugh Lenox Scott had urged Secretary Baker that conscription was "the only equitable, proper, and certain way to raise an army." If the War Department waited to draft, he warned, "you will already have lost this war."[15] On March 28, Wilson announced his decision to rely exclusively on the draft—rather than volunteers like those Roosevelt pledged—to raise the army.[16] Less than two months later, Wilson signed the Selective Service Act into law.

With the Selective Service Act in place, the War Department now faced the daunting task of organizing, equipping, and training the country's civilians within six months. The judge advocate general of the Army, Major General Enoch Crowder, was made provost marshal in order to oversee the Selective Service at the national level. The system relied on a broad coalition of local and state authorities, including governors, mayors, chambers of commerce, and local Councils of National Defense to organize (and, if necessary, coerce) young men to register for conscription.[17] In a public announcement in June 1917, Wilson also called upon "the patriotism of the press" to support the official public relations effort to educate the public.[18] The result was a flood of newspaper articles, posters, advertisements, and popular jingles urging registration as an act of civic duty. In three months, the Regular Army expanded from under 100,000 to nearly 250,000 men. The National Guard, some 150,000 strong at the April declaration of war, grew to nearly 260,000 men.[19]

Local control of the registration process shielded the Wilson administration from popular opposition to a coercive policy. Wilson, Baker, and Crowder built a decentralized registration system reliant on local resources and intended to minimize conflicts of interest. By keeping the process at the local level, planners hoped to maintain popular trust in the system. Moreover, local officials' knowledge of their communities would ease the process of identifying appropriate accommodations to maintain fairness and ease the burden on families and local economies. Hoping to hit the ground running, Crowder and Baker secretly printed and mailed millions of registration forms to 40,000 sheriffs across the nation.[20]

---

[15] Hugh Lenox Scott, *Some Memories of a Soldier*, New York: The Century Co., 1928, p. 559.

[16] Chambers, 1987, p. 138.

[17] Kennedy, 1980, p. 150. On the issue of coercion, see Christopher Capozzola, "The Only Badge You Need Is Your Patriotic Fervor: Vigilance, Coercion, and the Law in World War I America," *Journal of American History*, Vol. 88, No. 4, March 2002. For the relationship between America's state and society during World War I, see Christopher Capozzola, *Uncle Sam Wants You: World War I and the Making of the Modern American Citizen*, Oxford, UK: Oxford University Press, 2008; Michael S. Neiberg, *The Path to War: How the First World War Created Modern America*, New York: Oxford University Press, 2016.

[18] "10,000 Men a Day," *Washington Post*, June 24, 1917.

[19] "500,000 Join Colors," *Washington Post*, June 25, 1917.

[20] Kennedy, 1980, p. 150.

The registration process worked well and quickly gained wide popular support. Potential registrants would present themselves to the local registration panel (one of the 4,647 established nationwide, or one for approximately every 30,000 people), which consisted of a three-man panel, including at least one physician.[21] The local and press campaign was a dramatic success, and nearly 10 million men reported for registration on June 5, 1917.[22] In addition to voluntary enlistments, mass conscription allowed the Army to balloon from a strength of approximately 200,000 men in early 1917 to nearly 3.7 million by November 1918.[23]

Government officials leveraged official and unofficial methods to ensure compliance with the Selective Service Act. The Justice Department ordered those who did not register or report for mobilization to be arrested.[24] Young men who chose not to appear for their draft registration faced social condemnation, legal action, and, in some cases, violence. The government's media campaign cultivated an intense patriotism and stirred anger and calls for retribution. Not surprisingly, the campaign had ugly side effects, and newspapers published accounts of vigilante violence against nonregistrants, often directed against immigrants who were suspected of exploiting loopholes in the exemption process.[25] Newspapers promised to publish and maintain updated public lists of all local registrants (with comparisons across states and localities) to stir local competition and induce public shaming of "slackers." As one *New York Times* headline in October 1917 helpfully read, "DRAFTED MEN WARNED: Those Who Fail to Report Will Be Punished, Though Not with Death."[26] By mid-1918, 10,000 men were prosecuted for failure to register.[27] This number likely underestimated the phenomenon. Aware of the necessity for rapid mobilization, draft boards often did not spare dodgers and deserters from military service—instead, the men were often delivered straight to training camps under military escort.[28]

Even with Selective Service firmly in place as a source of manpower for Army expansion, the War Department encountered significant issues processing inductees into service. All male civilians were obliged to register for service, but conscription was selective and staggered to ensure fitness for military service, minimize economic and social disruption, and avoid overburdening an already strained logistical apparatus.

---

[21] Chambers, 1987, p. 182.

[22] Kennedy, 1980, p. 154.

[23] Richard W. Stewart, *American Military History*, Vol. II: *The United States Army in a Global Era, 1917–2008*, 2nd ed., Washington, D.C.: U.S. Army Center of Military History, 2010, p. 21.

[24] Weigley, 1962.

[25] Kennedy, 1980, p. 151.

[26] "Drafted Men Warned," *New York Times*, October 4, 1917, p. 8.

[27] Chambers, 1987, p. 213; Kennedy, 1980, p. 165.

[28] Carter, 1903; Jessup, 1938.

The Selective Service Act forced military planners to confront many thorny issues: How many men should (or could) be called up? At what rate? Who should be called first? How could the military's manpower needs be balanced with industry's need for workers?

Another key issue was deferment from military service. From late July through August 1917, local boards fielded nearly 1 million deferment cases.[29] Eligibility for service was determined by a range of factors, including physical fitness, mental and "moral" health, number of dependents, family income, criminal record, and country of origin. In theory, an individual could be exempted or deemed ineligible for military service if he were a resident alien, married, or had dependents. Yet the law provided few specific guidelines, and interpretations varied between, or even within, states. In the absence of federal oversight, local boards were often vulnerable to corruption, patronage, and racism.[30] For example, during the first call in 1917, local boards made 51.65 percent of African-Americans eligible for immediate induction, compared with 32.53 percent of whites. The trend of overdrafting African-Americans was particularly pronounced in the South and remained constant throughout the war; the provost marshal later estimated that local boards declared 33 percent of white registrants and 52 percent of black registrants eligible.[31] Legislative loopholes complicated the mobilization process by creating unintended consequences and ambiguities. For example, the high approval rate of deferments for married registrants with dependents produced a sudden spike in weddings; by the war's end, marriage would be cited as the reason for 43 percent of all deferments.[32] Military planners were shocked by the level of fraud. After early estimates found that 80 percent of married men had filed for deferments rather than fulfill their military service, Lieutenant General S. B. M. Young, president of the National Association for Universal Military Training, complained that Americans' shirking was "a condition which is not only surprising, but which is full of menace."[33] If trends held, the United States would soon run out of eligible men. Either deferments would have to be cancelled or the age of eligibility would have to be lowered.

---

[29] Chambers, 1987, p. 185.

[30] Kennedy (1980, p. 156) notes that "in Fulton County, Georgia, a board proved so flagrantly discriminatory—it exempted 526 of 815 whites, and only 6 of 202 blacks—that its members had to be removed."

[31] Arthur E. Barbeau and Henri Florette, *The Unknown Soldier: Black American Troops in World War I*, Philadelphia, Pa.: Temple University Press, 1974.

[32] Jennifer D. Keene, *Doughboys, the Great War, and the Remaking of America*, Baltimore, Md.: Johns Hopkins University Press, 2003, p. 18.

[33] Quoted in Barr, 1998.

Bringing the National Guard into Federal Service

Initially, the swell of patriotism, and the threat of conscription, boosted voluntary enrollment into National Guard units. Recruiters exploited uncertainty over conscription to sell the National Guard as an appealing alternative, and they promised that Guardsmen would be allowed to serve in units alongside their family members and friends. As a result, National Guard units nearly doubled in size between April and July 1917.

To meet wartime demands, the Army had to alter its peacetime force structure to better fit the operational demands for the war in Europe. Planners in the War Department, along with the newly designated commander of the American Expeditionary Force, General John Pershing, and his staff, developed a new organizational structure. The initial design expanded the overall size of the Army to 38 Infantry Divisions: six Regular Army, 16 National Guard, and 16 National Army (new federal divisions that had not been part of the Regular Army or National Guard). Once these plans were in place, on August 5, 1917, Wilson federalized the entire National Guard specifically under the provisions of the Selective Service Act and in accordance with Section 111 of the 1916 NDA.[34] Guard units subsequently departed their state mobilization points for federal training camps in the West and South, where the weather was warmer and more moderate during winter months. Pershing's new organizational structure for the infantry division caused a significant amount of restructuring, which generated much turmoil and disruption, especially in Guard units.

Guardsmen reacted to these changes with frustration, anger, and confusion. After decades of lobbying to gain recognition as the nation's first-line reserve, it appeared to some Guardsmen that the federal government was looting the state militia for men. "The necessity of drawing on some regiments to increase the ranks of others caused a very general disorganization of the National Guard," the *New York Times* noted at the time. "For example," the *Times* continued, "only about 400 men are left of what was the Fifth Massachusetts, one of the oldest militia regiments in the country."[35] Reorganizing to meet the new divisional structure also meant that some units were forced to convert to different types, which the Militia Bureau characterized as "a proceeding fraught with considerable difficulty."[36] Angered by what they believed to be an undue burden and disregard for the Guard's autonomy, many elected to go absent without leave in protest. In one camp, Guard cavalrymen held a mock funeral to bury their dis-

---

[34] "War Department General Orders No. 90 (July 12, 1917): Call into Federal Service and Draft of the National Guard by the President of the United States of America," in *War Department General Orders and Bulletins, 1917*, Washington, D.C.: U.S. Government Printing Office, 1918, pp. 1–4.

[35] Quoted in Cantor, 1963.

[36] *Report of the Chief of the Militia Bureau Relative to the National Guard of the United States, 1917*, Washington, D.C.: U.S. Government Printing Office, 1917, p. 10.

tinctive state uniforms before converting peacefully to a federal artillery unit.[37] At the same time Guard units were being reorganized, they began to receive new men drafted into the Army by the Selective Service Act. Since all Guard units (and Regular Army units, for that matter) were below war strength, the Army used newly drafted men to fill out their ranks.

The War Department's shuffling of National Guard men and units was an intentional element of its strategy to build a unified force.[38] On paper, the National Guard in 1917 was organized into divisions, but only two—New York and Pennsylvania—were organizationally complete and ready for quick deployment.[39] The remaining divisions required significant restructuring. The War Department revised the National Guard's organizational and numbering scheme, and announced an expansion of Army divisions to support the divisional structure adopted by General Pershing. Having recently returned from the punitive expedition in Mexico, and after spending a few weeks in Europe, the commander of what was to be called the American Expeditionary Force (AEF) had a new appreciation for Western Front combat that stressed firepower, supply, and command and control over mobility. As a result, the new "square" divisions each consisted of four infantry regiments.[40] The purpose of divisional renumbering was to ease standardization and coordination and symbolize the creation of a new, truly *national* force. Under the new protocol, the War Department designated numbers 1 through 25 for Regular Army divisions, 26 through 75 for National Guard divisions, and 76 and above for national Army (i.e., newly formed with varying combinations of Organized Reserves, Regular Army troops, and conscripts) divisions. For example, the New York Guard became the 27th Division under Major General O'Ryan, and the Pennsylvania Guard became the 28th under General Charles H. Muir.[41]

The War Department dispensed with titles such as National Guard and Regular Army to emphasize the creation of a single national Army, known as the American Expeditionary Force. As General Peyton C. March told the *New York Times*, the United States had constructed

---

[37] Coffman, 1998, p. 65.

[38] The President was authorized to "organize the land forces of the United States into brigades and divisions . . . as he may deem necessary" by legislation passed in the months leading up to the outbreak of war in Europe (Public Law 63-90, An Act to Provide for Raising the Volunteer Forces of the United States in Time of Actual or Threatened War, April 25, 1914).

[39] Henry Joseph Reilly, *Americans All; the Rainbow at War: Official History of the 42s Rainbow Division in the World War*, 2nd ed., Columbus, Ohio: The F. J. Heer Printing Company, 1936; Reilly, 1936.

[40] John B. Wilson, *Maneuver and Firepower: The Evolution of Divisions and Separate Brigades*, Washington, D.C.: United States Army Center of Military History, 1998, pp. 49–64; Reilly, 1936, p. 25.

[41] By the end of the war in 1918, the War Department had not used all of the designated numbers for the respective component divisions. See Wilson, 1998, pp. 59, 61.

a great democratic army, in which we do not propose to have any difference, in the public estimation, in any branch of it. They are all to be on an equality—the men who have come from the regular army, from the National Guard, and from civil life—and as the war proceeds and the training and experience all these recruits require becomes more nearly equal, they will in fact be on an absolutely equal basis.[42]

The War Department issued standard uniforms for Regulars, National Army personnel, and Guardsmen, and directed all officers to wear the same "U.S." insignia on their collars.[43]

As conscription continued apace, the War Department struggled to find sufficient officers to lead the expanded expeditionary force. The Army trained approximately 182,000 civilian officers by the war's end, but was in constant need of more.[44] The War Department compounded the problem by favoring white, college-educated, civilian men over more-capable blue-collar workers or National Guard officers, whose inclination toward long-term service some Regular Army officers continued to question.[45] The supposed lack of suitable Guard officers, and the apparent discrimination against them, was also partly the legacy of a failed Root reform. Beginning in 1904, the War Department had opened the Army's service schools to applicants from the National Guard to provide the officers with enhanced military skills and to foster cooperation between regulars and militiamen. Even for those who passed the difficult admissions requirements, however, few militia officers could dedicate a year away from their families and civilian jobs. Before 1916, only three managed to graduate from the School of the Line at Fort Leavenworth, a course known among Guardsmen for its instructors' seeming bias against citizen-soldiers; no Guard officers would attend the program after 1906. Major General O'Ryan was the only Guardsman to graduate from the Army War College in this era, while only one other Guard officer graduated from both the Line School and the Leavenworth Staff College. The service school experience bolstered many Regular Army officers' existing doubts about the abilities of their militia counterparts. For National Guardsmen, it substantiated a common suspicion that Regulars were prejudiced against them. It is reasonable to assume that both sentiments carried over into World War I mobilization.[46]

The shortage of capable officers did not dissuade the Army from removing Regulars and Guardsmen from leadership roles if they did not meet exacting standards.

---

[42] Quoted in Paul Thompson, "Only One U.S. Army: An Interview with General March on the Great Change That Merges Regulars, National Army Men, and Guardsmen," *New York Times*, August 11, 1918.

[43] Thompson, August 11, 1918; Coffman, 1998, pp. 61–62.

[44] Keene, 2003, p. 16.

[45] Keene, 2003, pp. 16–17; Coffman, 1998, p. 61.

[46] Nenninger, 1986, p. 220.

General Pershing's review of officers, both Regular Army and National Guard, was complex and ruthless, consisting of a multistage examination that included a physical evaluation. Regardless of their impeccable peacetime records and accomplishments, many Regular Army generals and colonels were in their late 50s and 60s and did not meet Pershing's fitness standards. Eleven Guard generals who had recently served on the Mexican border were considered physically unfit once they arrived in Europe. More than 12,000 Guard officers entered active duty in 1917, but within a year nearly 1,500 were reassigned or sent home. The issue became controversial enough that Pershing ordered the AEF Personnel Bureau to prepare dossiers on the Regular and Guard officers relieved. Historians have found that, just as evidence suggests Regular Army bias did exist, it also reveals that reliefs were harsh but ultimately done with justification.[47]

Despite difficulties, the National Guard played an important role in the creation of the AEF, comprising 40 percent of the AEF's divisions.[48] The Guard's participation in the war effort served to popularize its promise to serve as an efficient and loyal manpower reserve.

Training the U.S. Army for War

The AEF's training and combat record in World War I illustrates the uneven effect of early 20th century reforms on the Army. On the one hand, Root's reforms and the new institutions established by the 1916 NDA provided the institutional apparatus necessary to prepare the Army for expansion and combat operations. The General Staff, Army War College, and other institutions allowed the Army to avoid pitfalls that had hampered efficiency during the Spanish-American War. On the other hand, significant problems remained. Military planners had sought to standardize and improve training through new initiatives. In practice, however, the reforms did little to prepare the Army for the challenges of mass mobilization on the scale needed for World War I. Given that the most recent and consequential reform, the 1916 NDA, was barely a year old when the United States declared war, time was not an abundant commodity.

Mobilization strained the understaffed and underfunded War Department. By August 1917, overwhelmed military planners determined that existing mobilization

---

[47] Timothy K. Nenninger, "'Unsystematic as a Mode of Command': Commanders and the Process of Command in the American Expeditionary Forces, 1917–1918," *Journal of Military History*, Vol. 64, No. 3, July 2000, pp. 747–753; James J. Cooke, *Pershing and His Generals: Command and Staff in the AEF*, Westport, Conn.: Praeger, 1997, p. 63; Coffman, 2004, p. 208; Coffman, 1998, p. 330; Hill, 1964, pp. 261–286; Mark Ethan Grotelueschen, *The AEF Way of War: The American Army and Combat in World War I*, Cambridge, UK: Cambridge University Press, 2007, pp. 26–27; Edward M. Coffman, "American Command and Commanders in World War I," in Russell F. Weigley, ed., *New Dimensions in Military*, San Rafael, Calif.: Presidio Press, 1975, pp. 183–184.

[48] Anne Cipriano Venzon, ed., *The United States in the First World War: An Encyclopedia*, New York: Routledge, 2012, p. 404.

plans could not be implemented. Rail traffic congestion, supply shortages, and difficulties setting up the necessary cantonments required delaying and then staggering draftees' training.[49] Although planners originally intended for 30 percent of men with military experience to mobilize on September 5, delays and disorganization meant that only 5 percent of men mobilized on schedule. These were the unlucky few; according to a *New York Times* report, the first round of draftees was assigned the burden of building camps and assimilating later contingents in addition to undertaking training of their own.[50] A second mass wave arrived two weeks later, and a third in early October.

Despite disorganization, the draftees' induction proceeded amidst great public fanfare.[51] New York's "Draft Army" exemplified the common experience. At 7:30 a.m. on September 10, 1917, men from 139 state legislative districts gathered at Long Island Station to await transportation by designated trains to divisional training cantonments upstate. They arrived individually by ferry or automobile, often in the company of family and friends. After roll call, boards appointed a person from each district to be in charge until arrival at training camp. Two more rolls were read at 8 and 10 a.m. Soon after, amid "cheering like soldiers after a victory, waving flags, hats, and handkerchiefs," the 1,942 men left for Camp Upton (on Long Island, New York, and named for the late Regular Army Brevet Major General Emory Upton), where they continued training and awaited orders to deploy abroad. Three men who did not appear were arrested, and their names—and purported excuses—were reported in mocking detail in the *New York Times*.[52]

Despite the War Department's extensive preparations and efforts to stagger the arrival of trainees, few camps were ready on time, and many trainees were required to build trenches, shooting ranges, and company streets before instruction could begin.[53] In addition, camps suffered from shortages in clothing, equipment, and housing, a problem that further complicated training efforts. This problem grew worse over time as the General Staff expanded the number of training areas to meet the demand. Military planners had envisioned 16 training areas located near areas of dense population, so that camps could fill quickly with draftees from the area. By early 1918, however, the number of "mushroom cities" had doubled to 32 to meet the training demand. Each housed approximately 30,000 men and was equipped with wooden barracks, hospitals, storehouses, offices, modern plumbing and heat, and society outposts, such

---

[49] Weigley, 1971.

[50] Machoian, 2006.

[51] Huntington, 1985. On September 4, President Wilson, flanked by congressmen, diplomats, administration officials, and residents of Washington, D.C., marched down Pennsylvania Avenue from the Capitol to the White House to honor the district's first quota of men.

[52] Hewes, 1975.

[53] Keene, 2003, p. 37.

as the Knights of Columbus and the Young Men's Christian Association.[54] The lack of prewar planning, preparations, and congressional appropriations was evident in nearly every facet of Army mobilization and expansion.

Similar problems plagued many units of the National Guard, which were still deployed along the U.S.-Mexican border. Individual nondeployed Guardsmen first reported to their local armories in June, but they often waited weeks before complete units could be organized and transported to initial training sites. After a month of small unit instruction, Guardsmen traveled to a second training site for integration into multistate regiments. The new regiments would then move to a tent cantonment, often out of state, where they would receive several weeks of intensive training. Eventually, they would travel to encampments near ports of embarkation, where they remained until orders for overseas deployment arrived.[55]

Some military commanders took matters into their own hands to avoid the cumbersome mobilization process. For example, Major General Clarence R. Edwards, a 58-year old Regular Army officer in command of the newly formed 26th "Yankee" Division, an amalgamation of New England National Guards, refused to move his division to its designated training camp in North Carolina and decided to deploy directly to France. The division entered into a series of unilateral agreements with port authorities in New York City and Montreal. Edwards reorganized his regiments into a square division while still at state mobilization camps and, in early October 1917, moved directly to ports of embarkation. By the time a surprised War Department learned of Edward's initiative, the 26th Division had already sailed for France.[56]

The mobilized divisions continued to train upon their deployment to France. Pershing imposed strict training requirements for all units, regardless of origin or component.[57] This proved to be a sound decision, since many units consisted of new recruits with little training or experience. As Pershing later recalled, "such a large percentage of them were ignorant of practically everything pertaining to the business of the soldier in war." Pershing's critique extended even to the officers, who "had to learn the interior

---

[54] Stewart, 2010, p. 21; Coffman, 1998, pp. 29–31.

[55] For an illustrative example, see the diary of Indiana Guardsman Vernon E. Kniptash: Vernon E. Kniptash, *On the Western Front with the Rainbow Division: A World War I Diary*, Norman, Okla.: University of Oklahoma Press, 2009.

[56] The 26th saw extensive combat action one year later between August and November 1918 (Doubler, 2001, p. 157).

[57] For examinations of Army training and doctrine, see Grotelueschen, 2007; James W. Rainey, "The Questionable Training of the AEF in World War I," *Parameters: Journal of the U.S. Army War College*, Vol. 22, Winter 1992–1993; James W. Rainey, "Ambivalent Warfare: The Tactical Doctrine of the AEF in World War I," *Parameters: Journal of the U.S. Army War College*, Vol. 13, September 1983; Kretchik, 2011; Timothy K. Nenninger, "American Military Effectiveness in the First World War," in Allan R. Millett and Williamson Murray, eds., *Military Effectiveness*, Vol. 1: *The First World War*, Boston, Mass.: Allen and Unwin, 1988; Mark Ethan Grotelueschen, *Doctrine Under Trial: The American Artillery Employment in World War I*, Westport, Conn.: Greenwood Press, 2001.

economy of their units—messing, housing, clothing, and, in general, caring for their men—as well as methods of instruction and the art of leading them in battle."[58]

Pershing's emphasis on training, although justified, delayed the movement of units to the front line. The 1st Infantry Division, for example, trained for six months before its assignment to a quiet sector of the Western front in mid-January 1918.[59] At that point, it was the only American division on the front lines.[60] "The practical effect," Chief of Staff March lamented,

> was that the large bodies of American troops, divisions whose morale was at the highest point, who had had from four to six months' training, and often more in camps in America, and who expected on arrival in France to be thrown into battle immediately, found the keen edge of their enthusiasm dulled by having to go over again and again drills and training which they had already undergone in America.[61]

The delay frustrated British and French planners, who were desperate to relieve some of the pressure on their exhausted men. To expedite the process, the Allies pushed Wilson to integrate U.S. forces into French and British "amalgamation" units that could be quickly built, trained, and deployed while Pershing oversaw the gradual buildup of an independent American Army in France. Both Wilson and Pershing, fearful that amalgamation would undermine U.S. negotiating power after the war, insisted that American soldiers would serve exclusively under American commanders. Wilson, with Pershing in agreement, later walked back this position after a German offensive threatened Paris in late spring 1918, but by then the AEF was nearly ready.[62]

---

[58] John J. Pershing, *My Experiences in the World War*, Vol. 1, New York: Frederick A. Stokes, 1931, p. 150; Stewart, 2010, p. 47.

[59] Stewart, 2010, p. 46.

[60] Weigley, 1967, p. 372.

[61] Quoted in Weigley, 1967, p. 376.

[62] "Note for Colonel Fagalde, French Military Attaché in London, from French Ambassador, Washington, Received December 20, 1917," *United States Army in the World War, 1917–1919: Policy-Forming Documents of the American Expeditionary Force*, Washington, D.C.: U.S. Army Center of Military History, 1989, p. 123; "Extract from Minutes of a Meeting of the War Cabinet Held at 10 Downing Street, S.W., on Friday, December 21, 1917 at 11:30 A.M.," *United States Army in the World War, 1917–1919: Policy-Forming Documents of the American Expeditionary Forces*, Washington, D.C.: U.S. Army Center of Military History, 1989; Stewart, 2005, 2010. Also see David F. Trask, *The AEF and Coalition Warmaking, 1917–1918*, Lawrence, Kans.: University Press of Kansas, 1993; David F. Trask, *The United States in the Supreme War Council: American War Aims and Inter-Allied Strategy, 1917–1918*, Westport, Conn.: Greenwood Press, 1978; Robert B. Bruce, *A Fraternity of Arms: America & France in the Great War*, Lawrence, Kans.: University Press of Kansas, 2003; Kevin D. Stubbs, *Race to the Front: The Material Foundations of Coalition Strategy in the Great War*, Westport, Conn.: Praeger Publishers, 2002.

The U.S. entry into the war helped ensure Allied victory.[63] After years of bloody conflict that had taken an enormous toll on all belligerents, the AEF's arrival provided an important psychological boost to the Allies and a much-needed infusion of fresh troops to help drive back Germany's final advances. Moreover, the United States harnessed its enormous industrial capacity, providing crucial supplies and reinforcements at a time when Allied civilian and military morale was plummeting.[64]

Despite facing a mauled and tired German Army, the AEF's battle record was marred by some of the same issues that had plagued mobilization. Significant delays and logistical challenges weakened U.S. forces, which struggled to maintain the pace necessary to sustain lengthy offensives. U.S. forces fought well enough during the spring of 1918 to provide vital support for French and British efforts to halt German advances. Yet the AEF did not fight as an independent army until September 1918, a full 17 months after the United States' formal entry into the war.[65] Even then, Pershing was forced to borrow over half of the AEF's artillery, tanks, and aircraft from the French and man them with American troops.[66] Inexperienced U.S. forces struggled to sustain lengthy offensives, despite Allied assistance.[67] Pershing clung to outdated tactical methods that proved deadly for U.S. forces in combat, and progress slowed as casualties mounted. As a result, the inexperienced U.S. divisions did not contribute as much as they may have to speeding up the progress of the Allied offensive, which met strong German defenses and poor weather.[68]

Despite the many problems, the AEF improved greatly by the end of the war. General Hunter Ligget's assumption of command of the First Army in October 1918 during the Meuse-Argonne Offensive brought new strategy and leadership.[69] At the time, the AEF was locked in a stalemate and badly needed to reorganize and replen-

---

[63] Allan R. Millett, "Over Where? The AEF and the American Strategy for Victory, 1917–1918," in Kenneth J. Hagan and William R. Roberts, eds., *Against All Enemies: Interpretations of American Military History from Colonial Times to the Present*, Westport Conn.: Greenwood Press, 1986; Timothy K. Nenninger, "Tactical Dysfunction in the AEF, 1917–1918," *Military Affairs*, Vol. 51, October 1987; Trask, 1993.

[64] Stewart, 2010, pp. 51–52.

[65] Stewart, 2010.

[66] Stewart, 2010; James H. Hallas, *Squandered Victory: The American First Army at St. Mihiel*, Westport, Conn.: Praeger, 1995.

[67] Paul F. Braim, *The Test of Battle: The American Expeditionary Forces in the Meuse-Argonne Campaign*, Shippensberg, Pa.: White Mane Publishing, 1998; Edward G. Lengel, *A Companion to the Meuse-Argonne Campaign*, Malden, Mass.: Wiley Blackwell, 2014; Peter L. Belmonte, *Days of Perfect Hell: The U.S. 26th Infantry Regiment in the Meuse-Argonne Offensive, October–November 1918*, Atglen, Pa.: Schiffer Military History, 2014; Robert H. Ferrell, *Collapse at Meuse-Argonne: The Failure of the Missouri-Kansas Division*, Columbia, Mo.: University of Missouri Press, 2004; Robert H. Ferrell, *America's Deadliest Battle: Meuse-Argonne, 1918*, Lawrence, Kans.: University Press of Kansas, 2007.

[68] Stewart, 2010. For Pershing's reflections on World War I, see Pershing, 1931.

[69] Stewart, 2010, p. 51.

ish stockpiles of equipment and supplies. If the war had ended in late October, the American war effort might have appeared to be a failed one.[70] U.S. forces returned to the battlefield on November 1 with new vigor, but by then the war was nearly over; ten days after the AEF's resumption of fighting, on November 11, 1918 the war ended.

Although the principal campaign in which the AEF was involved had mixed results, World War I was a triumph of managerial improvisation and innovation for the United States. The civilian and military leadership tasked with the largest military mobilization in the nation's history to that point fielded a 1.5 million-man army less than a year and a half after Wilson ordered its formation. However, the AEF struggled to train, equip, and use its citizen-soldiers. The memory of these difficulties would spur further reforms once the war ended.

Demobilizing the Army and the War's Aftermath

The demobilization of U.S. forces after World War I was as disorganized as the mobilization had been. Planning did not begin until a month before the war's end, a fault that reflected Army planners' surprise at the sudden German collapse and Wilson's rush to the treaty table. The process was often chaotic, but it achieved the objective of drawing down the massive wartime force. Returning units reported to one of 30 demobilization stations around the country, and were typically discharged together. By the end of 1919, the Regular Army had been reduced from a wartime high of approximately 2 million at the time of the armistice to 19,000 officers and 205,000 enlisted men. The exodus created a new problem: how to replace discharged men with new enlistments. The Army needed new enlistees to provide essential services, such as transportation, supply, and medical support, and to maintain the ranks of combat units. In short, the nation still needed an Army, albeit one significantly reduced in size, to meet present and future security requirements. Congress focused on this problem starting in February 1919.[71]

The mobilization and demobilization also wreaked havoc on National Guard units. The conscription of individual Guardsmen for federal service in the AEF, as outlined in the 1916 NDA, meant that only the state adjutants general and small cadres of Guardsmen remained in place at home. In response to complaints regarding the lack of Guard forces to support domestic crises (e.g., labor unrest), the War Department authorized states to organize backfill units, but this solution was ineffective at best. The adjutant general of Virginia reported to the Militia Bureau in January 1918 that "at present there is no national guard in this State, all of the units having been mustered

---

[70] Beaver, 2006, p. 115.

[71] Public Law 65-309, An Act to Authorize the Resumption of Voluntary Enlistment in the Regular Army, and for Other Purposes, February 28, 1919.

into federal service."[72] National Guard loyalists viewed the wartime mobilization and conscription of Guardsmen as threatening the health and survival of their institution.[73]

After the problems of mobilization, the Guard underwent further personnel turbulence during the demobilization process. Although some returning Guard units reformed for parades and welcome-home ceremonies, most units returning from Europe turned in their equipment and were discharged as individuals—not, as the National Guard had expected, demobilized back into prewar units. As such, they retained neither federal nor state obligations.[74] Moreover, the 1916 NDA made no provision for individual Guardsmen's return to the state units from which they originated.

Guard leaders recognized that rapid reorganization was critical, but their efforts were stymied by a shortage of men willing to enlist (or reenlist) in the National Guard. The law did not prevent demobilized Guardsmen from voluntarily rejoining their former units. Many returning soldiers, however, exhausted by war and believing their civic duty fulfilled, lacked enthusiasm for continued military service. The Chief of the Militia Bureau, Major General Jesse McIlvane Carter, explained to the House Committee on Military Affairs in 1919 that the National Guard reorganization's slow pace was because "men who have come back from overseas are rather fed up on military work, and do not care to rejoin the guard at this time," and the adjutants general were not pushing hard to reorganize either.[75] National Guard leaders blamed the War Department for this state of affairs. As the adjutant general of Georgia grimly concluded in his 1920 report, there existed "a most determined feeling against rejoining the National Guard on the part of the officers and men who served in the war, the reasons for which . . . may be attributed to the unpopularity of the federal law and the regulations promulgated thereunder by the War Department."[76] The paradoxical effect of these charges was that the more National Guardsmen lamented their postwar realities, the less likely they were to inspire recruits to join an organization that was, by their own telling, impaired by unfair War Department policies.[77]

The animosity caused by demobilization and other issues during World War I had a powerful influence on Guardsmen for many years. In public statements and con-

---

[72] *Report of the Adjutant General of the Commonwealth of Virginia for the Year Ending December 31, 1918*, Richmond, Va., 1919, p. 20.

[73] "Need Not Return to National Guard," *New York Times*, December 25, 1918, p. 4; "Official Proceedings of the National Guard Association of the United States," paper presented at Sixty-Sixth Annual Convention of the National Guard Association of the United States, Baltimore, Md., May 3–6, 1944.

[74] Elbridge Colby and James F. Glass, "The Legal Status of the National Guard," *Virginia Law Review*, Vol. 29, No. 7, May 1943, pp. 849–850.

[75] *National Guard Reorganization Status: Hearings Before the House of Representatives Committee on Military Affairs, Sixty-Sixth Congress, First Session, September 23, 1919*, Washington, D.C.: U.S. Government Printing Office, 1919, p. 16.

[76] *Report of the Adjutant General for the State of Georgia, Atlanta*, 1920, p. 9.

[77] See Fitzhugh Lee Minnigerode, "Crippled Militia's Needs," *New York Times*, February 6, 1921, p. X5.

gressional testimony, Guardsmen highlighted their perceived mistreatment during the war and argued for a range of new reforms. In his 1944 address at the National Guard Association of the United States' annual convention, National Guard Association President Major General Ellard Walsh—a Minnesotan who had deployed to Europe as a second lieutenant in the 34th Infantry Division, which arrived just as the Armistice was signed—cited Wilson's federalization of the Guard and subsequent drafting of individual Guardsmen to discharge them from the militia on August 5, 1917, as the moment when, "at one fell swoop the National Guard utterly and completely ceased to exist." He condemned the War Department and Regular Army for their roles in the Guard's destruction, alleging that both seized whatever "opportunity presented itself to break up a National Guard Organization and to scatter its personnel to the wind. . . . When they held the whip they never lost the opportunity to let us know who was master for it was then that their undiluted and undigested hate of us came to the surface."[78]

Though Guard leaders such as Walsh lamented the consequences, attributing their grievances to willful War Department and Regular Army designs, they almost certainly tended to overlook the realities of mobilization and demobilization. The drafting of Guardsmen into federal service as individuals, rather than units, under the Selective Service Act was not a policy devised by President Wilson or the Regular Army. Rather, it was in accordance with the 1916 NDA, which prescribed that individuals when federalized ceased to be a member of the organized militia.[79] To the extent that the provision's usage damaged the National Guard at home during and after the war, it seems apparent that it was more the result of flawed legislation than by arrangement, evidenced by postwar debate and subsequent changes in law.[80]

With regard to demobilization, the discharge of Guardsmen as individuals to regional camps rather than returning home as complete units was not unique to the National Guard. Rather, after weighing economic and military considerations the War Department determined that this was the quickest and most orderly method given the circumstances. The War Department judged that the administrative overhead required to support the near-simultaneous demobilization of Guard units in every town and city across America was unaffordable and infeasible, and would actually significantly delay demobilizations if attempted. Instead, the department established 30 regional demobilization sites across the nation, at which all administrative assistance could be provided to demobilizing soldiers who were given transportation vouchers to return home. Some

---

[78] "Official Proceedings of the National Guard Association of the United States," 1944. Also see "Attacks on Officers of the Regular Army," *New York Times*, May 18, 1919, p. 54; "Kill National Guard Declared Army Plan," *Los Angeles Times*, December 12, 1918, p. I6; "National Guard Entirely Wiped Out," *Boston Daily Globe*, December 25, 1918, p. 12.

[79] The relevant provision is Section 111 of the 1916 NDA, "National Guard When Drafted into Federal Service."

[80] John Dickinson, *The Building of an Army*, New York: The Century Co., 1922, pp. 369–370; Colby and Glass, 1943, pp. 849–850.

soldiers no doubt traveled home as units if so organized by their leaders and communities, while many others used their separation pay in more celebratory ways. City government leaders in large cities, such as New York, bemoaned the influx of young postwar GIs with pockets full of cash in pursuit of entertainment. The same discharge practices were employed for all servicemen that made up the emergency Army with the exception of Regular Army units, which were the last to return home due to occupation and demobilization duties.[81]

The Army Reorganization Act of 1920

The end of the war brought renewed debate on the structure of the Army. Believing that the experience of mass mobilization provided an opportunity for significant reforms, the War Department again made the case for a large standing Army. Chief of Staff March and Secretary of War Baker presented their proposal to Congress in January 1919. The Baker-March bill would have overhauled the Army in ways similar to the reforms proposed in the 1915 General Staff Plan. The bill called for a 21-division, 509,900-man Regular Army, expandable to over a million troops through the creation of a federal reserve of men who had undergone compulsory military training. Additionally, it proposed a supplementary role for the National Guard and provided for training. March justified the diminished role by arguing that, during the war, the National Guard had "gone out of existence" in all but a few states."[82]

Despite their joint authorship, Baker and March approached the task of selling the bill to Congress differently. Baker introduced the legislation during his presentation to the House as a temporary, emergency measure that sought to resolve an unintended consequence of U.S. involvement in the war, namely that the majority of enlistments would soon expire and leave the Army undermanned to meet its peacetime obligations.[83] The chief of staff was less subtle. March aimed to use the expediency of an emergency bill, slipped through Congress six weeks before its adjournment, to fix

---

[81] John C. Sparrow, *History of Personnel Demobilization in the United States Army*, Washington, D.C.: Department of the Army Pamphlet No. 20-210, July 1952, pp. 11–19; E. Jay Howenstine, Jr., "Demobilization After the First World War," *Quarterly Journal of Economics*, Vol. 58, No. 1, November 1943, pp. 91–105; Benedict Crowell and Robert F. Wilson, *Demobilization: Our Industrial and Military Demobilization after the Armistice, 1918–1920*, New Haven, Conn.: Yale University Press, 1921.

[82] Crossland and Currie, 1984. The Baker-March bill was introduced in the First Session of the Sixty-Sixth Congress as S. 2715 on August 4, 1919, and as H.R. 8287 on August 15, 1919.

[83] *Army Reorganization: Hearings Before the House of Representatives Committee on Military Affairs House, Sixty-Fifth Congress, Third Session on H.R. 14560, To Reorganize and Increase the Efficiency of the Regular Army (January 16, 1919)*, Washington, D.C.: Government Printing Office, 1919; Holley, 1982, p. 413; Dickinson, 1922, pp. 330–334.

the standing army at over half a million men and permanently reorganize the military establishment.[84]

Neither man, however, was able to convince a majority in Congress. Many members believed that World War I had sapped public appetite for military reform. The war did not erase Americans' distrust of large standing forces; on the contrary, many believed that European militarism had *produced* the war, and that the United States should avoid falling into a similar trap by reducing military expenditures.[85] Noted one congressional opponent,

> I am frank enough to say . . . that I do not believe that any bill providing for an Army of 500,000 men in time of peace will ever get through the House. . . . I do not believe the people of this country will stand for the sized Army which you provide for in this bill in time of peace.[86]

The Baker-March Bill generated intense antipathy in influential parts of Congress and angered even former advocates of military reform. Former chairman of the Senate Military Affairs Committee Senator George E. Chamberlain, a vocal critic of the Army's mobilization during the war, now denounced the legislation as evidence of the General Staff's "militaristic despotism" and threatened dramatic action *against* the reformers, including a reduction in the General Staff's power and potential removal of the Secretary of War.[87]

By fall 1919, congressional rejection of the Baker-March bill appeared inevitable. The defection of respected authorities such as Chamberlain and Pershing doomed the bill's chances for popular support, and the press circulated negative testimony widely.[88] Moreover, the nation was no longer at war, and the new Republican administration was not inclined to authorize a massive, peacetime expansion of the Army. Focused on domestic and economic matters, Congress was not about to approve an expensive peacetime force.[89]

---

[84] Beaver, 2006, pp. 196–200; Edward M. Coffman, *Hilt of the Sword: The Career of Peyton C. March*, Madison, Wis.: University of Wisconsin Press, 1966; Hewes, 1975, pp. 52–53; Weigley, 1967, p. 396.

[85] John Braeman, "Power and Diplomacy: The 1920s Reappraised," *The Review of Politics*, Vol. 44, No. 3, July 1982.

[86] U.S. House of Representatives, *Army Reorganization: Statements of Hon. Newton D. Baker and Gen. Peyton C. March, H.R. 14560: Hearing Before the Committee on Military Affairs*, Washington, D.C., U.S. Government Printing Office, January 16, 1919.

[87] *Army Reorganization: Hearings before the Senate Committee on Military Affairs, Remarks by George E. Chamberlain (September 5, 1919)*, 66th Congress, 1st Session, Washington, D.C.: U.S. Government Printing Office, 1919, p. 16; "Our 'Militaristic Peril,'" *Literary Digest*, Vol. 62, No. 13, September 27, 1919, pp. 9–10.

[88] "Senate Declares Army Bill Sets Up Staff Despotism," *New York Times*, September 14, 1919, p. 1. On this event, see Bernard L. Boylan, "Army Reorganization 1920: The Legislative Story," *Mid-America XL*, April 1967, pp. 117–118.

[89] "Baker Offers New Army Plan for 21 Division," *Chicago Daily Tribune*, January 16, 1919, p. 5.

Congress still had to consider the issue of universal military training, which had gained new momentum as a grassroots movement following the war. Since its founding in 1915, the Military Training Camps Association had evolved into an effective lobby, including an effective outlet for its agenda in *National Service Magazine*. The association helped draft the 1919 Kahn-Chamberlain bill to implement universal military training and establish a federal reserve component. The bill proposed a six-month training period for all males in their 19th year, with an additional three months of education for illiterate and non-English speakers.[90] *National Service Magazine* noted that, on completing the training, all able American men "would be organized territorially . . . into a Reserve of the United States Army in which they" would remain for a ten-year period.[91]

In keeping with the National Guard's opposition to creating a federal reserve that might supplant its perceived status within the military establishment, the National Guard Association of the United States (NGAUS) publicly denounced the Kahn-Chamberlain bill. Its denunciation provoked an angry response by the Military Training Camps Association, which accused the NGAUS of willfully misrepresenting its legislation.[92] The NGAUS had the advantage, however, due to its grassroots membership in virtually every congressional district, and its very close association with many key members of Congress. Congress rejected the bill.[93]

By the end of 1919, the military reform effort had stalled. The key remaining issues concerned the peacetime size of the Regular Army, and the potential creation of a federal Organized Reserve for the Army.[94] These were precisely the questions confronting the country concerning its Army. Should the Regular Army be a small force whose main mission was to train and prepare the National Guard and Organized Reserves, which would, in turn, become the nucleus of a mass wartime army built on universal military training? Or should the Regular Army be a larger force able to defend the nation until the larger citizen-soldier mass army could be mobilized? Who would lead an expanded wartime army—Regular Army officers, National Guard officers, or those commissioned from civilian life? After nearly two decades of debate, the nation had made little progress in resolving these thorny issues.

---

[90] Perry, 1921, p. 236.

[91] Tompkins McIlvaine, "A People's Army: Plan of M.T.C.A. to Congress," *National Service Magazine*, Vol. 6, No. 3, September 1919, p. 151.

[92] "Editorial," *National Service Magazine*, Vol. 6, No. 3, September 1919, p. 134.

[93] The NGAUS was formed in 1911 from the older National Guard Association, which was first established in 1878. The new NGAUS was a more centralized lobbying organization in terms of its shared vision for the National Guard as a dual constitutional reserve to the Army as part of the first-line defenses.

[94] James W. Wadsworth, "Address by the Honorable James W. Wadsworth Delivered to the Military Training Camps Association of the United States, New Willard Hotel, Washington, D.C., August 1, 1919," *National Service Magazine*, Vol. 6, No. 3, September 1919, pp. 155–156.

Congress considered three options. First, the United States could establish a federal reserve under the armies clause of the Constitution and absorb National Guard veterans. A second option would be to retain, but federalize, existing National Guard units and individuals under the armies clause. General O'Ryan, adjutant general of New York, supported this approach, saying before Congress in 1919 that not only would it "provide a maximum of preparedness at a minimum of cost," but it "would be free from constitutional limits affecting the militia, if that is thought to be desirable."[95] General Palmer, also testifying before Congress in 1919, claimed that "it is impossible to organize an efficient army for war purposes under the militia clause of the Constitution."[96] The Regular Army, meanwhile, could support either option, but preferred aligning the Guard against domestic missions and establishing a new federal reserve.

A third option, opposed by the War Department based on its recent operational experience, was to retain the National Guard as a dual-status force. In this framework, the National Guard would continue to exist as the states' organized militia under the militia clause, but, when federalized, would be part of the Army under the armies clause, as the 1916 NDA had stipulated. Unsurprisingly, the National Guard and its association backed this position. Additionally, it sought a legislative guarantee that Guardsmen be discharged from federal service as units rather than as individuals.[97]

The Guard wanted both to preserve its independence from the Regular Army and to solidify itself as the nation's primary reserve force. As O'Ryan summarized in a March 1920 letter to Palmer, the majority of adjutants general were "strenuously opposed to any Bill which does not give the National Guard control of itself and does not vest in the states."[98] O'Ryan's thoughts had not changed appreciably from his *North American Review* piece five years earlier. A lawyer in civilian life, he envisioned a military policy that organized the National Guard as a federal reserve force under the armies clause, but would be available as a state force that could answer the call of governors when needed for state duties. He envisioned dual utility, not dual status. In contrast with many of his colleagues, O'Ryan believed that the National Guard's link to the militia clause should be severed and that it should become an exclusive federal reserve force. Consistent with the 1915 General Staff Plan, O'Ryan reasoned that National Guard units should have only one political master, not two, to simplify

---

[95] *Reorganization of the Army: Hearings Before the Subcommittee of the Committee on Military Affairs of the United States Senate*, Sixty-Sixth Congress, Session I on S. 2691, S.2693, S.2715, September 2, 1919, Washington, D.C.: U.S. Government Printing Office, 1919, pp. 517–518.

[96] Quoted in Lee, 1940; U.S. Senate, *Politics of Our Military National Defense: History of the Action of Political Forces Within the United States Which Has Shaped Our Military National Defense Policies from 1783 to 1940*, Washington, D.C.: U.S. Government Printing Office, Document No. 274, August 28, 1940, p. 94.

[97] Holley, 1982.

[98] John F. O'Ryan, "Letter from John F. O'Ryan to John McAuley Palmer," Palmer Papers, Library of Congress, Box 5, Folder 4, March 5, 1920.

command channels and allow greater synchronization of training across state lines. As O'Ryan noted in the same letter, revising military policy along the lines he was recommending took on new importance in the postwar period, when National Guard units were struggling to rebuild after demobilization. With much sympathy for their wartime hardships, he lamented the growing separation between veteran Guardsmen, who focused on reestablishing their civilian lives and businesses, and the state adjutants general, who wielded most of the influence and demanded the link to the states through the militia clause remain in place.[99]

In February 1920, the Senate and the House Military Affairs Committees produced separate bills for reorganizing the Army. The Senate's proposal, named after its sponsor and Chairman of the Military Affairs Committee, James W. Wadsworth, himself a former Guardsman, outlined a sweeping reorganization of the Army that would replace rather than amend the 1916 NDA. The bill proposed organizing the National Guard under the armies clause, but allowing governors to call out their Guard units for state and local emergencies as "state troops," rather than militias. The phrase referenced the constitutional prohibition against states maintaining "state troops" without the explicit permission of Congress.[100] The Wadsworth Bill thus endeavored to strike a balance between proponents of federal and state forces. The bill mandated four months of compulsory military training for able men between the ages of 18 and 45. These provisions proved to be highly controversial, especially on university and college campuses which believed that universal military training would delay and perhaps impede students' education.[101]

In contrast, the House bill, sponsored by California Republican and Chairman of the House Military Affairs Committee, Julius Kahn, called only for amending the 1916 NDA, rather than replacing it with an entirely new law. Unlike the Wadsworth bill, Kahn's bill kept in place many of the provisions of the 1916 NDA. It organized the National Guard under the militia clause of the Constitution and allowed the President to call National Guard units into federal service to repel invasions, suppress insurrection, and execute the laws of the Union. Furthermore, and in keeping with the 1916 NDA, National Guard units would be trained under state authority and, under the armies clause, could be federalized in the event of a national emergency. Whereas the Senate Bill had increased the power of the General Staff, the House Bill further reduced it. House Democrats had already overwhelmingly voted against compulsory military training, a clear signal to the House Military Affairs Committee that they would not tolerate such a measure within the evolving legislation.[102]

---

[99] O'Ryan, 1920.

[100] This rule was written into the Constitution to prevent states from creating their own armies of state troops.

[101] See, for example, "The Wadsworth Bill," *The Vassar Miscellany News*, Vol. 4, No. 33, February 21, 1920.

[102] Boylan, 1967, p. 121.

Both bills sparked controversy. Opponents framed the Wadsworth Bill as too militaristic, especially in its stance on universal military training, and they feared the General Staff would supplant civilian leadership. In the press and in Congress, comparisons to the militancy of Germany and Russia were common. One campus newspaper alleged that the General Staff sought to "think and plan for its 'next war' in terms of our entire man power, docile and mobilized, ready to be flung into battle at a moment's notice."[103] This sentiment was echoed in Congress, where the bill's opponents were vocal and consistent. Senator Kenneth McKellar asked melodramatically:

> Shall America be ruled by a military oligarch more powerful, more expensive, and more subversive of freedom than the German military oligarchy ever was? Or shall we continue to be ruled under our constitution by the representatives of a democratic people? The issue is unmistakable. The lines are clearly drawn. The fight is on.[104]

Having drafted much of the Wadsworth Bill, Palmer strongly supported it. He anticipated the difficulty of reaching consensus and acknowledged "we have a long fight before us in establishing a sound military policy." Still, he believed that the Wadsworth bill was "a very sound solution of the National Guard problem" because it provided provisions to incorporate the organized militia as "a real part of the National Citizen Army" while "preserv[ing] their use to the State for State purposes." In the end, however, Palmer underestimated the extent of National Guard opposition and overestimated the inclination of Guardsmen who had served in World War I to support the bill.[105]

Because the National Guard sought to maintain its link to the militia clause in order to retain its independence of the Regular Army, the NGAUS rejected the Wadsworth proposal. The bill's affirmation of the National Guard's first-line reserve role was appealing, but the constitutional issue remained front and center. Palmer's belief that World War I veterans would support the Wadsworth Bill was ill-founded, as few had rejoined the National Guard after the war. Moreover, the adjutant generals, who had since 1918, from their point of view, railed against the federal government's abuses during the war, had strong influence over the National Guard lobby.

The "long fight" Palmer predicted between February and May 1920 came to pass. By May, the Senate and the House had reached a deadlock. The legislators disagreed on the issue of compulsory military service or, at minimum, universal training, which proponents of an all-volunteer system opposed. They also disagreed over the National

---

[103] "The Wadsworth Bill," 1920.

[104] Boylan, 1967, p. 121.

[105] John McAuley Palmer, Palmer Papers, Library of Congress, Box 5, Folder 1, 1920.

Guard's role and its organization. Both issues influenced the debate on the Army's peacetime strength, another divisive issue.[106]

The Passage and Provisions of the Army Reorganization Act of 1920

Congress finally reached a compromise in the first week of June. As the bill's authors acknowledged, the resulting Army Reorganization Act of 1920 was "the result of prolonged study" and "exhaustive hearings . . . after weighing the view of many persons, both within and without the Army."[107] The sweeping legislation amended—but did not replace—the 1916 National Defense Act, yet it remains a critical turning point in the history of U.S. military policy.[108] It remedied shortcomings in the 1916 NDA and included provisions to avoid problems in training, planning, and organization that manifested during World War I. In the process, it enshrined a new relationship between the federal government, National Guard, and reserves based on the principle that citizen-soldiers or conscript armies would fight America's wars.

The Army Reorganization Act's provisions are listed in Table 4.1. The law reaffirmed that the United States would maintain a small Regular Army backed by a civilian force of Guardsmen and reservists. It defined the Army of the United States as consisting of the Regular Army, National Guard while in the service of the United States, and an Organized Reserves, including the Officers' Reserve Corps and the Enlisted Reserve Corps. Congress determined that the Regular Army would form the "professional component of a larger national force and not a cadre or skeleton to be expanded in time of war."[109] The act abolished the Regular Army Reserve and defined the Organized Reserves as consisting of federally organized reserve forces, Officers' Reserve Corps, and the Enlisted Reserve Corps. It restated the 1916 NDA provisions establishing the ROTC. It fixed troop strength at 435,000 men for the National Guard and increased Regular Army enlisted end strength to 280,000 men, both to be achieved over the course of five years.

The act included provisions for the federal government to regulate and standardize both the National Guard and Reserve units. The bill's authors believed that peacetime organization was essential for efficient mobilization in the event of war. Accordingly, they prescribed that

---

[106] Boylan, 1967, p. 125.

[107] U.S. Senate, Committee on Military Affairs, *Statement of Subcommittee of the Committee on Military Affairs of the United States Senate to Accompany the Proposed Bill 'To Reorganize and Increase the Effectiveness of the United States Army, and for Other Purposes,'* Washington, D.C.: U.S. Government Printing Office, 1919, p. 1.

[108] Public Law 66-242, An Act to Amend an Act Entitled "An Act for Making Further and More Effectual Provision for the National Defense, and for Other Purposes," June 4, 1920.

[109] Holley, 1982, p. 478.

Table 4.1
Key Provisions of the Army Reorganization Act of 1920 (Public Law 66-242)

- Defined the Army of the United States as consisting of the Regular Army, the National Guard while in the service of the United States, and the Organized Reserves, including the Officers' Reserve Corps and the Enlisted Reserve Corps
- Abolished the Regular Army Reserve (while creating the Officers' and Enlisted Reserve Corps), but retained the National Guard reserve
- Maintained the on-campus ROTC program
- Mandated that National Guardsmen, upon termination of federal service, would resume their membership in the militia/National Guard
- For administration, training, and tactical control, directed the organization of the continental area of the United States into corps areas, each with at least one division from the National Guard or Organized Reserves, as well as other such troops as the President may direct
- Determined that National Guard officers could accept reserve commissions without prejudice to their Guard status[a]
- Elevated the rank of Chief of the Militia Bureau to major general; specified that the Chief of the National Guard Bureau be appointed by the President from the list of present and former National Guard officers who attained at least the grade of major

[a] Shaw, 1966, pp. 77–78.

the Organized peace establishment, including the Regular Army, the National Guard and the Organized Reserves, shall include all of those divisions and other military organizations necessary to form the basis for a complete and immediate mobilization for the national defense in the event of a national emergency.[110]

The new law divided the country into corps areas; each would include at least one division from the National Guard or the Organized Reserves.[111] Outside the continental United States, Regular Army forces were allotted to territorial departments in the Panama Canal Zone, Hawaii, and the Philippines.[112] To promote readiness and coordination, the Regular Army, augmented by a training staff, would train the civilian formations in the corps areas. In this vein, the act also reorganized the Militia Bureau and permitted National Guardsmen to serve on the General Staff, a move designed to improve coordination and provide Guardsmen with exposure to the Regular Army's traditions and techniques.

These were all noteworthy improvements, but some important issues remained unresolved. For instance, the Army had no institutional method of providing routine information and guidance to Organized Reserve units, and such units had few opportunities to receive adequate training. Both problems had hampered mobilization during World War I.[113] Despite the improvements, preparedness advocates were disappointed. The legislation failed to extend conscription and rejected the principle

---

[110] Public Law 66-242, 1920, Section 3.

[111] Public Law 66-242, 1920, Section 3.

[112] Stewart, 2010, p. 60.

[113] Crossland and Currie, 1984.

of universal military training, although it continued to support the MTCA's Citizens' Military Training Camps and the ROTC programs nationwide. Also, the act limited the Regular Army to 280,000 enlisted men, well below what the preparedness advocates had wanted.[114]

The 1920 act secured many of the National Guard's preferences, illustrating the NGAUS's power as a political lobby.[115] It reaffirmed a military policy premised on the use of a civilian army in war and ensured that the Regular Army's authorized size in peacetime remained below that of the National Guard. Moreover, the act maintained the Guard's prominence among the reserve components by mandating that the National Guard would be the first reserve component activated in the event of a national emergency.[116] The act guaranteed the National Guard a larger share of the Army's budget than the Organized Reserve. That said, the law did not specify how the components would implement these changes or the amount of resources the Army would apply toward the National Guard and Organized Reserves.

Despite its appeal to Guardsmen, the act had one major drawback from their perspective. It stipulated that the National Guard would be a part of the Army when federalized and in the service of the United States. When not federalized, however, the Guard performed its duties as the states' organized militia under the militia clause. In practice from the Guard's point of view, these provisions enabled the Regular Army and War Department to bypass the National Guard when not federalized and to create a federal reserve force. If the National Guard was an Army component only when federalized, Guardsmen reasoned, then what would stop the War Department from creating a different federal reserve for all other times? This issue would prove to be a source of major importance for the National Guard in the future and would lead to a pivotal piece of legislation passed by Congress in 1933.

Conclusion

World War I was an important test for the 1916 NDA, especially regarding the Army's mobilization and expansion for modern warfare. Compared with the Army's modest expansion to fight the Spanish in 1898, the Army's expansion for World War I was impressive, although mobilization processes continued to be highly inefficient. In two decades, the Army had learned to mobilize, equip, and train millions of citizen-

---

[114] *Annual Report of the Chief of Staff of the United States Army, 1921*, Washington, D.C.: Government Printing Office, 1921, p. 11.

[115] Notably, the 1920 bill was presented as an amendment to the 1916 NDA (a popular legislation among the Guard's membership) because congressional proponents estimated that this would help ensure the NGAUS's approval (Holley, 1982).

[116] *Report of the Secretary of War to the President, 1922*, Washington, D.C.: U.S. Government Printing Office, 1922, p. 139.

soldiers, evacuate and replace casualties, and maintain the organizational flexibility to adapt peacetime structures for combat.

Regardless, U.S. military policy was still far from perfect. Exhausted by the horrors of World War I and eager to focus on domestic and economic policy, Congress echoed the attitudes of many Americans and rejected calls for a larger peacetime Army and the concomitant changes to military policy that would need to be put in place. Nonetheless, in the two decades following World War I, Congress would continue to adjust the laws that governed the Army. The next chapter will address the history of the most important of these acts, which finally gave the National Guard what it had been seeking for nearly 50 years.

CHAPTER FIVE

Refining Military Policy in the Interwar Years

Introduction

The 1920 amendment to the 1916 National Defense Act increased the size of the Regular Army peacetime enlisted force from 175,000 to 280,000 men (including the Philippine Scouts), and strengthened the Army's reserve forces. By summer 1922, every state except Nevada had organized Guard units, 20 states had reached the maximum number of authorized units by then, and the Guard's end strength totaled nearly 160,000 men, having increased by just over 40 percent in the previous 12 months.[1] Progress was limited towards its total end strength authorized by the 1916 NDA, however, by a series of financial and force reductions that weakened the entire Army. Although the U.S. economy boomed in the 1920s, Congress was parsimonious toward the military.[2] In 1921, it cut the Regular Army to 150,000 men; six years later, it capped the Regular Army's end strength at 118,750 men—significantly below the 280,000 men codified in the 1920 amendment. Unable to field the nine fully manned divisions authorized by the law, the Regular Army resorted to skeleton cadres for all of its divisions and brigades and largely abandoned the defense of the overseas territories. Even then, resources were scarce, which led the Regular Army to downsize regional training centers that had been created to train the Guard and Organized Reserves in peacetime.[3]

In the midst of these changes, the National Guard pushed for legislation that would ensure it a position as a reserve component of the Army at all times. Through persistent lobbying by the NGAUS, the Guard secured congressional passage of the National Guard Act in 1933.[4] The act codified in federal law the Guard's dual constitutional status, one of the institution's most cherished goals, and recognized the National Guard as a part of the Army when in federal service *and*—in a significant break from 1920—a permanent federal reserve component of the Army. The 1933 act established

---

[1] *Report of the Secretary of War to the President, 1922*, 1922, p. 139.

[2] Braeman, 1982.

[3] Weigley, 1967, p. 401.

[4] Public Law 73-64, An Act to Amend the National Defense Act of June 3, 1916, June 15, 1933.

in federal law that National Guardsmen now served two political masters in war *and* in peace: State governors would control the appointment of Guard officers and be responsible for the Guard's training when not in federal service, while the President, through the War Department, would be responsible for equipping and specifying the discipline, organization, and training standards of the National Guard for its role as a reserve component of the Army. In making these changes, Congress struck a balance between the militia and armies clauses as a basis for structuring the Army.

The Aftermath of the 1920 Amendment and the National Guard's Drive for Dual Status

Public opposition to military spending and widespread antimilitary sentiment after the experience of World War I led Congress to keep Army manpower below the levels authorized in the 1920 Army Reorganization Act.[5] As a result, the War Department considered two schemes for the Army's reorganization. The first would cut the number of Regular Army divisions from nine to four, but keep them at full strength. In this plan, the National Guard would keep its number of divisions at 18 at close to full strength, and the Army would do its best to fill the Organized Reserve divisions in manpower. This first proposal was predicated on the assumption that reducing the number of Regular Army divisions would free resources to sustain and train the National Guard and Organized Reserve divisions. The second scheme would retain the Regular Army's nine divisions, but slash end strength across each of the three components. It would also, to the National Guard's dismay, eliminate the Regular Army's training programs for National Guard units; all Regular Army trainers would be needed to keep the nine-division force structure in place.

The two War Department schemes reflected a new twist in the arguments that had been made by the professionalists in the long-running debate over the appropriate distribution of roles and responsibilities among the Regular Army, National Guard, and Organized Reserves. The first proposal represented the view, shared by one aspect of the professionalist reformers, such as Palmer and Guardsmen, that training the National Guard and Organized Reserves was one of the Regular Army's most important peacetime missions, even if it drew resources away from the Regular Army's

---

[5] These reductions were driven by both economic and political considerations. The war's devastation drove thousands of Americans to join pacifist organizations, such as the National Council for the Prevention of War and the Women's International League for Peace and Freedom, that rejected organized military forces altogether. Many Americans also blamed arms dealers and military reformers for the outbreak of World War I, and viewed any investment with suspicion. Robert H. Ferrell, "The Peace Movement," in Alexander DeConde, ed., *Isolation and Interests in Twentieth-Century American Foreign Policy*, Durham, N.C.: Duke University Press, 1957, pp. 84–106; Robert H. Ferrell, *Peace in Their Time: The Origins of the Kellogg-Briand Pact*, New Haven, Conn.: Yale University Press, 1952; Braeman, 1982.

manpower, training, and equipping.⁶ In this thinking, the Regular Army's immediate combat readiness was second in priority to the training of the National Guard and Organized Reserve Divisions. The second proposal was embraced by another aspect of the professionalist school, which maintained that the Army should be centered on the Regular Army, at the expense, if necessary, of the National Guard and Organized Reserves. They envisioned the Regular Army as the priority, with the National Guard and Organized Reserves receiving less emphasis, especially if budgets became tighter. To maintain Regular Army force structure, resources for and men to staff the regional training centers would come at the expense of the National Guard and Organized Reserves.⁷

Ultimately, the War Department chose to implement parts of both schemes. To the dismay of reformers such as Palmer, the Regular Army's nine divisions were retained but in skeletonized form. The decision to maintain force structure came at the expense of Regular Army trainers for the National Guard and Organized Reserve divisions. Palmer noted that, to retain sufficient soldiers and leaders for Regular Army divisions, the training centers for the Army's two reserve components were "broken up and their officers and men were scrambled into their Regular Army Division force structure."⁸

Palmer later argued that Congress's intention in 1920 had been for the Regular Army—not the National Guard or Organized Reserve—to be reduced in times of fiscal austerity. Thus, in Palmer's view, the skeletonized Regular Army nine-division organization weakened the readiness of all three components in a misguided effort to preserve Regular Army force structure. The War Department used a different logic.⁹

---

⁶ John McAuley Palmer, *Washington, Lincoln, Wilson: Three War Statesmen*, Garden City, N.Y.: Doran & Company, Inc., 1930.

⁷ Palmer, 1930.

⁸ Palmer, 1930, p. 368.

⁹ During the interwar years, few people would be as influential in the debates over U.S. military policy as Brigadier General Palmer. It was not uncommon during this time for Army officers and policymakers to cite Palmer's work. As discussed in Volume III, Army Chief of Staff General George C. Marshall called Palmer back onto active duty in 1940 to work on important matters of military policy. In his *Washington, Lincoln, Wilson: Three War Statesmen*, Palmer explained to his readers his recent archival discovery of George Washington's *Sentiments of a Peace Establishment*, which would heavily influence his thinking and writings. Palmer claimed that Washington's views on military policy aligned with his own. To make that claim believable, he dismissed Washington's belief in the primacy of a professional standing army as the lynchpin to the American security system. Palmer's flawed 1930 criticism of Upton remains the most cited component of his historical reasoning. Palmer incorrectly argued that Upton, due to poor research, had missed Washington's 1783 *Sentiments of a Peace Establishment* and, because of that omission, pursued the wrong track in his advocacy for the expansible army policy. In fact, Upton's original handwritten manuscript cites Washington's writings. Palmer, who continuously deployed historical counterfactual reasoning, argued that if Upton had read Washington's plan, he would have pursued a very different military policy of his own. Palmer seems to have the ignored the facts that did not comport with his ideas. Additionally, Palmer felt that Upton's work was responsible for misguiding generations of policymakers. The importance of Palmer's arguments, even though many of them were flawed, would become quite apparent in

Their experience with mass mobilization for World War I suggested that maintaining as much divisional force structure as possible in all three components would best facilitate expansion, through volunteers or conscription, if the nation had to fight another industrial war again.

The National Guard and the Regular Army could both find fault with meager congressional appropriations in the apparent security of interwar peace. Annual reports from the chief of the Militia Bureau during this time detail the fiscal shortfalls that hampered the institution, reporting deficiencies in the past year and forewarning of troubles ahead. Guardsmen did not save their criticism for those in control of the purse strings, but also criticized the War Department for its decision. By the mid-1920s, the National Guard had begun to harness the lobbying power of the NGAUS. The organization had become one of the most influential lobbying groups in the United States, with representatives in nearly every congressional district. Through annual conventions and ties to prominent congressmen, the NGAUS sought to influence future legislation and help shape U.S. military policy. At its 1926 annual convention, it focused on two core issues: the National Guard's ambiguous constitutional status and its relationship with the Army. These two issues influenced the whole range of challenges the National Guard was confronting, from the difficulty of procuring Army commissions for its officers to continued funding concerns. Despite the NGAUS's initial support for the 1920 amendment, attendees at the convention now criticized the act's stipulation that the Guard was an official reserve component only when *federalized*. This legal arrangement reflected Congress's intent to preserve the relevance of both the armies and militia clauses, but it failed to satisfy many Guardsmen. As one colonel explained during the convention, the Guard's primary problem was that it was only part of the Army, and thus only a "first-line defense," when ordered to federal service. It was not a legal component of the Army during peacetime. "I wonder if most of you know—and I'm convinced you don't—" he cautioned convention goers,

> that we are not part of the Army of the United States, not a component part of the national defense. The present National Defense Act, which we are telling the people is such a wonderful measure, provides that the [National Guard] is not a part of the Army of the United States. . . . that the troops who, when called, will constitute the first line, are not part of the Army.[10]

The NGAUS conferees increasingly characterized the Guard's distinction as part of the Army of the United States *only* when federalized (according to the 1920 amend-

---

the years ahead, as his 1930 book and other writings on U.S. military policy were read by many Army officers, legislators, and policymakers.

[10] National Guard Association of the United States, *NAGAUS Annual Convention Report*, Washington, D.C., November 17–19, 1926, p. 82.

ment) as at best, "folderol" and, at worst, an "insidious outrage."[11] Either way, from their perspective, the act was an affront to the National Guard's proud tradition in American military history.[12] Consequently, they focused on amending the amendment to make the National Guard a permanent reserve component and thus clarify its roles and obligations under the armies clause. Still, they were careful not to seek a wholesale replacement of the militia clause, as they wanted to retain their links to the several states. Accordingly, the NGAUS conferees approved Resolution 14, which stated preference for amending the NDA so that:

> the federally recognized National Guard shall at all times, whether in peace or war, be a component of the Army of the United States, its status under the Constitution being preserved, so that its government when not in the service of the United States shall be left to the respective States and that all federally recognized officers thereof shall be duly appointed and commissioned therein.[13]

The resolution focused the NGAUS's lobbying effort in the years ahead and laid the groundwork for the eventual passage of the National Guard Act of 1933 amendment to the 1916 NDA.

The Challenge of Fiscal Restraint for the Organized Reserves and the National Guard

The Organized Reserves

Like the National Guard, the Organized Reserves grew during the interwar period. General Pershing's appointment as Army Chief of Staff in 1921 was a boon for federal reservists, as he prioritized reform of that component. He established a separate Reserve Office in 1923 and soon after transferred the office's responsibilities to the Army Chief of Staff's office, under the supervision of the newly established Executive for Reserve Affairs. The creation of an independent Reserve Affairs agency and its access to a sympathetic chief of staff enabled the Organized Reserves to establish itself on par with the other two components of the Army. In practice, however, the Reserve Office had few resources and little authority to develop, decide, or enact relevant policy. Instead, the Executive for Reserve Affairs served as a liaison between the Organized Reserves and the Chief of Staff.[14]

---

[11] National Guard Association of the United States, 1926, pp. 83–84.

[12] National Guard Association of the United States, 1926, pp. 83–84.

[13] Quoted in U.S. House of Representatives, Committee of the Whole House on the State of the Union, *National Guard Bill*, Washington, D.C.: U.S. Government Printing Office, June 9, 1932.

[14] Crossland and Currie, 1984.

The War Department viewed the Officers' Reserve Corps as the Army's primary source of officers for expansion in wartime.[15] Although the Corps lacked sufficient funds to expand to full strength, there was no shortage of potential recruits. Officers were commissioned through ROTC programs on college campuses and Citizens' Military Training Camps, the product of Plattsburgers' hard work before World War I. These programs flourished in the interwar years. By 1928, 325 ROTC programs operated at civilian colleges and universities and produced large numbers of trained reserve officers, many of whom would serve in World War II.[16] In addition to civilian students, the Officers' Reserve Corps recruited combat veterans of World War I, who contributed experience to the officer ranks. Together, these recruitment initiatives produced a deep and relatively well-trained pool of junior officers for potential service in time of war.[17]

Despite the successes of the ROTC programs, the problem of maintaining, training, and especially manning Organized Reserve divisions remained.[18] Fiscal shortfalls reduced training opportunities and forced drastic cuts in the Enlisted Reserve Corps through the late 1930s. From a decade-high 5,028 ERC personnel in 1933, the number had fallen to 3,054 by the end of the decade.[19] Reserve officers could receive training by participating in exercises with the Regular Army, Citizens Military Training Camps, or the Civilian Conservation Corps, and could get credit for inactive duty training with a Reserve unit or completion of a correspondence course.[20] Even with this range of options, barely a third of eligible reservists received training each year.[21] Unlike Guardsmen, who received federal drill pay, members of the Organized Reserves received no such compensation. Efforts to resolve this problem made little headway, as Congress justified its refusal to allocate additional funds by contending that payment would undermine the reserve forces' status as "amateurs."[22]

---

[15] West Point provided only a small fraction of the officers necessary to lead a wartime army. In 1917, the graduating class numbered only 139 men. This number rose slightly during the war, but the graduating class of 1920 included only 227 men. *Biographical Register of the Officers and Graduates of the U.S. Military Academy at West Point, N.Y.: From Its Establishment, in 1802, to 1890*, Vol. 6, New York: Houghton Mifflin, 1920.

[16] Stewart, 2010, p. 63.

[17] Crossland and Currie, 1984.

[18] Robert K. Griffith, *Men Wanted for the U.S. Army: America's Experience with An All-Volunteer Army Between the World Wars*, Westport, Conn.: Greenwood Press, 1982.

[19] *Annual Report of the Secretary of War to the President, 1933*, Washington, D.C.: U.S. Government Printing Office, 1933, p. 168; *Annual Report of the Secretary of War to the President, 1939*, Washington, D.C.: U.S. Government Printing Office, 1939, p. 70; Crossland and Currie, 1984, p. 296.

[20] Crossland and Currie, 1984, p. 40.

[21] Crossland and Currie, 1984, pp. 40–54.

[22] Crossland and Currie, 1984, p. 49.

The National Guard

Fiscal austerity measures adversely affected the entire Army, including the National Guard units of the states. The shortage of federal and state appropriations meant that National Guard units were forced to limit recruitment below its authorized, nationwide level of 435,800.[23] Regardless, National Guard units made important strides in other ways. The National Guard expanded its physical infrastructure and established a more visible presence in American communities. After decades of reorganization, it now mustered units in every state.[24] Ironically, this expansion was facilitated by the type of federal intervention the National Guard had once opposed, such as the introduction of standardized recruitment methods and training. National Guard units also benefited from the influx of federal funds, which replaced dwindling state appropriations. National Guard units established powerful local and national ties to other influential community organizations, such as Rotary and Lions clubs, the Association of Mayors, and local mayors and sheriffs. This network of private and civic organizations and individuals provided National Guard units credibility and a powerful coalition capable of helping to protect its interests.

The Guard's interaction with the Regular Army was bolstered by a resumption of officer training at Fort Leavenworth. Although Guardsmen did not typically attend the one-year-long Command and General Staff Course, the three-month-long Special Command and General Staff Course was a more realistic investment of time than the pre–World War I year-long course. For as many as 50 Guard and Reserve officers each spring, and for those who could not physically attend, there was a three-year correspondence course that accomplished the same goal: fundamental instruction in doctrine and methodology.[25] Regardless of its success, the National Guard continued to worry about budget gaps. In 1923, Arizona's adjutant general argued that a shortage of federal funding made it difficult for his state to complete the reorganizations directed by the War Department and Militia Bureau.[26] He noted again in 1924 that annual fed-

---

[23] *Annual Report of the Chief of the Militia Bureau*, Washington, D.C.: Government Printing Office, 1922, p. 6; Weigley, 1967, p. 401.

[24] The Arizona National Guard's experience is illustrative. In 1920, Arizona's adjutant general complained in his annual report that the state had provided only one armory. He boasted, however, of efforts to remedy this problem, and described new construction under way in Flagstaff and plans for additional armories in Williams and Phoenix. In 1922, he noted that his headquarters had received federal recognition, and five new companies in Phoenix, Tucson, Casa Grande, Flagstaff, and Mesa, as well as an additional artillery battery for the state. In addition to the plans outlined in 1920, he now described proposals to build armories in Casa Grande and Mesa. By 1929, the Arizona Guard would report a total of 1,101 enlisted men and officers—more than double its size in 1923. *Report of the Adjutant General for the State of Arizona*, Phoenix, Ariz., 1920, 1922, and 1928.

[25] Jonathan M. House, "Officer Education and the Fort Leavenworth Schools, 1881–1940," in James H. Willbanks, ed., *Generals of the Army: Marshall, MacArthur, Eisenhower, Arnold, Bradley*, Lexington, Ky.: University Press of Kentucky, 2013, p. 12; Timothy K. Nenninger, "Leavenworth and Its Critics: The U.S. Army Command and General Staff School, 1920–1940," *Journal of Military History*, Vol. 58, No. 2, April 1994, p. 202.

[26] *Report of the Adjutant General for the State of Arizona*, 1923, p. 1.

eral appropriations to his state were not "sufficient for the maintenance of the National Guard at its present strength."[27] The lack of sufficient federal funding continued in each of his remaining reports for the decade, which bemoaned "woefully insufficient" funds and budgets that were "more inadequate" each year.[28] In general, Guardsmen criticized the War Department's parsimony in distributing federal funds. The Chief of the Militia Bureau noted in 1930, for example, that, despite the increases in enlisted men, officers, warrant officers, and support installations, the benefits to the National Guard "could have been materially extended had appropriations and War Department policies permitted."[29]

Despite these complaints and their insinuations, the Regular Army was not reaping the benefits of budgetary manipulation during the 1920s. The 1925 budget offers useful context, as in the words of the Secretary of War that year in his annual report, the Regular Army received "considerably less than a first reading of the appropriation bill" seemed to suggest.[30] Of the $334 million in the total 1925 budget, nearly $51 million went to the civilian components through direct and indirect support. Around $220 million was earmarked for the Regular Army, spread across training, equipping, and not only supporting a military force in the continental United States, but garrisoning overseas possessions far from home. A considerable amount of that was siphoned off for the support of the entire Army of the United States. Answering intimations of favoritism when determining expenditures, the Secretary of War wished to "correct an erroneous impression, which seems prevalent, as to the actual disposition" of military funds. Using the numbers for the following budget cycle, he claimed that after the estimates were collected and the size of the Army decided upon, "the only amount over whose allocation to items" he had "any real influence" over was not even 10 percent of the total.[31]

The 1933 Amendment to the 1916 National Defense Act

The National Guard was not alone in suffering from limited federal funding. The stock market's collapse in 1929 and the ensuing Great Depression brought fiscal austerity

---

[27] *Report of the Adjutant General for the State of Arizona*, 1924, p. 1.

[28] *Report of the Adjutant General for the State of Arizona*, 1926. The funding shortfalls were not unique to Arizona. The adjutant general of North Carolina would note a "shortage of funds" in his state reports in the 1920s as well. The 1929 report attributed reductions in drill pay to insufficient appropriations.

[29] *Annual Report of the Chief of the Militia Bureau*, Washington, D.C.: U.S. Government Printing Office, 1930, p. 1.

[30] *Annual Report of the Secretary of War, 1925*, Washington, D.C.: Government Printing Office, 1925, p. 8.

[31] *Annual Report of the Secretary of War, 1925*, 1925, p. 10.

measures to the entire Army.³² Still, National Guard reformers were undeterred in their determination to achieve their goals. Thanks to the rapid expansion of National Guard units during the 1920s, in spite of limited federal funding, and the NGAUS's growing influence, the organization increased its pressure for new legislation to safeguard its desired status as a permanent reserve component of the Army while maintaining its links to the states through the militia clause.

In 1930, the NGAUS drafted a proposal to amend the 1920 amendment. Eager to preserve the Guard's link to the states while gaining the prestige (and resources) afforded by federal status even during peacetime, the NGAUS sought to redefine the National Guard as a permanent reserve component of the Army in peace and war. "The National Guard are desirous of becoming a real component, instead of just a make-believe component of the national defense," General Alfred E. Foote, president of the NGAUS, explained to the House Committee on Military Affairs in 1930. "We desire such changes in the national defense act which will assure to us a certain place for ourselves and our organizations in this great scheme of national defense."³³

The House Committee proved a receptive audience. Many committee members shared the Guard's new found criticism of the 1920 amendment and were sympathetic to Guardsmen's complaints that they had been poorly treated by the War Department during World War I. Representatives repeatedly referenced the "injustices" done to the "splendid" Guardsmen, and questioned few of the NGAUS's proposals.³⁴ The amendment was referred to the House for debate, and passed easily on June 15, 1933.³⁵

The 1933 amendment to the 1916 National Defense Act, which at the time was referred to as "The National Guard Act," remains one of the most important laws in Army history (see Table 5.1). The legislation created a new reserve component of the Army defined as the National Guard of the United States, distinct from the existing National Guard of the states and territories.³⁶ The amendment stipulated that the Army of the United States shall "consist of the Regular Army, the National Guard of the United States, the National Guard while in the service of the United States, the Officers' Reserve Corps, the Organized Reserves, and the Enlisted Reserve Corps."³⁷

---

[32] Herring, 2008, pp. 484–486.

[33] U.S. House of Representatives, 1930, p. 12.

[34] Quoted in U.S. House of Representatives, 1930, pp. 32, 34, 38, 41.

[35] Public Law 73-64, 1933.

[36] Public Law 73-64, 1933.

[37] U.S. Senate, Committee on Military Affairs, *Amend the National Defense Act*, Washington, D.C.: U.S. Government Printing Office, June 9, 1933; Griffith, 1982. A note on terminology: Established by the 1916 NDA, the Enlisted Reserve Corps was composed of prior enlisted men from the Regular Army and new enlistees who would receive specialty skills training in the Regular Army. It was similar to the Officers' Reserve Corps in that it was intended to provide a manpower replacement pool of enlisted soldiers with special skills for Engineers, Signal, Quartermaster, and Medical Corps to expand the Regular Army when needed. Unlike the Officers' Reserve Corps, however, Enlisted Reserve Corps members could be assigned by the President as reservists to the Regular

Table 5.1
Key Provisions of the National Guard Act of 1933 (Public Law 73-64)

- Replaced Section 1 of the 1916 NDA and inserted "That the Army of the United States shall consist of the Regular Army, the National Guard of the United States, the National Guard while in the service of the United States, the Officers' Reserve Corps, the Organized Reserves, and the Enlisted Reserve Corps."
- Stipulated that "all policies and regulations affecting the organization, distribution, and training" of the National Guard be prepared by General Staff committees, "to which shall be added an equal number of officers from the National Guard of the United States."
- Stipulated that "all policies affecting the organization, distribution, training, appointment, assignment, promotion, and discharge" of the Officers' Reserve Corps, Organized Reserves, and the Enlisted Reserve Corps shall be prepared by General Staff committees, "to which shall be added an equal number of officers from the Officers' Reserve Corps."
- Renamed the Militia Bureau as the National Guard Bureau.
- Empowered the Chief of Staff to "exercise the same supervision and control of the reserve components of the Army of the United States as he does over the Regular Army."

The 1933 amendment contained an important change in statutory approach and terminology that increased reliance on the armies clause to mobilize the National Guard. The 1916 NDA and 1920 amendment had stipulated that Guardsmen would be drafted for federal service as individuals and "stand discharged from the militia." The use of the term *draft* in the 1916 and 1920 laws was to sidestep constitutional limits on using federalized militia units overseas organized under the militia clause. Therefore, the 1933 amendment substituted the word *ordered* for the word *drafted*.[38] Accordingly, the law reaffirmed the practice of the post-1916 laws and firmly tied the mobilized Guard to the armies clause to ensure that Guard members and forces could be deployed overseas.[39] The 1933 amendment noted that

> All persons so ordered into the active military service of the United States shall from the date of such order stand relieved from duty in the National Guard of their

---

Army or to form new reserve organizations. In 1920, Congress clarified that the Enlisted Reserves were one component of a new umbrella apparatus, the Organized Reserves, which also included the Officers' Reserve Corps and the Enlisted Reserve Corps. The 1920 law added this new term for organizational purposes in recognition of the War Department's intention to maintain in peacetime an organized army reserve, under the armies clause, with corps, divisions, regiments, etc. Unlike the National Guard, Organized Reserve units were skeletal and comprised only officers. The 1920 law stipulated that each corps area would have one Regular Army division, two National Guard divisions, and the Organized Reserve divisions. This force structure would become the nucleus for a greater Army expansion in World War II.

[38] On the "twinning" of the two constitutional clauses, see H. Richard Uviller and William G. Merkel, "The Second Amendment in Context: The Case of the Vanishing Predicate," *Chicago-Kent Law Review*, Vol. 76, January 2000; Stephen I. Vladeck, "The Field Theory: Martial Law, the Suspension Power, and the Insurrection Act," *Temple Law Review*, Vol. 80, No. 2, 2007; Richard Allen Epstein, "Executive Power, the Commander-in-Chief, and the Militia Clause," *Hofstra Law Review*, Vol. 34, No. 2, 2005.

[39] For a clear articulation of the important difference in terminology between *call*, *draft*, and *order* in U.S. military policy, see Edgar C. Erickson and Ellard A. Walsh, "Address to the Army War College (February 17, 1954)," *The Nation's National Guard*, Washington, D.C.: National Guard Association of the United States, 1954.

respective States, Territories, and the District of Columbia so long as they shall remain in the active military service of the United States.

The amendment legislated that "The organization of said units existing at the date of the order into active Federal service shall be maintained intact insofar as practicable" and "Upon being relieved from active duty in the military service of the United States all individuals and units shall thereupon revert to their National Guard status."

The 1933 amendment bolstered the armies clause at the expense of the militia clause.[40] Now more than ever, the Guard would be "well regulated," as required by the militia clause, empowering the chief of staff to "exercise the same supervision and control of the reserve components of the Army of the United States as he does over the Regular Army." Equally important, it would be an integral part of the Army, and thus fall under the armies clause. Significantly, the 1933 law's definition of the National Guard as a reserve component of the Army—premised on the armies clause—also accepted that, when the Guard was not in federal service and thus under state control, it was still recognized under the Constitution's militia clause. Hence, the 1933 act in effect *joined* the two clauses in law. The 1933 House Committee on Military Affairs report pointed out that the act established a National Guard with two political masters: the states and the federal government. In stressing the importance of the Guard's dual role as a reserve component of the Army while maintaining its links to the states, the report noted:

> the National Guard of the United States . . . [is] a reserve organization of the Army of the United States, under the [armies clause] provisions of the Constitution, leaving the National Guard of the States . . . organized under the militia provisions of the Constitution, intact and unaffected by such amendments.[41]

The irony was that, even though by 1933 the armies clause had eclipsed the militia clause when it came to raising and organizing the Army to fight wars (a sentiment reinforced by the previously mentioned 1917 Supreme Court decision), the 1933 act maintained the militia clause on an equal statutory footing with the armies clause.[42]

---

[40] Todd, 1941, p. 170.

[41] U.S. House of Representatives, Committee of the Whole House on the State of the Union, *National Guard Bill: Report to Accompany H.R. 5645*, Washington, D.C.: U.S. Government Printing Office, Document No. 141, 1933, p. 3.

[42] Interestingly, observers at the time, such as lawyer Frederick Todd and others decades after the act, did not see the potential political power of this mechanism. For example, Martha Derthick argued in her 1965 *The National Guard in Politics* that the Guard's power as a political force was waning significantly, to the point where the Guard "would cease to be powerful" as a force in American politics (p. 179). What these observers saw in the 1933 amendment was a winnowing of state control to the point where the federal government virtually owned the National Guard under the armies clause, just as it did the Regular Army and Organized Reserves. However, what observers like Todd and Derthick missed was that having this dual constitutional status allowed the Guard

This elevation of the militia clause occurred despite the fact that the federal government was, by 1933, providing nearly 70 percent of all Guard funding and was likely to provide virtually all of the Guard's funding by 1940. Although the Guard's historical identity was founded on its association with the militia clause, federal funding and the Guard's future were now based on the Guard's status as a reserve component of the Army under the armies clause of the Constitution.

Equally important to the National Guard was legal recognition as a *voluntary* reserve for the U.S. Army. As early as 1926, the NGAUS had as its primary political goal for Congress to pass a new law recognizing the National Guard as a voluntary, federal reserve component of the Army at all times. It pushed for this legislation because the Guard had come to fundamentally disagree with the 1920 amendment. To federalize the Guard, it had stipulated that each individual member of the Guard had to be "drafted" into federal service, although they had previously volunteered to be so drafted when they accepted federal funding for drills and annual training and through their expanded oath of allegiance. Guardsmen started to ask why they should be drafted into federal service when they had already made a voluntary commitment to serve when federalized. Two prominent National Guard officers made this argument pointedly to Congress during their consideration of new legislation. Major General Benson Hough of the Ohio National Guard told members of the House Committee on Military Affairs that the current law required individual Guardsmen to be "drafted into federal service" and thereby discharged from their duty as state militia. In contrast, Hough recommended a bill that would make the National Guard a reserve component to the Army at all times under the armies clause of the Constitution, as had Palmer and O'Ryan. Doing so would then eliminate the need for individual Guardsmen to be "drafted" into federal service. General Hough went on to note that the proposed bill "will in no way change" a Guardsman's status "as a citizen," nor would it

> alter his volunteer military obligation to his state and will in no way change his obligation to respond to the call of the President; but will, by his voluntary consent, prepare the way in advance for his future active Federal service and thus obviate the necessity of subjecting him to the draft without his consent.[43]

Milton Reckord, the adjutant general of Maryland who had commanded a National Guard infantry regiment in World War I, reinforced General Hough's testimony:

> We in the National Guard desire to be a part of the Army of the United States at all times, in peace as well as in war, and yet we also desire to serve in a dual capac-

---

to play both political masters in ways that gave them influence and clout to protect their institutional interests much beyond what the Regular Army and Organized Reserves could do.

[43] Quoted in U.S. House of Representatives, 1930.

ity under the militia clause of our respective States. . . . [W]e provide a method by which to create another reserve force similar in every respect to the present Organized Reserves, to be known as the National Guard of the United States; and then . . . we provide, in case of war or emergency declared by Congress, the President may then order this new reserve force into the Federal service . . . under the Army clause, rather than the militia clause.[44]

Thus, the 1933 act afforded the Guard precisely what it sought: dual allegiance to the states and the federal government. Indeed, when the act was discussed on the House floor on June 5, 1933, Congressman William Patrick Connery, Jr. of Massachusetts stated that "the National Guard has been trying to get this legislation since 1926. Seven years the Guard has favored this type of bill." Connery further noted that the bill and "its passage will greatly help the morale of the Guard."[45]

The Road to War, 1939–1940

The gathering of war clouds in the late 1930s prompted Congress to reconsider the needs of the Army. The push for Army reform and expansion was led by top officials in the War Department, most notably including newly appointed Army Chief of Staff General Marshall, as of September 1, 1939. Thanks to his persistence, the United States implemented new initiatives to develop manpower, mobilize industry, increase defense spending, restore focus on training and readiness exercises, and develop mobilization plans that would ultimately serve as the foundation for the U.S. war effort. Marshall's efforts as the key architect of Army expansion contributed to the United States' ultimate ability to effectively mobilize, fight, and win World War II.[46]

In early 1939, the U.S. Army remained ill-prepared to conduct major combat operations. The Great Depression had forced cuts to the military's already insufficient budgets, and the Regular Army continued to rely on weapons, equipment, and organizations it had used 20 years earlier in Europe. This changed when Germany, after months of annexations and threats, finally invaded Poland on September 1. Four days later, President Franklin D. Roosevelt issued a proclamation of neutrality.[47] On Sep-

---

[44] Quoted in U.S. House of Representatives, 1930.

[45] U.S. Senate, "Patrick Connery of Massachusetts," *Congressional Record*, Washington, D.C.: U.S. Government Printing Office, 1933. The U.S. House of Representatives' *National Guard Bill* (U.S. House of Representatives, Committee of the Whole House on the State of the Union, 1933) states that the origins of the 1933 act came out of the NGAUS Annual meeting in 1926, hence the congressman's claim that the bill had been "seven years" in the making. For the original rationale by the National Guard for the act, see National Guard Association of the United States, 1926.

[46] Stewart, 2010.

[47] Franklin D. Roosevelt, "Executive Order 8233: Prescribing Regulations Governing the Enforcement of the Neutrality of the United States," Gerhard Peters and John T. Woolley, eds., American Presidency Project, 1939a.

tember 8, he declared a "limited" national emergency and issued an executive order authorizing an immediate increase in Army, Navy, and Marine Corps manpower.[48] The impact, however, was modest: Congress authorized the Regular Army to grow by only 17,000 men, to a total strength of 280,000 men.

As Britain and France entered the war against Germany, Congress expanded the Regular Army to 330,000 men. Additionally, it increased training funds to improve readiness, although the appropriations fell far short of President Roosevelt's initial $2.25 billion, which amounted to a quarter of the federal budget.[49] Meanwhile, military planners developed war plans and began implementing modernization efforts to update the Army's equipment and munitions.[50] In June 1940, Congress approved a new munitions program that provided for the procurement of sufficient equipment, weapons, and munitions to equip and maintain a 1.2 million-man army.[51]

The National Guard seized the opportunity to secure increases in funding, manpower, and training. It had begun preparations as early as 1935, when it participated in the first joint maneuvers with Regular units in nearly 20 years. That same year, Congress authorized an annual expansion of 5,000 Guard troops per year, and by 1939 the National Guard reached nearly 200,000 men. This number grew dramatically over the next year, when Congress approved an additional increase of 43,000 Guardsmen. The increases in personnel allowed National Guard divisions to fill out their organizations and to create combat and support units to serve at the corps and army levels once the war began. By the time President Roosevelt federalized the National Guard in August 1940, it had reached 242,402 soldiers.[52]

---

[48] Franklin D. Roosevelt, "Proclamation 2352: Proclaiming a National Emergency in Connection with the Observance, Safeguarding, and Enforcement of Neutrality and the Strengthening of the National Defense Within the Limits of Peace-Time Authorizations," Gerhard Peters and John T. Woolley, eds., American Presidency Project, 1939b.

[49] Walter Trohan, "Roosevelt Asks 2 1/4 Billion Fund for U.S. Defense: Requests Total Quarter of Entire Budget," *Chicago Daily Tribune*, January 5, 1940, p. 8.

[50] Stewart, 2010; Paul A. C. Koistinen, *Planning War, Pursuing Peace: The Political Economy of American Warfare, 1920–1939*, Lawrence, Kans.: University Press of Kansas, 1998; Henry G. Gole, *The Road to Rainbow: Army Planning for Global War, 1934–1940*, Annapolis, Md.: Naval Institute Press, 2003; Williamson R. Murray and Allan R. Millett, *Military Innovation in the Interwar Period*, Cambridge, UK: Cambridge University Press, 1996; Russell Weigley, "The Interwar Army, 1919–1941," in Kenneth J. Hagan and William R. Roberts, eds., *Against All Enemies: Interpretations of American Military History from Colonial Times to the Present*, Westport, Conn.: Greenwood Press, 1986; David E. Johnson, *Fast Tanks and Heavy Bombers: Innovation in the U.S. Army, 1917–1945*, Ithaca, N.Y.: Cornell University Press, 1998; Timothy Moy, *War Machines: Transforming Technologies in the U.S. Military, 1920–1940*, College Station, Tex.: Texas A&M University Press, 2001; Harold R. Winton and David R. Mets, eds., *Military Institutions and New Realities, 1918–1941*, Lincoln, Neb.: University of Nebraska Press, 2000; William O. Odom, *After the Trenches: The Transformation of U.S. Army Doctrine, 1918–1939*, College Station, Tex.: Texas A&M University Press, 1999.

[51] Stewart, 2010.

[52] Franklin D. Roosevelt, "Executive Order 8530: Calling Out the National Guard," Gerhard Peters and John T. Woolley eds., American Presidency Project, August 31, 1940.

In contrast, and generally due to congressional disinterest and lack of an effective political lobbying arm, the Organized Reserves were less prepared when war broke out in Europe in 1939. As discussed previously in Chapter Four, the federal reserves had successfully recruited veteran officers from World War I and college and university students via the growing ROTC program. The Organized Reserves remained popular during the Great Depression, and reservists drilled regularly, served periodically on active duty, and assisted with public works programs, although they did not receive any compensation, as their National Guard counterparts did.[53] However, the lack of congressional funding left most reserve units undermanned, undertrained, and poorly equipped.[54] When hostilities in Europe began, the Regular Army turned to the Officers' Reserve Corps to help lead the expanding force.[55] It soon became clear, however, that many were unfit for duty, and in February 1940 the War Department announced a nationwide "combing" of the "nation's second-line of defense" to weed out thousands of reserve officers who had failed to complete required training or meet physical standards.[56] The Enlisted Reserves Corps was in even worse shape. While the Officers' Reserve Corps numbered 104,228 members eligible for active duty by 1940, the Enlisted Reserve Corps contained only 3,233 men.[57] The same "combing" occurred across the Regular Army and mobilized National Guard units. In retrospect, it is admirable that so many Americans joined the Officers' and Enlisted Reserve Corps without compensation and limited access to training to retain their proficiency.

In addition to its plans to expand the National Guard, Organized Reserves, and Regular Army, Congress approved the Selective Service Act in 1940, the first peacetime national conscription in the nation's history. Recall that Congress had passed a similar act in April 1917 to increase the size of the Army for World War I; however, that act was passed after the United States declared war on Germany, whereas in 1940, the United States was still at peace and would not declare war on Japan and Germany until December 1941.

Even though establishing a new Selective Service process to increase the size of the Army through conscription was the main thrust of the 1940 law, it also contained a new and profound statement about U.S. military policy. The act declared that

> . . . in accordance with our [American] traditional military policy as expressed in the National Defense Act of 1916, as amended, that it is essential that the strength

---

[53] John W. Killigrew, *The Impact of the Great Depression on the Army*, New York: Garland, 1979.

[54] Crossland and Currie, 1984; Donald M. Kington, *Forgotten Summers: The Story of Citizen's Military Training Camps, 1921–1940*, San Francisco, Calif.: Two Decades Publishing, 1995.

[55] Crossland and Currie, 1984.

[56] John G. Norris, "Army Orders Laggard Officers Ousted from Reserve Corps," *Washington Post*, February 3, 1940.

[57] Kington, 1995; Crossland and Currie, 1984.

and organization of the National Guard, as an integral part of the first-line defenses of this Nation, be at all times maintained and assured.[58]

The inclusion of the phrase "traditional military policy" in the act was no accident; that same year, Chief of Staff Marshall had brought out of retirement Army reformer Brigadier General Palmer to assist Army planners in mobilization planning and eventually in writing postwar military policy. Along the way, he also provided his ideas and assistance to various members of Congress. Palmer worked with the writers of the 1940 Selective Service Act to insert the passage on "traditional military policy," to suggest, albeit counterfactually, that there had been one such policy for governing the Army and the key role of the National Guard since the Constitution.

Unfortunately, the 1940 Selective Service Act's use of the phrase "traditional military policy" gave the legislation and the policy it charted the feel of a culmination of history, with the implication that, after so many years, the United States had finally settled on the right military policy. Indeed, after the passing of the 1940 act, Palmer spoke in April 1942 at the annual convention of the Adjutant Generals Association of the United States, asserting that, had Congress in 1920 accepted all his proposals, it would have settled "our military policy forever."[59] But there was nothing in the years from 1903 to 1940 to suggest that the history of U.S. military policy had come to an end, that a plan to settle "forever" U.S. military policy was available to decisionmakers, or that all the historical forces that had shaped U.S. military policy over time had culminated in the 1940 act and required no more fundamental changes or adjustments.

Conclusion

In the decade following the end of World War I, Congress and policymakers vigorously debated whether to completely replace the 1916 NDA or to revise it based on the experience of the U.S. Army in World War I. The result was the 1920 amendment to the 1916 NDA, which revised some important provisions of the 1916 NDA. After the passing of the 1920 amendment, it seemed to many Army reformers that they might, with the revised law Congress just passed, build an Army with an overarching military policy that might be prepared in a serious way for America's next war. Unfortunately for these reformers, almost as soon as the ink was dry on the 1920 act, Congress moved away from providing the Army the funding it needed to achieve the manning, equipping, and training levels that the act established. It was also during the early and

---

[58] Public Law 76-783, An Act to Provide for the Common Defense by Increasing the Personnel of the Armed Forces of the United States and Providing for Its Training, September 16, 1940.

[59] John McAuley Palmer, "Address of Brigadier General John McAuley Palmer: Excerpts from the Transcript of the Shorthand Report of the Proceedings of the Adjutants General Association Annual Meeting," Palmer Papers, Library of Congress, April 21, 1942.

middle years of the 1920s that the National Guard formulated a lobbying platform that sought to fundamentally alter its relationship to the Army as stipulated in the 1916 NDA and 1920 amendment. The 1933 amendment maintained the National Guard's link to the states through the militia clause, but also created a new reserve component—the National Guard of the United States—under the armies clause. The upcoming global conflict would provide the crucible for the Army and its governing military policy.

CHAPTER SIX

Volume Conclusion

The modern U.S. Army took shape during the first four decades of the 20th century. The Spanish-American War of 1898 exposed weaknesses in U.S. military policy, as established by Congress, that had plagued the Army for nearly a century and triggered a flurry of legislative activity that sought to resolve them. The war forced American military planners and political leaders to acknowledge the inconvenient truth that 19th century laws were ill-equipped to manage 20th century challenges. As the United States' global interests and security requirements grew, Congress expanded, modernized, and reorganized the nation's defenses for the new century, albeit incrementally and typically behind the need.

For those driving legislative change between 1898 and 1940, the tradition of maintaining a Regular Army of insufficient strength to bear the initial brunt of battle, was continued. Defending the nation would require the mobilization of citizen-soldiers. A new National Guard movement had since the end of the 19th century acquired considerable political influence. Spearheaded by the National Guard Association of the United States, advocates of the "organized militia" sought to expand the National Guard's resources, responsibilities, and status while opposing initiatives to build and, after 1916, strengthen, new federal reserve components.

The National Guard's status and relationship to the Army changed considerably in this period. The Dick Act of 1903 recognized the National Guard as the "organized militia" of the several states, but did not establish it as a reserve component of the Army or even establish the relationship between the Army and the National Guard. The 1916 NDA did recognize the National Guard as part of the Army, but only when in the service of the United States (i.e., federalized), and it increased both federal support and oversight. When not federalized, as the 1916 NDA stipulated, the National Guard was under state control, in accordance with the militia clause. Accordingly, the 1903 and 1916 laws (and the 1920 amendment to the 1916 NDA) treated the National Guard and the two constitutional clauses like an on-off switch: Either the Guard was federalized under the armies clause and part of the Army, or it was not federalized and remained under the militia clause, but not part of the Army. The 1933 amendment did what no other legislation had done: It created the statutory framework for the National

Guard's dual status without violating the limitations imposed by Constitution's militia clause.

The 1903 Dick Act and the 1916 NDA enabled the Army to mobilize adequately for World War I, yet the conflict revealed many lingering problems in U.S. military policy. The Army's plodding mobilization and reliance on British and French support revealed the clear need for better personnel, logistical planning, and resources. As the National Guard's status evolved, the division among military reformers deepened. Until the 1933 amendment, Upton-inspired professionalists accepted the constitutional limitations on the federal use of the militia (National Guard) as nonnegotiable, as specified in the 1912 legal opinion of the attorney general of the United States. The 1933 amendment provided for the National Guard's dual status, paving the way for reliance on the National Guard of the United States as one of the Army's reserve components. Meanwhile, militia advocates worked to enshrine the National Guard's status as an integral element of the nation's military policy. The end result was a set of compromises, codified in 1920 and 1933, that strengthened the nation's ability to raise large war armies through the combined use of the Regular Army and its reserve components, volunteerism, and conscription. In stark contrast to the 19th century, when militia advocates opposed efforts to expand federal authority, the National Guard now agreed to federal regulation—and funding—designed to regulate and improve readiness. In exchange, the National Guard received recognition of its dual role as a federal and state force.

APPENDIX A
Summary Table of 19th Century Militias and Volunteer Forces

Table A.1 summarizes the various types of militias and volunteer forces that existed in the 19th century.

Table A.1
Summary Table of 19th Century Militias and Volunteer Forces

Type of Force	Organization	Legal Basis	Use	Period of Existence	Links to Present Day
Militia manpower pool	Was not organized and is referred to in current law as the "unorganized militia." It comprised all free able-bodied males between 18 and 45 years of age.	1792 Uniform Militia Act and state laws stipulating all adult free men's liability for militia service.	Was the manpower base for the various militias described below, both voluntary and compulsory.	Originated in the first American settlements in Virginia and Massachusetts and runs to the present day.	Title 32 (The National Guard) and Title 10, Subtitle A (The Army) both stipulate that American men ages 18–45 are in the "unorganized militia."
Compulsory or common militias	Individual states required all men to be on militia musters and to meet for training as part of a militia company of approximately 60 men several times per year. Militia companies were often formed into regiments. By state and federal law, the common militia's service was limited to 3 months.	1792 Uniform Militia Act and state laws stipulating all adult free men's liability for militia service.	States used the compulsory militias for local law enforcement, defense, and fighting against Native Americans. In times of war or insurrection, the federal government would assign quotas to states for militia units. Local militia captains would muster their men and organize a small number of volunteers or conscripts. The newly formed militia unit would be in federal service for up to 3 months.	Began in the first American settlements of Virginia and Massachusetts but had severely atrophied to the point that fewer and fewer states required men to muster regularly for training; by the 1840s, compulsory militia muster drill was a rarity, especially in the North.	None.

Table A.1—continued

Type of Force	Organization	Legal Basis	Use	Period of Existence	Links to Present Day
State-sanctioned volunteer militias for federal service	Men interested in military affairs and the camaraderie of other like-minded men formed volunteer militia units independent of the state-generated common militias. They could be used in federal service for longer than 3 months.	State and local laws authorized governors, mayors, magistrates, etc., to utilize volunteer militia units. Their service on foreign soil during the Mexican-American War was founded on the Constitution's "raise and support armies" clause because they were brought into federal service as individual volunteers.	These volunteer militias were often called on by state governors for a variety of uses, including law enforcement and the escorting of dignitaries. Equally important, state governors offered these volunteer militias to meet federal quotas for the Mexican-American War and the Civil War.	The first volunteer militia was established in Boston in 1638. More developed in the 18th century. Volunteer militias were used extensively in the Mexican-American War and were the first militia units to respond to President Lincoln's call in the spring of 1861. Starting in the late 1870s, new volunteer militias began to form and call themselves "Guards" or "National Guards," increasingly under state control.	The modern National Guard traces its historical roots to the volunteer militias that emerged in the 1870s after the Civil War.
State-formed volunteer militias for federal service	The federal government issued calls to states to organize a quota of volunteers into regiments for federal service. These volunteer militias could serve for longer than 3 months in times of war.	1792 Uniform Militia Act, state militia laws, and the Constitution's "raise and support armies" clause.	Volunteer militias were used inconsistently during the War of 1812, but constitutional barriers to their use beyond U.S. borders limited their utility. During the Mexican-American War, volunteer militias were locally organized, but the states could use them to meet federal quotas in times of war for 1–3 years.	The apex for volunteer militias and volunteer forces was during the Civil War, when the early armies of the war from the North and South consisted overwhelmingly of volunteer units.	None.

Table A.1—continued

Type of Force	Organization	Legal Basis	Use	Period of Existence	Links to Present Day
Civil War volunteer regiments, Union Army *(The sheer number of volunteers relative to other U.S. wars makes this a separate category.)*	Through Lincoln's executive order, the federal government issued quotas to states for "volunteers." States then relied on local systems to organize regiments of infantry, cavalry, artillery, etc. These volunteer units were technically "militias" because, under the 1792 Uniform Militia Act, all men ages 18–45 were part of the "unorganized militia."	The 1792 Uniform Militia Act was amended twice during the Civil War. The authority to call on the militia was based on Article 1, Section 8's provisions to suppress insurrection. With the March 1863 Enrollment Act, volunteers (and draftees) were brought into federal service under the "raise and support armies" clause.	After organizing volunteer regiments and, in some cases, providing initial training, states sent them to rendezvous points where the regiments were brought into federal service and assigned to higher brigades for service in the various theaters of war. Terms of service ranged from 6 months to 3 years to the full duration of the war.	The Civil War. Although the states produced these kinds of volunteer units for the Mexican-American War and, in a more limited sense, the War of 1812, the aggregate size of the Union Army, made up largely of volunteer regiments, makes the Civil War distinct from previous U.S. wars.	None.
Federal volunteers for the Spanish-American War	The 1898 Volunteer Army Act authorized the federal government to organize, directly, volunteers with "special qualifications." As a result, three federal cavalry regiments were raised (one of which was Leonard Wood's and Teddy Roosevelt's 1st Volunteer Cavalry). These regiments were formed in territories rather than states to encourage volunteerism beyond state political limitations.	The 1898 Volunteer Army Act stipulated that these federal volunteer cavalry regiments would be organized in the territories directly by the federal government under the Constitution's armies clause. They were intentionally formed in the territories to bypass problems with the individual states and their governors, who were forming militia units for volunteering into federal service.	Only one volunteer cavalry regiment was actually formed: Wood and Roosevelt's 1st Volunteer Cavalry, which deployed with Regular Army forces to Cuba, was brigaded with a Regular Army cavalry division, and fought heroically at the Battle of San Juan Hill.	The Spanish-American War from April to August 1898. They were formed using existing territorial militia companies and individual volunteers in the territories of Arizona, New Mexico, and Oklahoma, as well as volunteers from across the nation, and consolidated their training in San Antonio, Texas. Men from the northeast who were friends of Roosevelt also volunteered as enlisted men and officers.	None.

APPENDIX B

Summary Table of Legislation Pertaining to the Evolution of U.S. Military Policy

Table B.1
Summary Table of Legislation Pertaining to the Evolution of U.S. Military Policy

Statute/Act	Historical Context	Significance	Links to Titles 10 and 32
U.S. Constitution: Militia, Raise/Support Armies, and President as Commander in Chief Clauses	• 1787: Framers want small standing army • Framers envision a select portion of the militia as a federal reserve • Framers also envision the militia as the military force to deal with domestic issues such as insurrection and enforcement of laws	• The constitutional basis for Regular Army, federal army reserve, and militias • No constitutional link between Regular Army and militia • Future policy—laws enacted—would therefore define roles of militia and Regular Army	• Title 32 states National Guard is trained and has its officers appointed under militia clause • Title 10 organized current U.S. Army under raise/support armies clause
1792 Uniform Militia Act	• George Washington wants militia organized on his 1783 "Sentiments on a Peace Establishment"	• Congress passes militia law with no mechanism for federal enforcement • Is based on militia clause of Constitution • Only militia law until 1903	• Title 32 acknowledges 1792 act and that National Guard is organized under the militia clauses of the Constitution
1795 Amendment to the 1792 Calling Forth Act	• Concern over 1794 Whiskey Rebellion and possible future rebellions • Congress's trust in Washington allows them to give Executive control over militia to deal with domestic problems	• Gives President power to call forth militia without restrictions placed by the 1792 act • Starts the statutory movement away from the militia envisioned in Constitution	• Title 10 gives President authority to either "call forth" or "order" National Guard without congressional authorization per 1795 act
1799 "Augment the Army" Act	• Failure of negotiations with France increased fear of war between the two nations • Domestic unrest at home over taxes to pay for military mobilization increases need for expanded military to deal with insurrections	• Gives President power to expand temporarily the Regular Army by 24 regiments • President given authority to accept organized companies of volunteers from the militia into federal service • 1799 act gives President authority to use this expanded Army for the same purposes when "calling forth" the militia	• Title 10 gives President power to expand Regular Army and use it for domestic problems in combination with National Guard per the 1795 act

Table B.1—continued

Statute/Act	Historical Context	Significance	Links to Titles 10 and 32
1807 Insurrection Act	• With frontier expanding and continuing domestic unrest, there is need for Regular Army for internal problems in addition to Militias	• Gives President authority to use the Regular Army and Navy for internal rebellions and other problems • Completes the statutory movement away from militia envisioned in Constitution	• Title 10 gives President authority to use Regular forces for domestic problems
1863 Enrollment Act	• American Civil War. Union Army having trouble relying on states to bring men and units under federal control to meet manpower demand after two years of war with high casualties	• First federal statutory law that authorized a federal draft premised on universal military duty under the "raise and support armies" clause	• Title 10 relies on the Constitution to give it the statutory means to raise and support an army • Implicit is the assumption that a national draft might be necessary to do so, as stipulated in Title 50
1898 Act to Provide for Temporarily Increasing the Peace Establishment of the United States in Time of War	• Spanish-American War. Regular Army and state National Guards largely unprepared for expeditionary warfare • Debacle of deploying the Army to Cuba to fight Spain spurs significant postwar Army reforms	• Continues Congress on path increasing reliance on armies clause to organize army for war and maintains precedent for American men liable for service in "national forces"	• Same as 1863 Enrollment Act
1903 Act to Promote Efficiency of Militia (Dick Act)	• Spanish-American War reveals problems expanding Army and its readiness • Secretary of War (Elihu Root) implements major reforms for U.S. Army • United States enters world stage as new global power • Perceived need for major Army reform to fight 20th century industrial wars	• First update to Uniform Militia Act for federal organizing of militia since 1792 • Is based on militia clause • Is statutory birthday of modern Guard • Federal government recognizes state Guards as "organized militia" • Directs state Guards to be organized like Regular Army • Establishes federal oversight • Formalizes process of trading autonomy for federal aid • Directs Guard units to train for a minimum of 24 drill periods per year, including a 5-day summer encampment • Funds Guard 5-day encampments	• Title 32 refers to Guard as "organized militia" and directs state Guards to be organized like Regular Army • Title 32 is premised on militia clause and armies clause of Constitution

Table B.1—continued

Statute/Act	Historical Context	Significance	Links to Titles 10 and 32
1908 Army Medical Department Act (April)	• Experience In Spanish-American War with casualties because of poor sanitation and health issues drives need for reform in Army medical care	• Establishes Medical Reserve Corps • Statutory birthday of Army Reserve	• Title 10 Army Reserve premised on armies clause
1908 Dick Act Amendment	• Growing tension between Regular Army and War Department and state Guards • Constitutional debate over use of state Guards in foreign wars as organized militia • State Guards worry federal volunteers will eclipse their desire to be in first line of defense	• Establishes state National Guards as Organized Militia of Several States when called to federal service before any volunteers (individuals or units) and can deploy overseas • Further stokes legal debate over constitutionality of deploying the state Guards, organized on the militia clause, outside of United States	• Title 32 stipulates state Guards are trained and have their officers appointed under the militia clause
1916 National Defense Act	• World War I underway for two years • Mexican border issues • Debate over whether to have federal-only reserve or state National Guards as reserve in first line of defense • Need to reorganize Army for industrial-age warfare • Preparedness movement led by Elihu Root and other leading progressives argues for centralization of Army, universal military training for all American adult males, and rejection of state Guards as reserve force to Army, calls for federal reserve force envisioned in the War Department's "Continental Army Plan"	• Establishes National Guard as component of Army when federalized and in service of the United States • Constitutional premise is armies clause • Directs state Guards to be organized like Regular Army • Gives detailed organization direction for Army • Establishes Organized Reserves and Reserve Officers' Training Corps (ROTC) • Funds Guard for weekly armory training • Is major increase of federal oversight and control of Guard • Sets end strength goal for state Guards at 435,000 and Regular Army at 280,000 • States that Guards when federalized will be drafted as individuals • Establishes Militia Bureau under Secretary of War, not Army Chief of Staff	• Title 10 recognizes the Army National Guard of the United States as a standing reserve component of the Army • Virtually all funding for National Guard under Title 10 is based on Congress organizing the Guard for war under the armies clause • Title 10 allows for Reserve Officers Training

Table B.1—continued

Statute/Act	Historical Context	Significance	Links to Titles 10 and 32
1917 Selective Service Act	• U.S. enters World War I, needs to form quickly a mass citizen-based war army • Selective Service national draft is the means to provide manpower	• First major national draft in American history • Draws on 1898 act and 1863 Enrollment Act that virtually all adult males are susceptible to federal military service • First time Army receives major amounts of manpower without using the state militia systems	• Title 10 is statutory framework to carry out constitutional provision to raise and support armies • National conscription is an implicit mechanism in Title 10 and explicitly stated in Title 50, to carry out that function, if needed • Conscription into federal forces premised on armies clause
1920 Army Reorganization Act (amendment to 1916 National Defense Act)	• End of World War I yields more debate on how to organize peacetime army • War Department produces plan similar to 1915 Continental Army Plan that calls for federal-only reserve to Army • Backlash from Congress • John M. Palmer becomes key adviser to Senate Military Affairs Committee • Demobilization of Guard as individuals not units embitters Guard toward Regular Army	• Continues much of 1916 National Defense Act • Sets end strength goal for Guard 435,000, Regular Army 280,000 (but over next 20 years, neither is funded to those levels) • Word *draft* used to bring Guard to federal service but says Guard can be used for any mission (implying foreign wars) • Makes Chief of Militia a Guard officer (formerly a Regular Army officer); also says if Guard demobilized from federal service will be by units, not individuals	• Title 10 National Guard Bureau headed by Guard officer
1933 National Guard Act (amendment to 1916 National Defense Act)	• Main problem is how to mobilize mass citizen-based war army • Both Regular Army and Guard at 50% • Organized Reserve units are manned at skeleton levels • Based on World War I experience, National Guard Association of the United States and Guard lobby Congress hard for Guard to be made reserve component of Army at all times. • National Guard had sought this kind of legislation since the years following end of World War I	• Is statutory birth of modern guard as dual state and federal reserve force • Establishes U.S. Army as the Regular Army, the National Guard of the United States, the National Guard while in the service of the United States, the Officers Reserve Corps, the Organized Reserves, and the Enlisted Reserve Corps • Says Guard is reserve component of U.S. Army at all times; because Guard is permanent reserve of Army the word *ordered* is used for first time • The statutory birthday of the modern Army Total Force	• Title 10 defines U.S. Army as Regular Army, Army National Guard of the Several States, the Army National Guard while in the Service of the United States, and the Army Reserve • Title 10 uses "call forth" and "order" to federalize Guard • Joins the armies and militia clauses into statutory law. • Title 32 reflects "joining" by stating Guard is trained and has officers appointed under militia clause; however, it is organized and equipped under the armies clause

Table B.1—continued

Statute/Act	Historical Context	Significance	Links to Titles 10 and 32
1940 Selective Service Act	• World War II looms • Regular Army, Guard, and Organized Reserves mobilizing and preparing • Palmer brought back by Marshall to think about postwar military policy • Guard worries again about being eclipsed by War Department relying on Army Reserve before Guard	• Stipulates explicitly the term "traditional military policy of the United States" is to maintain "at all times" the National Guard as "integral part of first line defenses"	• Title 32 (as does Title 50) stipulates almost verbatim the term "traditional military policy" as stated in the 1940 Selective Service Act

APPENDIX C
Taxonomy of Important Terms

Active component: This term is often used as a substitute for the Regular component of any of the military Services, and is often confused with *active duty*.

Active duty: The term *active duty* means full-time duty in the active military service of the United States. The term includes full-time training duty, annual training duty, and attendance, while in the active military service, at a school designated as a service school by law or by the Secretary of the military department concerned. The term does not include full-time National Guard duty (10 USC 101(d)(1)).

Armies clause: Article I, Section 8, of the U.S. Constitution states that Congress "shall have the power to," among other things, "raise and support Armies, but no Appropriation of Money to that Use shall be for a longer Term than Two Years."

Army National Guard (ARNG): ARNG is defined in 32 USC 101 as "that part of the organized militia of the several States and Territories, Puerto Rico, and the District of Columbia, active and inactive that a) is a land force; b) is trained, and has its officers appointed, under the 16th clause of section 8, article I, of the Constitution; c) is organized, armed, and equipped wholly or partly at Federal expense; and d) is federally recognized." The National Defense Act of 1916 introduced the use of the term *National Guard* for the organized militia. After the National Security Act of 1947 created the Air Force, the term *Army National Guard* was established to distinguish the land force. When referring to the Army National Guard as a reserve component of the Army, either of the terms *reserve component* (singular) or *reserve components* (plural) should be used. Title 10 of the U.S. Code generally uses the plural term, but it also uses the singular term, which is why either of the two can be used. See also *Army National Guard of the United States* and *National Guard*.

Army National Guard of the United States (ARNGUS): The ARNGUS is the reserve component of the Army all of whose members are members of the Army National Guard (10 USC 101(c)(3)). See also *Army National Guard* and *National Guard*.

Army of the United States divisions, World War II: Formed by the War Department starting in 1943, these were divisions formed in excess of what the 1920 amendment had established: 9 Regular Army, 18 National Guard, and 36 Organized Reserve divisions.

Army Total Force Policy: This is a formal term adopted in DoD and Department of the Army policy (not statutory law) documents starting in 1970 with Secretary of Defense Melvin Laird's "Total Force Policy" for the entire DoD. It would be incorrect to apply this term to the U.S. Army of 1936, or even 1966, since it is a specific historical term that emerged in a specific historical context. This term was created in an attempt to characterize a shift in DoD thinking, which included higher expectations for the annual investments made in reserve forces and resulting higher levels of readiness.

Calling forth militia clause: Article 1, Section 8, of the U.S. Constitution states that Congress "shall have the power to," among other things, "provide for calling forth The militia to execute the Laws of the Union, suppress Insurrections and repel Invasions."

Chief of the National Guard Bureau (CNGB): The CNGB is responsible for the organization and operation of the National Guard Bureau but does not exercise command over the Army and Air National Guards of the States and Territories. The CNGB serves as a principal adviser to the Secretary of Defense, the Chairman of the Joint Chiefs of Staff, and the Secretaries and Service Chiefs of the Army and Air Force on issues related to the nonfederalized National Guard. In 2011, Congress revised 10 USC 10502 to include the CNGB as a four-star general and as a member of the Joint Chiefs of Staff.

Commander-in-chief clause: Article II, Section 2, of the U.S. Constitution states that "The President shall be Commander in Chief of the Army and Navy of the United States, and of the Militia of the several States, when called into the actual service of the United States . . ."

Director of the Army National Guard (DARNG): Since 1948 and under 10 USC 10506, the DARNG is appointed by the President and is tasked with assisting the Chief of the National Guard Bureau in carrying out the functions of the National Guard Bureau related to the Army National Guard. To be eligible for this four-year post, the officer must be an active member of the Army National Guard and have been nominated for selection by his or her governor or, in the case of the District of Columbia, the commanding general of the District of Columbia National Guard. The President may, with or without the Secretary of Defense's recommendation, appoint the DARNG from general officers of the Army National Guard.

Enlisted Reserve Corps (ERC): Established in federal law by the 1916 National Defense Act, the ERC comprised prior enlisted men from the Regular Army and new enlistees who would receive specialty skills training in the Regular Army. It was similar to the Officers' Reserve Corps in that it was intended to provide a manpower replacement pool of enlisted soldiers with special skills for Engineers, Signal, Quartermaster, and Medical Corps to expand the Regular Army when needed. But, like the Officers' Reserve Corps, the law allowed the President to assign ERC members as reservists to the Regular Army or to form new reserve organizations. Only a handful of men came into the ERC.

First-line defenses and **second-line defenses:** *First-line defenses* refers to U.S. ground and naval forces that will first meet an enemy of the United States in combat. *Second-line defenses* refers to follow-on forces that will take much longer to mobilize and prepare for battle. For example, in the 19th century, the first line of ground defenses against an invasion from a foreign power was the small Regular Army scattered throughout the country alongside the state militias. The second line in this context would have been a larger volunteer army that would be mobilized by the several states and provided for federal service. In the 20th century, which ground forces were in the first and second lines of defense became the subject of debate among the War Department, Regular Army, and National Guard proponents. Guardsmen saw their organized state militia units as being a part of the first-line defense with the Regular Army. In their view, the Regular Army would respond first but would be quickly joined by ready National Guard units. In this view, the second line would have been the larger volunteer or conscript army. Many Regular Army officers contested this view, arguing that the first-line defenses ought to comprise only the Regular Army and a federal reserve force. The second line of defense, in their view, would have been the larger militia and volunteer army that would take time to mobilize and train. In this view, the state National Guards would be dedicated to state missions, and not typically part of the larger war army, which many Regular Army officers believed must be under the command of one commander-in-chief, namely the President, and not subordinate to state governors, as were the state National Guards.

Inactive Duty for Training (IDT): First codified in 1952, this term refers to authorized training performed by a member of the Army Reserve or National Guard not on active duty or active duty for training. Commonly known as "weekend drill," IDT includes regularly scheduled unit training assemblies, equivalent or additional training, and any special duties authorized for reserve component personnel by the Secretary concerned.

Medical Reserve Corps: Established in federal law on April 23, 1908, in response to capability shortfalls during the 1898 Spanish-American War, the Medical Reserve Corps was the first federal reserve to the U.S. Army organized under the armies clause.

It was to be made up of certified medical doctors who had volunteered to serve in the Medical Reserve Corps and be called to active service when the need was determined by the Secretary of War. This Medical Reserve Corps was the forerunner of the modern Army Reserve of today.

Military policy: Refers to the foundational laws that govern the U.S. Army by defining what the Army consists of—its component parts—and the relationship between those component parts. The first true legal statement of a military policy to govern the Army was the 1916 National Defense Act, although that law did not use the term explicitly. See also *traditional military policy*.

Militia: See Appendix A: Summary Table of 19th Century Militias and Volunteer Forces. Also see *organized militia*.

Militia clause: Article 1, Section 8, of the U.S. Constitution states that Congress "shall have the power to," among other things, "provide for organizing, arming, and disciplining, the Militia, and for governing such Part of them as may be employed in the Service of the United States, reserving to the States respectively, the Appointment of the Officers, and the Authority of training the Militia according to the discipline prescribed by Congress."

Mobilize or mobilization: Refers to either calling forth militias of the several states or ordering the reserve components to federal service to augment the Regular Army.

National Army divisions, World War I: Established by the War Department in 1917 to designate newly formed Army divisions that were made up of draftees (and cadres from Regular Army and National Guard formations) that were created in addition to Regular Army and National Guard divisions.

National Guard: The National Guard evolved out of the volunteer uniformed militias that developed prior to the Civil War. After the Civil War, starting in the 1870s, volunteer uniformed militia units increasingly called themselves National Guard or National Guards. Until the early 20th century, these National Guard units were state entities unto themselves with little or no federal oversight or authority. With the Dick Act in 1903 came federal recognition of the National Guard units as the "organized militia" of the several states. Over the course of the 20th century, the level of federal funding for the National Guard increased to the point that, today, virtually all of the funding for the National Guard comes from the federal government. See also *Army National Guard* and *Army National Guard of the United States*.

Officers' Reserve Corps: Established in federal law by the 1916 National Defense Act to facilitate the rapid expansion of the Army, the Officers' Reserve Corps was to consist of men who had volunteered to be in it, had received the appropriate level of training as further stipulated by the 1916 act, and would be liable to be ordered by the President to federal service to fill out and expand the ranks of the Regular Army. The Officers' Reserve Corps was premised on the armies clause. Its historical use was generally during the period between 1916 and 1941.

Organized militia and **unorganized militia:** The first use of the term *organized militia* in federal law was in the 1903 Dick Act, which recognized the National Guards of the several states as the "organized militia" and premised on the militia clauses. This statutory term should not be confused with various militia units in 18th and 19th century America that were organized, either under compulsory service or volunteerism.

The term *unorganized militia* was first stipulated in federal law in the 1903 Dick Act to refer to men between ages 18 and 45 who were not members of the state National Guards or "organized militia."

Organized Reserve Corps: This term is often used in post–World War II writings to describe the "Organized Reserves" during the interwar years from 1920 to 1940. The term *Organized Reserve Corps* was not used during those interwar years unless someone was referring to an actual "corps" formation in the Organized Reserves. The term *Organized Reserve Corps* came into use during the World War II years, especially when planners were writing about postwar Army organizations. However, the term was first stipulated in federal law in the Army Organization Act of 1950. The 1952 Armed Forces Reserve Act then stipulated the term *Organized Reserve Corps* would be replaced with *Army Reserve*. Therefore, the term *Organized Reserve Corps* should be used carefully and only when referring to the years between roughly 1944 and 1952. Unfortunately, many secondary sources use *Organized Reserve Corps* interchangeably with *Organized Reserves* to describe the Organized Reserves during the interwar years. One other point of confusion is that the abbreviation *ORC* is also used for the Officers' Reserve Corps; the two organizations are obviously quite different and distinct.

Organized Reserves: Established in the 1920 amendment to the 1916 National Defense Act, the Organized Reserves consisted of the Officers' Reserve Corps and the Enlisted Reserve Corps. The 1920 law added this new term from the 1916 National Defense Act for organizational purposes, because when World War I ended in 1918, the Department of War intended to maintain in peacetime an organized Army reserve, under the armies clause, that had actual "in being" corps, divisions, regiments, etc. A big difference from the National Guard was that the Organized Reserve units were of skeletal strength, consisting only of officers. Importantly, the 1920 amendment designated nine corps regional areas in the United States responsible for training and recruiting for the Regular Army, National Guard, and Organized Reserve divisions in it. The 1920 amendment stipulated that each corps area would have one Regular Army division, two National Guard divisions, and three Organized Reserve divisions.

This force structure would become the nucleus for a greater Army expansion in World War II.

Regular Army: In continuous existence since 1788 as stipulated in federal law, the Regular Army is the full-time, standing component of the Army. The term *active duty* is often used as being synonymous with the Regular Army, but it is not. The confusion comes from the premise of the Regular Army being a full-time "active" force.

Reserve component: This singular term may refer to any of the reserve components of the military services or the Coast Guard described below under *reserve components*. With regard to the Army, *reserve component* may refer to either the Army Reserve or the Army National Guard of the United States. The term first appeared in the Code of Federal Regulations in 1926, when Title 32 defined the National Guard as the United States' reserve component. It has since expanded in line with the emergence of additional reserve forces.

Reserve components: As codified in 1994 in 10 USC 10101, *reserve components* is the collective term for the seven individual reserve components of the U.S. military: Army National Guard of the United States, Army Reserve, Marine Corps Force Reserve, Navy Reserve, Air National Guard of the United States, Air Force Reserve, and Coast Guard Reserve. Under 10 USC 10102, the purpose of the reserve components is to "provide trained units and qualified persons available for active duty in the armed forces, in time of war or national emergency, and at such other times as the national security may require, to fill the needs of the armed forces whenever more units and persons are needed than are in the regular components."

Reserve Officers' Training Corps (ROTC): The ROTC was established in statutory law by the 1916 National Defense Act. The law authorized the President, under the armies clause, to establish ROTC detachments at U.S. colleges granting four-year degrees. The law also mandated ROTC detachments at U.S. colleges and universities that were established by the 1862 U.S. land grant (Morrell Act), which provided federal land to newly formed states to build colleges and universities. A provision of the Morrell Act directed that military tactics and sciences be taught at these land grant institutions. Hence the connection between the 1916 National Defense Act establishing the ROTC and the 1862 Morrell Act.

Traditional military policy: A term created by an important Army reformer of the first half of the 20th century, John McAuley Palmer. Palmer first used the term in a report he wrote for the Secretary of War Henry Stimson in 1912. In Palmer's view, the "traditional military policy" of the United States was to have a small Regular Army in peacetime that would be expanded by mobilizing the mass of the citizenry into a war army that was also led by "citizen soldiers." Palmer also began, in the years prior to World War I, to add an additional tenet of this "traditional military policy," which was to have this citizen army in place in peacetime so that it could be equipped and trained. In 1940, Congress applied the term *traditional military policy* in statutory law to the National Guard, by stating "in accordance with the traditional military policy of the United States, it is essential that the strength and organization of the National Guard as an integral part of the first line defenses of the United States be maintained and assured at all times . . ."

U.S. Army or **Army:** The term *Army* refers to the totality of the U.S. Army at any given time in U.S. history—that is, the Regular Army and whatever type of force has been added to expand it. It is incorrect to assume that the term *Army* is synonymous with *Regular Army*; *Army* refers to the Regular Army *and* the actual or potential means to expand it. For example, one could use the term *Army* during the War of 1812 to mean the Regular Army, compulsory militia units provided by the several states to expand the overall size of the Army, and volunteer militia units from the several states. Or, by way of another example, the term *Army* in 1944 meant units of the Regular Army, Organized Reserves, the National Guards of the states and territories, and the Army of the United States. As a more recent example, the term *Army*, as stipulated in Title 10 of the U.S. Code, means the Regular Army, the Army National Guard of the United States, the Army National Guard while in the service of the United States, and the Army Reserve (i.e., the U.S. Army Reserve). The Army recognizes its birthday as occurring in 1775, when the Continental Congress established the American "Continental" Army.

U.S. Army Reserve: The 1952 Armed Forces Reserve Act, a major piece of legislation reforming all of the military services' reserve components, largely based on the experience of the partial mobilization during the Korean War, replaced older terms for the Army, such as *Organized Reserves* and *Organized Reserve Corps* with the new term *Army Reserve*. It is important to note that this legal title should be used in singular form and not in the plural—*Army Reserves*—since in its singular form, as stipulated in law, it refers to the individual members and units of the Army Reserve. At the Department of Defense (DoD) level, it is typical to refer to the *reserves* (plural and lowercase) when referring collectively to the Army Reserve, Navy Reserve, Air Force Reserve, Marine Corps Forces Reserve, and Coast Guard Reserve—but, importantly, not the Army National Guard. When referring to the Army Reserve as a reserve component of the Army, the term *reserve component* should be used; the *Army reserve components* are the U.S. Army Reserve and the Army National Guard of the United States.

Abbreviations

AEF	American Expeditionary Force
ARNG	Army National Guard
DMA	Division of Militia Affairs
JMSI	*Journal of the Military Service Institution of the United States*
MTCA	Military Training Camps Association
NCFA	National Commission on the Future of the Army
NDA	National Defense Act
NGAUS	National Guard Association of the United States
ROTC	Reserve Officers' Training Corps

References

"10,000 Men a Day," *Washington Post*, June 24, 1917.

"122,120 Volunteers in Service," *New York Times*, May 31, 1898.

1908 Militia Act—*See* U.S. Statutes at Large, An Act to Further Amend the Act Entitled 'An Act to Promote the Efficiency of the Militia, and for Other Purposes.'

"500,000 Join Colors," *Washington Post*, June 25, 1917.

Abrahamson, James L., *American Arms for a New Century: The Making of a Great Military Power*, New York: The Free Press, 1981.

Alexander, Arthur J., "Service by Substitute in the Militia of Northampton and Lancaster Counties (Pennsylvania) During the War of the Revolution," *Military Affairs*, Vol. 9, No. 3, Autumn 1945, pp. 278–282.

Alger, Russell Alexander, *The Spanish-American War*, New York: Harper & Brothers Publishers, 1901.

Ambrose, Stephen E., *Upton and the Army*, Baton Rouge: La: Louisiana University Press, 1992.

Anderson, Thomas M., "Nationalization of the State Guards," *Forum*, Vol. 30, 1901.

Annual Report of the Chief, Division of Militia Affairs, Washington, D.C.: U.S. Government Printing Office, 1908.

Annual Report of the Chief, Division of Militia Affairs, Washington, D.C.: U.S. Government Printing Office, 1909.

Annual Report of the Chief, Division of Militia Affairs, Washington, D.C.: U.S. Government Printing Office, 1911.

Annual Report of the Chief, Division of Militia Affairs, Washington, D.C.: U.S. Government Printing Office, 1913.

Annual Report of the Chief of the Militia Bureau, Washington, D.C.: Government Printing Office, 1922.

Annual Report of the Chief of the Militia Bureau, Washington, D.C.: U.S. Government Printing Office, 1930.

Annual Report of the Chief of Staff of the United States Army, 1921, Washington, D.C.: Government Printing Office, 1921.

Annual Report of the Secretary of War, 1904, Volume I, Washington, D.C.: U.S. Government Printing Office, 1904.

Annual Report of the Secretary of War, 1907, Volume I, Washington, D.C.: U.S. Government Printing Office, 1907.

Annual Report of the Secretary of War, Washington, D.C.: U.S. Government Printing Office, 1908.

Annual Report of the Secretary of War, 1925, Washington, D.C.: Government Printing Office, 1925.

Annual Report of the Secretary of War to the President, 1933, Washington, D.C.: U.S. Government Printing Office, 1933.

Annual Report of the Secretary of War to the President, 1939, Washington, D.C.: U.S. Government Printing Office, 1939,

Ansell, S. T., "Status of State Militia Under the Hay Bill," *Harvard Law Review*, Vol. 30, No. 7, 1917, pp. 712–723.

"Anxious to Volunteer," *Washington Post*, May 8, 1898.

"Army Desertion Causes," *Galveston Daily News*, October 30, 1907, p. 10.

"Army Desertion on the Increase," *Helena Independent*, August 10, 1905, p. 5.

"Army Desertions and the Remedy," *Washington Post*, October 16, 1903, p. 6.

"Army Desertions Increase," *Washington Post*, November 27, 1906, p. 15.

"Army Desertions," *Boston Daily Globe*, October 27, 1907, p. SM5.

"Army Gossip in Washington," *Daily Kennebec Journal*, August 12, 1904, p. 8.

Army Medical Department Act—*See* U.S. Statutes at Large, An Act to Increase the Efficiency of the Medical Department of the United States Army.

"Army Officers Uniting," *New York Times*, September 29, 1878, p. 5.

Army Reorganization Act—*See* Public Law 66-242.

Army Reorganization: Hearings Before the House of Representatives Committee on Military Affairs House, Sixty-Fifth Congress, Third Session on H.R. 14560, To Reorganize and Increase the Efficiency of the Regular Army (January 16, 1919), Washington, D.C.: Government Printing Office, 1919.

Army Reorganization: Hearings Before the Senate Committee on Military Affairs, Remarks by George E. Chamberlain (September 5, 1919), 66th Congress, 1st Session, Washington, D.C.: U.S. Government Printing Office, 1919.

Arnett, Alex Mathews, *Claude Kitchin and the Wilson War Policies*, New York: Russell & Russell, 1971.

"Attacks on Officers of the Regular Army," *New York Times*, May 18, 1919, p. 54.

Baer, George W., *One Hundred Years of Sea Power: The U.S. Navy, 1890–1990*, Stanford, Calif.: Stanford University Press, 1994.

"Baker Offers New Army Plan for 21 Division," *Chicago Daily Tribune*, January 16, 1919, p. 5.

Barbeau, Arthur E., and Henri Florette, *The Unknown Solider: Black American Troops in World War I*, Philadelphia, Pa.: Temple University Press, 1974.

Barr, Ronald J., *The Progressive Army: U.S. Army Command and Administration, 1870–1914*, New York: St. Martin's Press, 1998.

Beaver, Daniel R., *Modernizing the American War Department: Change and Continuity in a Turbulent Era, 1885–1920*, Kent, Ohio: Kent State University Press, 2006.

Beckett, I. F. W., *Britain's Part-Time Soldiers: The Amateur Military Tradition, 1558–1945*, Barnsley, UK: Pen & Sword Military, 2011.

Belmonte, Peter L., *Days of Perfect Hell: The U.S. 26th Infantry Regiment in the Meuse-Argonne Offensive, October–November 1918*, Atglen, Pa.: Schiffer Military History, 2014.

Betros, Lance, "Officer Professionalism in the Late Progressive Era," in Lloyd J. Matthews, ed., *The Future of the Army Profession*, New York: McGraw-Hill Primis Custom Publishing, 2002, pp. 271–290.

Biographical Register of the Officers and Graduates of the U.S. Military Academy at West Point, N.Y.: From Its Establishment, in 1802, to 1890, Vol. 6, New York: Houghton Mifflin, 1920.

Birkhimer, William E., "Congress and the National Guard," *Journal of the Military Service Institution of the United States*, Vol. 20, 1897.

Bjornstad, Alfred W., "The Military Necessities of the United States, and the Best Provisions for Meeting Them," *Journal of the Military Service Institution of the United States*, Vol. 42, May–June 1908, pp. 335–361.

Bliss, Tasker H., "Mobilization and Maneuvers," *Journal of the Military Service Institution of the United States*, Vol. 50, January–June 1912, pp. 180–182.

Boehm, Bill, *The Chiefs of the National Guard Bureau, 1908–2011*, Arlington, Va.: Historical Services Division, Office of Public Affairs, National Guard Bureau, 2011.

Boemeke, Manfred F., Roger Chickering, and Stig Förster, eds., *Anticipating Total War: The German and American Experiences, 1871–1914*, Cambridge, UK: Cambridge University Press, 1999.

Bonura, Michael A., *Under the Shadow of Napoleon: French Influence on the American Way of Warfare from the War of 1812 to the Outbreak of WWII*, New York: New York University Press, 2012.

Boylan, Bernard L., "Army Reorganization 1920: The Legislative Story," *Mid-America XL*, April 1967, pp. 115–128.

Braeman, John, "Power and Diplomacy: The 1920s Reappraised," *The Review of Politics*, Vol. 44, No. 3, July 1982, pp. 342–369.

Braim, Paul F., *The Test of Battle: The American Expeditionary Forces in the Meuse-Argonne Campaign*, Shippensberg, Pa.: White Mane Publishing, 1998.

Britton, Edward E., "In What Way Can the National Guard Be Modified So as to Make It an Effective Reserve to the Regular Army in Both War and Peace?" *Journal of the Military Service Institution of the United States*, Vol. 26, 1900.

Brown, Preston, "The Genesis of the Military Training Camp," *Infantry Journal*, December 1930.

Bruce, Robert B., *A Fraternity of Arms: America & France in the Great War*, Lawrence, Kans.: University Press of Kansas, 2003.

Byler, Charles A., *Civil-Military Relations on the Frontier and Beyond, 1865–1917*, Westport, Conn.: Praeger, 2006.

Cantor, Louis, *The Creation of the Modern National Guard: The Dick Militia Act of 1903*, PhD dissertation, Durham, N.C.: Duke University, 1963.

———, "Elihu Root and the National Guard: Friend or Foe?" *Military Affairs*, Vol. 33, No. 3, December 1969, pp. 361–373.

Capozzola, Christopher, "The Only Badge You Need Is Your Patriotic Fervor: Vigilance, Coercion, and the Law in World War I America," *Journal of American History*, Vol. 88, No. 4, March 2002, pp. 1354–1382.

———, *Uncle Sam Wants You: World War I and the Making of the Modern American Citizen*, Oxford, UK: Oxford University Press, 2008.

Carter, William H., "The Organized Militia: Its Past and Future," *The United Service*, Vol. 3, No. 3, 1903, pp. 791–794.

———, "The Militia Is Not a National Force," *The North American Review*, Vol. 196, No. 680, 1912, pp. 130–135.

———, "Army Reformers," *The North American Review*, Vol. 208, No. 755, 1918, pp. 548–557.

Chambers, John Whiteclay, *To Raise an Army: The Draft Comes to Modern America*, New York: The Free Press, 1987.

———, *The Eagle and the Dove: The American Peace Movement and United States Foreign Policy, 1900–1922*, Syracuse, N.Y.: Syracuse University Press, 1991.

Cirillo, Vincent J, *Bullets and Bacilli: The Spanish-American War and Military Medicine* (New Brunswick, N.J.: Rutgers University Press, 2004.

Clark, Jason Patrick, *The Many Faces of Reform: Military Progressivism in the U.S. Army, 1866–1916*, PhD dissertation, Durham, N.C.: Duke University, 2009.

———, *Preparing for War: The Emergence of the Modern U.S. Army, 1815–1917*, Cambridge, Mass.: Harvard University Press, 2017.

Clifford, John Garry, *The Citizen Soldiers: The Plattsburg Training Camp Movement, 1913–1920*, Lexington, Ky.: University Press of Kentucky, 2014.

Coffman, Edward M., *Hilt of the Sword: The Career of Peyton C. March*, Madison, Wis.: University of Wisconsin Press, 1966:

———, "American Command and Commanders in World War I," in Russell F. Weigley, ed., *New Dimensions in Military*, San Rafael, Calif.: Presidio Press, 1975.

———, *The War to End All Wars: The American Military Experience in World War I*, Lexington, Ky.: University Press of Kentucky, 1998.

———, *The Regulars: The American Army, 1898–1941*, Cambridge, Mass.: Belknap Press of Harvard University Press, 2004.

Colby, Elbridge, "Elihu Root and the National Guard," *Military Affairs*, Vol. 23, No. 1, Spring 1959, pp. 20, 28–34.

Colby, Elbridge, and James F. Glass, "The Legal Status of the National Guard," *Virginia Law Review*, Vol. 29, No. 7, May 1943, pp. 849–850.

Cooling, Benjamin Franklin, "The Missing Chapters of Emory Upton: A Note," *Military Affairs*, Vol. 37, No. 1, 1973, pp. 13–15.

Cooke, James J., *Pershing and His Generals: Command and Staff in the AEF*, Westport, Conn.: Praeger, 1997.

Cooper, Jerry, *The Militia and National Guard in America Since Colonial Times: A Reference Guide*, Westport, Conn.: Greenwood Press, 1993.

———, *The Rise of the National Guard: The Evolution of the American Militia, 1865–1920*, Lincoln, Neb.: University of Nebraska Press, 1997.

Cooper, John Milton, Jr., *Woodrow Wilson: A Biography*, New York: Vintage Books, 2009.

Cosmas, Graham A., *An Army for Empire: The United States Army in the Spanish-American War*, Columbia, Mo.: University of Missouri Press, 1971a.

———, "Military Reform After the Spanish-American War: The Army Reorganization Fight of 1898–99," *Military Affairs*, Vol. 35, No. 1, 1971b.

———, "San Juan Hill and El Caney, 1–2 July 1898," in C. E. Heller and W. A. Stofft, *America's First Battles, 1776–1965*, Lawrence, Kans.: University Press of Kansas, 1981.

Crane, Charles J., "Comment and Criticism: Democracy and Our Armies," *Journal of the Military Service Institution of the United States*, Vol. 38, 1906, pp. 353–356.

Crossland, Richard B., and James T. Currie, *Twice the Citizen: A History of the United States Army Reserve, 1908–1983*, Washington, D.C.: Office of the Chief, Army Reserve, 1984.

Crowell, Benedict, and Robert F. Wilson, *Demobilization: Our Industrial and Military Demobilization after the Armistice, 1918–1920*, New Haven, Conn.: Yale University Press, 1921.

Cunliffe, Marcus, *Soldiers and Civilians: The Martial Spirit in America, 1775–1865*, Boston: Little, Brown, and Company, 1968.

Davis, Richard Harding, *The Cuban and Puerto Rican Campaigns*, New York: Scribner and Sons, 1898.

Derthick, Martha, *The National Guard in Politics*, Cambridge, Mass.: Harvard University Press, 1965.

"Desertions from the Army," *Boston Daily Globe*, March 3, 1906, p. 10.

"Desertions Increasing," *Washington Post*, November 19, 1909, p. 6.

Dick Act—See U.S. Statutes at Large, An Act to Promote the Efficiency of the Militia, and for Other Purposes.

Dick, Charles, "Our Second Line of Defense," *Journal of the Military Service Institution of the United States*, Vol. 31, 1902, pp. 747–751.

Dickinson, John, *The Building of an Army*, New York: The Century Co., 1922.

Dierks, Jack Cameron, *A Leap to Arms: The Cuban Campaign of 1898*, Philadelphia, Pa.: J. B. Lippincott, 1970.

Doubler, Michael D., *I Am the Guard: A History of the Army National Guard, 1636–2000*, Washington, D.C.: Army National Guard, 2001.

"Drafted Men Warned," *New York Times*, October 4, 1917, p. 8.

"Editorial," *The Army and Navy Journal*, Vol. 52, January 30, 1915.

"Editorial," *National Service Magazine*, Vol. 6, No. 3, September 1919, p. 134.

Edwards, John Carver, *Patriots in Pinstripes: Men of the National Security League*, Washington, D.C.: University Press of America, 1982.

Ely, Hanson E., "The Military Policy of the United States," *Journal of the Military Service Institution of the United States*, Vol. 40, 1907.

Epstein, Richard Allen, "Executive Power, the Commander-in-Chief, and the Militia Clause," *Hofstra Law Review*, Vol. 34, No. 2, 2005.

Erickson, Edgar C., and Ellard A. Walsh, "Address to the Army War College (February 17, 1954)," *The Nation's National Guard*, Washington, D.C.: National Guard Association of the United States, 1954.

"Extract from Minutes of a Meeting of the War Cabinet Held at 10 Downing Street, S.W., on Friday, December 21, 1917 at 11:30 A.M.," *United States Army in the World War, 1917–1919: Policy-Forming Documents of the American Expeditionary Forces*, Washington, D.C.: U.S. Army Center of Military History, 1989.

"Fails to Win Kitchin," *New York Times*, November 9, 1915, p. 4.

Ferrell, Robert H., *Peace in Their Time: The Origins of the Kellogg-Briand Pact*, New Haven, Conn.: Yale University Press, 1952.

———, "The Peace Movement," in Alexander DeConde, ed., *Isolation and Interests in Twentieth-Century American Foreign Policy*, Durham, N.C.: Duke University Press, 1957, pp. 82–106.

———, *Collapse at Meuse-Argonne: The Failure of the Missouri-Kansas Division*, Columbia, Mo.: University of Missouri Press, 2004.

———, *America's Deadliest Battle: Meuse-Argonne, 1918*, Lawrence, Kans.: University Press of Kansas, 2007.

Finnegan, John Patrick, *Against the Specter of a Dragon: The Campaign for American Military Preparedness, 1914–1917*, Contributions in Military History, Westport, Conn.: Greenwood Press, 1974.

"Fit All for War—T.R.," *Washington Post*, August 26, 1915, pp. 1–2.

Fitzpatrick, David, *Emory Upton: Misunderstood Reformer*, Norman, Okla.: University of Oklahoma Press, 2017.

Foote, Stephen M., "Based on Present Conditions and Past Experience, How Should Our Volunteer Armies Fight?" *Journal of the Military Service Institution of the United States*, Vol. 22, 1898.

Ford, Nancy Gentile, *The Great War and America: Civil-Military Relations During World War I*, Westport, Conn.: Praeger Security International, 2008.

Frazier, Walter S., Jr., "The National Guard National in Name Only," *Journal of the Military Service Institution of the United States*, Vol. 20, 1897a, pp. 518–523.

———, "The National Guard National in Name Only," *Journal of the Military Service Institution of the United States*, Vol. 21, 1897b, pp. 419–420.

Galloway, Eilene Marie Slack, *History of United States Military Policy on Reserve Forces, 1775–1957*, Washington, D.C.: U.S. Government Printing Office, 1957.

"General Order 38: June 22, 1915," *General Orders and Bulletins*, Washington, D.C.: U.S. Government Printing Office, 1915.

General Staff Corps, War College Division, *Statement of a Proper Military Policy for the United States*, Washington, D.C., 1915.

Glenn, Edwin F., "The Militia Law and Some Remarks About the Maneuver Camp at Pine Planes, N.Y.," *Journal of the Military Service Institution of the United States*, Vol. 43, July–December 1908, pp. 359–360.

Gole, Henry G., *The Road to Rainbow: Army Planning for Global War, 1934–1940*, Annapolis, Md.: Naval Institute Press, 2003.

Goodenough, William Howley, and James Cecil Dalton, *The Army Book from the British Empire: A Record of the Military Forces and Their Duties in Peace and War*, London: Harrison & Sons, 1893.

Greene, Francis V., "The Capture of Manila," *Century Illustrated Monthly*, No. 57, 1898–1899.

Griffith, Robert K., *Men Wanted for the U.S. Army: America's Experience with An All-Volunteer Army Between the World Wars*, Westport, Conn.: Greenwood Press, 1982.

Grotelueschen, Mark E., *Doctrine Under Trial: The American Artillery Employment in World War I*, Westport, Conn.: Greenwood Press, 2001.

———, *The AEF Way of War: The American Army and Combat in World War I*, Cambridge, UK: Cambridge University Press, 2007.

Hagedorn, Hermann, *Leonard Wood: A Biography*, Vols. 1 and 2, New York: Harper and Brothers Publishers, 1931.

Hallas, James H., *Squandered Victory: The American First Army at St. Mihiel*, Westport, Conn.: Praeger, 1995.

Hammond, Paul Y., *Organizing for Defense: The American Military Establishment in the Twentieth Century*, Princeton, N.J.: Princeton University Press, 1961.

Harris, Charles H., and Louis R. Sadler, *The Great Call-Up: The Guard, the Border, and the Mexican Revolution*, Norman, Okla.: University of Oklahoma Press, 2015.

Heitman, Francis B., *Historical Register and Dictionary of the United States Army*, Vol.2, Washington, D.C.: Government Printing Office, 1903.

Herring, George C., Jr., "James Hay and the Preparedness Controversy, 1915–1916," *The Journal of Southern History*, Vol. 30, No. 4, November 1964, pp. 383–404.

Herring, George C., *From Colony to Superpower: U.S. Foreign Relations Since 1776*, New York and London: Oxford University Press, 2008.

Herwig, Holger H., "The Battlefleet Revolution, 1885–1914," in MacGregor Knox and Williamson Murray, eds., *The Dynamics of Military Revolution, 1300–2050*, Cambridge, UK: Cambridge University Press, 2001, pp. 114–131.

Hewes, James E., Jr., *From Root to McNamara: Army Organization and Administration, 1900–1963*, Washington, D.C.: U.S. Army Center of Military History, 1975.

Hill, Jim Dan, *The Minute Man in Peace and War*, Harrisburg, Pa.: The Stackpole Company, 1964.

Hill, Nancy Peterson, *A Very Private Public Citizen: The Life of Grenville Clark*, St. Louis, Mo.: University of Missouri Press, 2014.

Hitchman, James H., *Leonard Wood and Cuban Independence, 1898–1902*, The Hague: Martinus Nijhoff, 1971.

Hirsch, Alan, "The Militia Clause of the Constitution and the National Guard," *University of Cincinnati Law Review*, No. 59, 1988.

Hobbs, William H., *Leonard Wood: Administrator, Soldier, and Citizen*, New York: C. P. Putnam's Sons, 1920.

Holley, I. B., *General John M. Palmer, Citizen Soldiers, and the Army of a Democracy*, Westport, Conn.: Greenwood Press, 1982.

Holme, John G., *The Life of Leonard Wood*, New York: Doubleday, Page, and Company, 1920.

House, Jonathan M., "John McAuley Palmer and the Reserve Components," *Parameters*, Vol. 12, No. 3, September 1982.

———, "Officer Education and the Fort Leavenworth Schools, 1881–1940," in James H. Willbanks, ed., *Generals of the Army: Marshall, MacArthur, Eisenhower, Arnold, Bradley*, Lexington, Ky.: University Press of Kentucky, 2013.

Howenstine, E. Jay, Jr., "Demobilization After the First World War," *Quarterly Journal of Economics*, Vol. 58, No. 1, November 1943, pp. 91–105:

Hudson, Walter M., *Army Diplomacy: American Military Occupation and Foreign Policy After World War II*, Lexington, Ky.: University Press of Kentucky, 2015.

Hull, Isabel V., *Absolute Destruction: Military Culture and the Practices of War in Imperial Germany*, Ithaca, N.Y.: Cornell University Press, 2004.

Huntington, Samuel P., *The Soldier and the State: The Theory and Politics of Civil-Military Relations*, Cambridge, Mass.: Harvard University Press, 1985.

Huston, James A, *The Sinews of War: Army Logistics, 1775–1953*, Washington, D.C.: United States Army Center of Military History, 1997.

Interstate National Guard Association, *Proceedings of the Third Annual Convention*, Washington, D.C.: National Guard Association of the United States Museum, 1900.

———, *Proceedings of the Fifth Annual Convention*, Washington, D.C.: National Guard Association of the United States Museum, 1903.

Jessup, Phillip, *Elihu Root*, Vol. 1, New York: Dodd Mead, 1938.

Johnson, David E., *Fast Tanks and Heavy Bombers: Innovation in the U.S. Army, 1917–1945*, Ithaca, N.Y.: Cornell University Press, 1998.

Jones, Howard, *Crucible of Power: A History of U.S. Foreign Relations Since 1897*, Lanham, Md.: SR Books, 2001.

Katz, Friedrich, "Pancho Villa and the Attack on Columbus, New Mexico," *The American Historical Review*, Vol. 83, No. 1, February 1978, pp. 101–130.

Kaufman, Jason, *For the Common Good? American Civic Life and the Golden Age of Fraternity*, Oxford, UK: Oxford University Press, 2002.

Keene, Jennifer D., *Doughboys, the Great War, and the Remaking of America*, Baltimore, Md.: Johns Hopkins University Press, 2003.

Kennedy, David M., *Over Here: The First World War and American Society*, Oxford, UK: Oxford University Press, 1980.

Killigrew, John W., *The Impact of the Great Depression on the Army*, New York: Garland, 1979.

"Kill National Guard Declared Army Plan," *Los Angeles Times*, December 12, 1918, p. I6.

Kindvatter, Peter S., "Santiago Campaign of 1898: Joint and Combined Operations," *Military Review*, Vol. 73, No. 2, 1993, pp. 3–14.

King, C. W., "The National Guard, National in Name Only," *Journal of the Military Service Institution of the United States*, Vol. 21, 1897a, pp. 210–211.

———, "'The National Guard National in Name Only'—A Reply" *Journal of the Military Service Institution of the United States*, Vol. 21, 1897b, pp. 629–630.

Kington, Donald M., *Forgotten Summers: The Story of Citizen's Military Training Camps, 1921–1940*, San Francisco, Calif.: Two Decades Publishing, 1995.

Kniptash, Vernon E., *On the Western Front with the Rainbow Division: A World War I Diary*, Norman, Okla.: University of Oklahoma Press, 2009.

Kohn, Richard H., *Eagle and Sword: Federalists and the Creation of the Military Establishment in America, 1783–1802*, New York: Free Press, 1975.

———, *The United States Military Under the Constitution of the United States, 1789–1989*, New York: New York University Press, 1991.

Koistinen, Paul A. C., *Planning War, Pursuing Peace: The Political Economy of American Warfare, 1920–1939*, Lawrence, Kans.: University Press of Kansas, 1998.

Kreidberg, Marvin A., and Merton G. Henry, *History of Military Mobilization in the United States Army, 1775–1945*, Washington, D.C.: U.S. Department of the Army, 1955.

Kretchik, Walter E., *U.S. Army Doctrine: From the American Revolution to the War on Terror*, Lawrence, Kans.: University Press of Kansas, 2011.

Lane, Jack C., *Leonard Wood and the Shaping of American Defense Policy, 1900–1920*, PhD dissertation, University of Georgia, 1963.

———, *Armed Progressive: General Leonard Wood*, Lincoln, Neb.: University of Nebraska Press, 2009.

Langston, Thomas S., *Uneasy Balance: Civil-Military Relations in Peacetime America Since 1783*, Baltimore, Md.: Johns Hopkins University Press, 2003.

Lee, Edward Brooke, Jr., *Politics of Our Military's National Defense: History of the Action of Political Forces Within the United States Which has Shaped our Military National Defense Policies from 1783 to 1940 Together with the Defense Acts of 1916 and 1920 as Case Studies*, Washington, D.C.: U.S. Government Printing Office, Document No. 274, 1940.

Lengel, Edward G., *A Companion to the Meuse-Argonne Campaign*, Malden, Mass.: Wiley Blackwell, 2014.

Lerwill, Leonard L., *The Personnel Replacement System in the United States Army*, Washington, D.C.: U.S. Department of the Army, 1954.

Linderman, Gerald F., *The Mirror of War: American Society and the Spanish-American War*, Ann Arbor, Mich.: University of Michigan Press, 1974.

Link, Arthur, *Woodrow Wilson: Revolution, War, and Peace*, Arlington Heights, Ill.: AHM Publishing, 1979.

Linn, Brian McAllister, *Guardians of Empire: The U.S. Army and the Pacific, 1902–1940*, Chapel Hill, N.C.: University of North Carolina Press, 1997.

———, *The Philippine War, 1899–1902*, Lawrence, Kans.: University Press of Kansas, 2000.

———, *The Echo of Battle: The Army's Way of War*, Cambridge, Mass.: Harvard University Press, 2007.

Loss, Christopher, *Between Citizens and State: The Politics of American Higher Education in the Twentieth Century*, Princeton, N.J.: Princeton University Press, 2012.

Machoian, Ronald G., *William Harding Carter and the American Army: A Soldier's Story*, Norman, Okla.: University of Oklahoma Press, 2006.

Marchand, C. Roland, *The American Peace Movement and Social Reform: 1898–1918*, Princeton, N.J.: Princeton University Press, 1972.

Marcosson, Isaac F., *Leonard Wood: Prophet of Preparedness*, New York: John Lane Company, 1917.

Matheny, Michael R., *Carrying the War to the Enemy: American Operational Art to 1945*, Norman, Okla.: University of Oklahoma Press, 2011.

McCallum, Jack, *Leonard Wood: Rough Rider, Surgeon, Architect of American Imperialism*, New York: New York University Press, 2006.

McIlvaine, Tompkins, "A People's Army: Plan of M.T.C.A. to Congress," *National Service Magazine*, Vol. 6, No. 3, September 1919, p. 151.

McKenna Charles Douglas, *The Forgotten Reform: Field Maneuvers in the Development of the United States Army, 1900–1920*, PhD Dissertation, Duke University, 1981.

McKenney, Janice E., *The Organizational History of Field Artillery, 1775–2003*, Washington, D.C.: United States Army Center of Military History, 2007.

Melzer, Richard and Phyllis Ann Mingus, "Wild to Fight: The New Mexico Rough Riders in the Spanish-American War," *New Mexico Historical Review*, Vol. 59, No. 2, April 1984, pp. 109–136.

"Men Stick to Army," *Washington Post*, December 5, 1908, p. 11.

Militia Act—*See* U.S. Statutes at Large, An Act to More Effectually to Provide for the National Defense by Establishing a Uniform Militia Throughout the United States.

Millet, Francis Davis, *The Expedition to the Philippines*, New York: Harber & Brothers, 1899.

Millett, Allan R., "Over Where? The AEF and the American Strategy for Victory, 1917–1918," in Kenneth J. Hagan and William R. Roberts, eds., *Against All Enemies: Interpretations of American Military History from Colonial Times to the Present*, Westport, Conn.: Greenwood Press, 1986.

Millett, Allan R., Peter Maslowski, and William B. Feis, *For the Common Defense: A Military History of the United States from 1607–2012*, New York: Free Press, 2012.

Minnigerode, Fitzhugh Lee, "Crippled Militia's Needs," *New York Times*, February 6, 1921, p. X5.

Moore, Colin D., "State Building Through Partnership: Delegation, Public-Private Partnerships, and the Political Development of American Imperialism, 1898–1916," *Studies in American Political Development*, Vol. 25, April 2011, pp. 27–55.

Moy, Timothy, *War Machines: Transforming Technologies in the U.S. Military, 1920–1940*, College Station, Tex.: Texas A&M University Press, 2001.

Murray, Williamson R., and Allan R. Millett, *Military Innovation in the Interwar Period*, Cambridge, UK: Cambridge University Press, 1996.

National Commission on the Future of the Army, *Report to the President and the Congress of the United States*, Arlington, Va., January 28, 2016.

National Guard Act—*See* Public Law 73-64, An Act to Amend the National Defense Act of June 3, 1916, June 15, 1933.

National Guard Association of the United States, *Proceedings of the Convention of National Guards 1st & 3rd Conventions*, St. Louis, Mo.: John J. Daly & Company, 1879–1881.

———, *NAGAUS Annual Convention Report*, Washington, D.C., November 17–19, 1926.

"National Guard Entirely Wiped Out," *Boston Daily Globe*, December 25, 1918, p. 12.

National Guard Reorganization Status: Hearings Before the House of Representatives Committee on Military Affairs, Sixty-Sixth Congress, First Session, September 23, 1919, Washington, D.C.: U.S. Government Printing Office, 1919.

NCFA—*See* National Commission on the Future of the Army.

"Need Not Return to National Guard," *New York Times*, December 25, 1918, p. 4.

Neiberg, Michael S., *The Path to War: How the First World War Created Modern America*, New York: Oxford University Press, 2016.

Nenninger, Timothy K., "The Army Enters the Twentieth Century, 1904–1917," in Kenneth J. Hagan and William R. Roberts, eds., *Against All Enemies: Interpretations of American Military History from Colonial Times to the Present*, Westport, Conn.: Greenwood Press, 1986.

———, "Tactical Dysfunction in the AEF, 1917–1918," *Military Affairs*, Vol. 51, October 1987, pp. 177–181.

———, "American Military Effectiveness in the First World War," in Allan R. Millett and Williamson Murray, eds., *Military Effectiveness*, Vol. 1: *The First World War*, Boston, Mass.: Allen and Unwin, 1988, pp. 116–156.

———, "Leavenworth and Its Critics: The U.S. Army Command and General Staff School, 1920–1940," *Journal of Military History*, Vol. 58, No. 2, April 1994.

———, "'Unsystematic as a Mode of Command': Commanders and the Process of Command in the American Expeditionary Forces, 1917–1918," *Journal of Military History*, Vol. 64, No. 3, July 2000, pp. 747–753.

New York Evening Post, "The New Militia Law," *Journal of the Military Service Institution of the United States*, Vol. 34, 1904, p. 329.

New York Sun, "Comment and Criticism: Democracy and Our Armies," *Journal of the Military Service Institution of the United States*, Vol. 38, 1906, pp. 363–364.

New York Times, "Comment and Criticism: Democracy and Our Armies," *Journal of the Military Service Institution of the United States*, Vol. 38, 1906, pp. 364–365.

Norris, John G., "Army Orders Laggard Officers Ousted from Reserve Corps," *Washington Post*, February 3, 1940.

"Note for Colonel Fagalde, French Military Attaché in London, from French Ambassador, Washington, Received December 20, 1917," *United States Army in the World War, 1917–1919: Policy-Forming Documents of the American Expeditionary Force*, Washington, D.C.: U.S. Army Center of Military History, 1989.

Odom, William O., *After the Trenches: The Transformation of U.S. Army Doctrine, 1918–1939*, College Station, Tex.: Texas A&M University Press, 1999.

"Official Proceedings of the National Guard Association of the United States," paper presented at the Sixty-Sixth Annual Convention of the National Guard Association of the United States, Baltimore, Md., May 3–6, 1944.

O'Laughlin, John Callan, "Uncle Sam's Eyes on Evils in Army," *Chicago Daily Tribune*, January 22, 1906, p. 1.

O'Ryan, John F., "The Role of the National Guard," *The North American Review*, Vol. 202, No. 718, 1915, pp. 364–372.

———, "Letter from John F. O'Ryan to John McAuley Palmer," Palmer Papers, Library of Congress, Box 5, Folder 4, March 5, 1920.

"Our 'Militaristic Peril,'" *Literary Digest*, Vol. 62, No. 13, September 27, 1919, pp. 9–10.

"Our Washington Letter," *National Guard Magazine*, Vol. 8, 1907, p. 445.

Oyos, Matthew M., "Theodore Roosevelt, Congress, and the Military: U.S. Civil-Military Relations in the Early Twentieth Century," *Presidential Studies Quarterly*, Vol. 30, No. 2, June 2000, pp. 312–330.

Palmer, John McAuley, *Report on the Organization of the Land Forces of the United States*, Washington, D.C.: U.S. Department of War, 1912.

———, Palmer Papers, Library of Congress, Box 5, Folder 1, 1920.

———, *Washington, Lincoln, Wilson: Three War Statesmen*, Garden City, N.Y.: Doran & Company, Inc., 1930.

———, "Address of Brigadier General John McAuley Palmer: Excerpts from the Transcript of the Shorthand Report of the Proceedings of the Adjutants General Association Annual Meeting," Palmer Papers, Library of Congress, April 21, 1942.

Pappas, George S., *Prudens Futuri: The U.S. Army War College, 1901–1967*, Carlisle Barracks, Pa.: Alumni Association of the U.S. Army War College, 1967.

Pearlman, Michael David, *To Make Democracy Safe for America: Patricians and Preparedness in the Progressive Era*, Champaign, Ill.: University of Illinois Press, 1984.

Perry, Ralph Barton, *The Plattsburg Movement: A Chapter of America's Participation in the World War*, New York: E. P. Dutton & Company, 1921.

Pershing, John J., *My Experiences in the World War*, Vol. 1, New York: Frederick A. Stokes, 1931.

Pettit, James S., "How Far Does Democracy Affect the Organization and Discipline of Our Armies, and How Can Its Influence Be Most Effectively Utilized?" *Journal of the Military Service Institution of the United States*, Vol. 38, January–February 1906, pp. 1–32.

Pier, Douglas Carl, *Choosing War: Presidential Decisions in the Maine, Lusitania, and Panay Incidents*, Oxford, UK: Oxford University Press, 2016.

"The 'Preparedness' Flurry," *The Nation*, Vol. 99, No. 2579, December 3, 1914.

"Proposes an Army of 1,000,000 Boys," *New York Times*, August 15, 1915, p. 3.

Pruitt, James Herman, II, *Leonard Wood and the American Empire*, PhD dissertation, Texas A&M University, 2011.

Public Law 62-338, An Act Making Appropriation for the Support of the Army for the Fiscal Year Ending June Thirtieth, Nineteen Hundred and Thirteen, and for Other Purposes, August 24, 1912.

Public Law 63-90, An Act to Provide for Raising the Volunteer Forces of the United States in Time of Actual or Threatened War, April 25, 1914.

Public Law 64-85, An Act for Making Further and More Effectual Provision for the National Defense, and for Other Purposes, June 3, 1916, pp. 166–217.

Public Law 65-12, An Act to Authorize the President to Increase Temporarily the Military Establishment of the United States, May 18, 1917, pp. 76–83.

Public Law 65-309, An Act to Authorize the Resumption of Voluntary Enlistment in the Regular Army, and for Other Purposes, February 28, 1919.

Public Law 66-242, An Act to Amend an Act Entitled "An Act for Making Further and More Effectual Provision for the National Defense, and for Other Purposes," June 4, 1920.

Public Law 73-64, An Act to Amend the National Defense Act of June 3, 1916, June 15, 1933.

Public Law 76-783, An Act to Provide for the Common Defense by Increasing the Personnel of the Armed Forces of the United States and Providing for Its Training, September 16, 1940.

Public Law 113-291, National Defense Authorization Act for Fiscal Year 2015, December 19, 2014.

Rainey, James W., "Ambivalent Warfare: The Tactical Doctrine of the AEF in World War I," *Parameters: Journal of the U.S. Army War College*, Vol. 13, September 1983, pp. 34–46.

———, "The Questionable Training of the AEF in World War I," *Parameters: Journal of the U.S. Army War College*, Vol. 22, Winter 1992–1993.

Ramsey, Robert D., III, *Savage Wars of Peace: Case Studies of Pacification in the Philippines, 1900–1902*, The Long War Series, Fort Leavenworth, Kans.: Combat Studies Institute Press, 2007.

Reilly, Henry Joseph, *Americans All; the Rainbow at War: Official History of the 42s Rainbow Division in the World War*, 2nd ed., Columbus, Ohio: The F. J. Heer Printing Company, 1936.

Relative to the Organized Militia of the United States, Washington, D.C., War Department, Division of Military Affairs in the Office of the Chief of Staff, U.S. Government Printing Office, 1911.

Reorganization of the Army: Hearings Before the Subcommittee of the Committee on Military Affairs of the United States Senate, Sixty-Sixth Congress, Session I on S. 2691, S.2693, S.2715, September 2, 1919, Washington, D.C.: U.S. Government Printing Office, 1919.

Report of the Commission Appointed by the President to Investigate the Conduct of the War Department in the War with Spain, Washington, D.C.: U.S. Government Printing Office, 1899.

Report of the Adjutant General for the State of Arizona, Phoenix, Ariz., 1920–1929. As of June 7, 2017: http://azmemory.azlibrary.gov/cdm/ref/collection/statepubs/id/11776

Report of the Adjutant General for the State of Georgia, Atlanta, Ga., 1920.

"Report to the Adjutant General of the Commonwealth of Virginia for the Year Ending December 31, 1917," *Annual Reports of Officers, Boards and Institutions of the Commonwealth of Virginia for the Year Ending September 30, 1917*, Richmond, Va.: Superintendent of Public Printing, 1918.

Report of the Adjutant General of the Commonwealth of Virginia for the Year Ending December 31, 1918, Richmond, Va., 1919.

Report of the Chief of the Militia Bureau Relative to the National Guard of the United States, 1917, Washington, D.C.: U.S. Government Printing Office, 1917.

Report of the Secretary of War to the President, 1922, Washington, D.C.: U.S. Government Printing Office, 1922.

Report on the Mobilization of the Organized Militia and National Guard of the United States, 1916, Washington, D.C.: U.S. Government Printing Office, 1916.

Rice, James W., "The Present Congress and the National Guard," *Journal of the Military Service Institution of the United States*, Vol. 19, 1896.

Roosevelt, Franklin D., "Executive Order 8233: Prescribing Regulations Governing the Enforcement of the Neutrality of the United States," Gerhard Peters and John T. Woolley, eds., American Presidency Project, 1939a. As of March 5, 2020: https://www.presidency.ucsb.edu/node/210747

———, "Proclamation 2352: Proclaiming a National Emergency in Connection with the Observance, Safeguarding, and Enforcement of Neutrality and the Strengthening of the National Defense Within the Limits of Peace-Time Authorizations," Gerhard Peters and John T. Woolley, eds., American Presidency Project, 1939b. As of March 5, 2020: https://www.presidency.ucsb.edu/node/210003

———, "Executive Order 8530: Calling Out the National Guard," in Gerhard Peters and John T. Woolley, eds., American Presidency Project, August 31, 1940. As of March 5, 2020: https://www.presidency.ucsb.edu/node/209927

"Roosevelt Urges Nation to Prepare," *New York Times*, July 22, 1915, p. 1.

Root, Elihu, "Preface," in Emory Upton, ed., *The Military Policy of the United States*, Washington, D.C.: U.S. Government Printing Office, 1903.

———, *The Military and Colonial Policy of the United States: Addresses and Reports*, Cambridge, Mass.: Harvard University Press, 1916.

Root, Elihu, and William Cary Sanger, *Report on the Reserve and Auxiliary Forces of England and the Militia of Switzerland: Prepared in 1900 for President McKinley and the Hon. Elihu Root*, Washington, D.C.: U.S. Government Printing Office, 1903.

Sandos, James A., "Pancho Villa and American Security: Woodrow Wilson's Mexican Diplomacy Reconsidered," *Journal of Latin American Studies*, Vol. 13, No. 2, November 1981, pp. 293–311.

Scott, Hugh Lenox *Some Memories of a Soldier*, New York: The Century Co., 1928.

Sears, Joseph H., *The Career of Leonard Wood*, New York: D. Appleton and Company, 1920.

"Sees Militarism in Wilson's Plan," *New York Times*, November 19, 1915, p. 4.

Selective Draft Law Cases, 245 U.S. 366, 1918.

Selective Service Act—*See* Public Law 65-12.

Semsch, Philip L., "Elihu Root and the General Staff," *Military Affairs*, Vol. 27, No. 1, 1963, pp. 16–27.

"Senate Declares Army Bill Sets Up Staff Despotism," *New York Times*, September 14, 1919, p. 1.

Shaw, William L., "The Interrelationship of the United States Army and the National Guard," *Military Law Review*, Vol. 31, January 1, 1966, pp. 39–84.

Silbey, David J., *A War of Frontier and Empire: The Philippine-American War, 1899–1902*, New York: Hill & Wang, 2007.

Skowronek, Stephen, *Building a New American State: The Expansion of National Administrative Capacities, 1877–1920*, Cambridge, UK: Cambridge University Press, 1982.

Sparrow, John C., *History of Personnel Demobilization in the United States Army*, Washington, D.C.: Department of the Army Pamphlet No. 20-210, July 1952.

Steele, Matthew F., "Comment and Criticism: Democracy and Our Armies," *Journal of the Military Service Institution of the United States*, Vol. 38, 1906, pp. 358–361.

Stentiford, Barry M., *The American Home Guard: The State Militia in the Twentieth Century*, College Station, Tex.: Texas A&M University Press, 2002.

Stewart, Richard W., *American Military History*, Vol. I: *The United States Army and the Forging of a Nation, 1775–1917*, Washington, D.C.: U.S. Government Printing Office, 2005.

———, *American Military History*, Vol. II: *The United States Army in a Global Era, 1917–2008*, 2nd ed., Washington, D.C.: U.S. Army Center of Military History, 2010.

Stiehm, Judith Hicks, *U.S. Army War College: Military Education in a Democracy*, Philadelphia, Pa.: Temple University Press, 2010.

Stimson, Henry L., "What Is the Matter with Our Army?" *The Independent*, April 4, 1912.

Stubbs, Kevin D., *Race to the Front: The Material Foundations of Coalition Strategy in the Great War*, Westport, Conn.: Praeger Publishers, 2002.

Taylor, Daniel M., "In What Way Can the National Guard be Modified So as to Make It an Effective Reserve to the Regular Army in Both War and Peace?" *Journal of the Military Service Institution of the United States*, Vol. 26, 1900, pp. 239–240.

Thompson, Paul, "Only One U.S. Army: An Interview with General March on the Great Change That Merges Regulars, National Army Men, and Guardsmen," *New York Times*, August 11, 1918.

Tinsley, William H., *The American Preparedness Movement, 1914–1916*, PhD dissertation, Stanford University, 1939.

Todd, Frederick P., "Our National Guard: An Introduction to Its History," *Military Affairs*, Vol. 5, No. 3, 1941.

Trask, David F., *The United States in the Supreme War Council: American War Aims and Inter-Allied Strategy, 1917–1918*, Westport, Conn.: Greenwood Press, 1978.

———, *The AEF and Coalition Warmaking, 1917–1918*, Lawrence, Kans.: University Press of Kansas, 1993.

———, *The War with Spain*, Lincoln, Neb.: University of Nebraska Press, 1996.

Trohan, Walter, "Roosevelt Asks 2 1/4 Billion Fund for U.S. Defense: Requests Total Quarter of Entire Budget," *Chicago Daily Tribune*, January 5, 1940, p. 8.

U.S. Code, Title 32—National Guard, Section 102: General Policy, 2012.

U.S. House of Representatives, *Efficiency of the Militia, H.R. 15345: Hearing Before the Committee on Military Affairs*, Washington, D.C.: U.S. Government Printing Office, 1902.

———, *Army Reorganization: Statements of Hon. Newton D. Baker and Gen. Peyton C. March, H.R. 14560: Hearing Before the Committee on Military Affairs*, Washington, D.C., U.S. Government Printing Office, January 16, 1919.

———, *Officers' Reserve Corps–National Guard (Proposed Amendments to the National Defense Act), H.R. 10478: Hearing Before the Committee on Military Affairs*, Washington, D.C., U.S. Government Printing Office, April 14, May 15, May 16, 1930.

———, *Review of the Reserve Program: Hearing Before the Subcommittee No. 1 of the Committee on Armed Services*, Washington: D.C., U.S. Government Printing Office, February 4–8, 18–21, 1957.

U.S. House of Representatives, Committee of the Whole House on the State of the Union, *National Guard Bill*, Washington, D.C.: U.S. Government Printing Office, June 9, 1932.

———, *National Guard Bill: Report to Accompany H.R. 5645*, Washington, D.C.: U.S. Government Printing Office, 141, 1933.

U.S. Senate, *Efficiency of the Militia, H.R. 15345: Hearing Before the Committee on Military Affairs*, Washington, D.C.: U.S. Government Printing Office, December 4, 1902.

———, "Patrick Connery of Massachusetts," *Congressional Record*, Washington, D.C.: U.S. Government Printing Office, 1933, pp. 5000–5009.

———, *Politics of Our Military National Defense: History of the Action of Political Forces Within the United States Which Has Shaped Our Military National Defense Policies from 1783 to 1940*, Washington, D.C.: U.S. Government Printing Office, Document No. 274, August 28, 1940.

U.S. Senate, Committee on Military Affairs, *Statement of Subcommittee of the Committee on Military Affairs of the United States Senate to Accompany the Proposed Bill 'To Reorganize and Increase the Effectiveness of the United States Army, and for Other Purposes,'* Washington, D.C.: U.S. Government Printing Office, 1919.

———, *Amend the National Defense Act*, Washington, D.C.: U.S. Government Printing Office, June 9, 1933.

U.S. Statutes at Large, An Act to More Effectually to Provide for the National Defense by Establishing a Uniform Militia Throughout the United States, Second Congress, Session I, Chapter 33, May 8, 1792 (1 Stat. 271).

U.S. Statutes at Large, An Act Giving Eventual Authority to the President of the United States to Augment the Army, Fifth Congress, Session III, Chapter 31, March 2, 1799 (1 Stat. 725).

U.S. Statutes at Large, An Act for Enrolling and Calling Out the National Forces, and for Other Purposes, Thirty-Seventh Congress, Session III, Chapter 75, March 3, 1863 (12 Stat. 731).

U.S. Statutes at Large, An Act to Provide for Temporarily Increasing the Military Establishment of the United States in Time of War, and For Other Purposes, Fifty-Fifth Congress, Session II, Chapter 187, April 22, 1898 (30 Stat. 361).

U.S. Statutes at Large, An Act to Provide for a Volunteer Brigade of Engineers and an Additional Force of Ten Thousand Enlisted Men Specially Accustomed to Tropical Climates, Fifty-Fifth Congress, Session II, Chapter 294, May 11, 1898 (30 Stat. 405).

U.S. Statutes at Large, An Act to Promote the Efficiency of the Militia, and for Other Purposes, Fifty-Seventh Congress, Session II, Chapter 196, January 21, 1903 (32 Stat. 775).

U.S. Statutes at Large, "An Act to Increase the Efficiency of the Army," Fifty-Seventh Congress, Session II, Chapter 553, February 14, 1903 (32 Stat. 830).

U.S. Statutes at Large, An Act to Increase the Efficiency of the Medical Department of the United States Army, Sixtieth Congress, Session I, Chapter 150, April 23, 1908 (35 Stat. 66).

U.S. Statutes at Large, An Act to Further Amend the Act Entitled "An Act to Promote the Efficiency of the Militia, and for Other Purposes," Sixtieth Congress, Session I, Chapter 204, May 27, 1908 (35 Stat. 339).

U.S. Statutes at Large, An Act to Further Amend the Act Entitled "An Act to Promote the Efficiency of the Militia, and for Other Purposes," Approved January Twenty-First, Nineteen Hundred and Three, Sixty-First Congress, Session II, Chapter 185, April 21, 1910 (36 Stat. 329).

Upton, Emory, *The Military Policy of the United States*, 4th ed., Washington, D.C.: U.S. Government Printing Office, 1903.

Uviller, H. Richard, and William G. Merkel, "The Second Amendment in Context: The Case of the Vanishing Predicate," *Chicago-Kent Law Review*, Vol. 76, January 2000.

Venzon, Anne Cipriano, ed., *The United States in the First World War: An Encyclopedia*, New York: Routledge, 2012.

Vladeck, Stephen I., "The Field Theory: Martial Law, the Suspension Power, and the Insurrection Act," *Temple Law Review*, Vol. 80, No. 2, 2007.

———, *The Calling Forth Clause and the Domestic Commander In-Chief*, Washington, D.C.: American University Washington College of Law, 2008.

"The Volunteer Army," *Los Angeles Times*, May 22, 1898.

"The Wadsworth Bill," *The Vassar Miscellany News*, Vol. 4, No. 33, February 21, 1920.

Wadsworth, James W., "Address by the Honorable James W. Wadsworth Delivered to the Military Training Camps Association of the United States, New Willard Hotel, Washington, D.C., August 1, 1919," *National Service Magazine*, Vol. 6, No. 3, September 1919, pp. 155–156.

War Department Annual Reports, 1916, Vol. I, Washington, D.C.: U.S. Government Printing Office, 1916.

War Department Annual Reports, 1917: Reports of the Secretary of War, Washington, D.C.: U.S. Government Printing Office, 1918.

"War Department General Orders No. 90 (July 12, 1917): Call into Federal Service and Draft of the National Guard by the President of the United States of America," in *War Department General Orders and Bulletins, 1917*, Washington, D.C.: U.S. Government Printing Office, 1918, pp. 1–4.

Ward, Robert D., "The Origin and Activities of the National Security League, 1914–1919," *Mississippi Valley Historical Review*, Vol. 47, No. 1, June 1960, pp. 51–65.

Weigley, Russell Frank, *Towards an American Army: Military Thought from Washington to Marshall*, New York: Columbia University Press, 1962.

———, *History of the United States Army*, New York: Macmillan, 1967.

———, "The Elihu Root Reforms and the Progressive Era," paper presented at Command and Commanders in Modern Warfare: The Proceedings of the Second Military History Symposium, U.S. Air Force Academy, May 2–3, 1968, Office of Air Force History and U.S. Air Force Academy, 1971.

———, *The American Way of War: A History of United States Military Strategy and Policy*, New York: Macmillan, 1973.

———, "The American Military and the Principle of Civilian Control from McClellan to Powell, *Journal of Military History*, Vol. 57, No. 5, October 1993, pp. 27–58.

———, "The American Civil-Military Gap: A Historical Perspective, Colonial Times to the Present," in Peter D. Feaver and Richard H. Kohn, eds., *Soldiers and Civilians: The Civil-Military Gap and American National Security*, Cambridge, Mass.: MIT Press, 2001.

Weigley, Russell, "The Interwar Army, 1919–1941," in Hagan, Kenneth J. and William R. Roberts, eds., *Against All Enemies: Interpretations of American Military History from Colonial Times to the Present*, Westport, Conn.: Greenwood Press, 1986.

Whitehorne, Joseph W. A., *The Inspectors General of the United States Army, 1903—1939*, Washington, D.C.: Office of the Inspector General and the United States Army Center of Military History, 1998.

Willbanks, James H., ed., *America's Heroes: Medal of Honor Recipients from the Civil War to Afghanistan*, Santa Barbara, Calif.: ABC-CLIO, 2011.

Wilson, John B., *Maneuver and Firepower: The Evolution of Divisions and Separate Brigades*, Washington, D.C.: United States Army Center of Military History, 1998.

Wilson, Woodrow, *Message to Congress*, Washington, D.C.: U.S. Government Printing Office, Senate Document No. 566, 1914.

———, "Address to Naturalized Citizens at Convention Hall, Philadelphia," Gerhard Peters and John T. Woolley, eds., American Presidency Project, 1915. As of March 5, 2020: https://www.presidency.ucsb.edu/node/206560

Winthrop, William, *Military Law and Precedents*, Boston, Mass.: Little, Brown, and Company, 1896.

Winton, Harold R. and David R. Mets, eds., *Military Institutions and New Realities, 1918–1941*, Lincoln, Neb.: University of Nebraska Press, 2000.

Wood, Leonard, "What Is the Matter with Our Army? It Lacks Concentration," *The Independent*, February 8, 1912a.

———, "What Is the Matter with Our Army? The National Failure to Realize Its Purpose," *The Independent*, April 11, 1912b.

———, *The Military Obligation of Citizenship*, Princeton, N.J.: Princeton University Press, 1915.

———, *Our Military History: Its Facts and Fallacies*, Chicago, Ill.: The Reilly & Britton Company, 1916.

———, "The Plattsburg Idea," *National Service*, February 1917, pp. 12–14.

Woodward, David R., *The American Army and the First World War*, Cambridge, UK: Cambridge University Press, 2014.

Work, David K., "The Tenth U.S. Cavalry on the Mexican Border, 1913–1919," *The Western Historical Quarterly*, Vol. 40, No. 2, Summer 2009, pp. 179–200.

"Worst of Army Evils," *Washington Post*, October 15, 1905, p. JJ2.

"Young America as a Soldier," *Washington Post*, April 4, 1905, p. 6.